THE MAJOR GODS OF ANCIENT YUCATAN

KARL ANDREAS TAUBE

Dumbarton Oaks Research Library and Collection   Washington, D.C. 1992

Library of Congress Cataloging-in-Publication Data

Taube, Karl A.
    The major gods of ancient Yucatan / Karl Andreas Taube.
        p.   cm. — (Studies in pre-Columbian art & archaeology ;
no. 32)
    Includes bibliographical references.
    ISBN 0-88402-204-8
    1. Mayas—Religion and mythology. 2. Manuscripts, Maya.
I. Title. II. Series.
E51.S85   no. 32
[F1435.3.R3]
299'.79265—dc20   92-5435

Second Impression, 1997

Contents

Acknowledgments

This study is partly the result of linguistic and ethnographic fieldwork during the academic year 1983–84. My research was supported by the following granting agencies affiliated with Yale University: the Josef Albers Travelling Fellowship, the Concilium on International and Areal Studies, and the Tinker Foundation Travel Grant, administered by the Council on Latin American Studies of Yale University. Two individuals were of great help during my stay in Yucatan: I wish to thank Joann Andrews and Edward Kurjack for their hospitality and frequent assistance during my trips to Merida. A major portion of this study was composed during a year of residence as a Junior Fellow in Pre-Columbian Studies at Dumbarton Oaks. I am grateful to Dumbarton Oaks for its support during the academic year 1986–87. Stephen Houston, David Stuart, and Bruce Love kindly provided me with unpublished manuscripts as well as their personal expertise. Over the years, Barbara and Justin Kerr have given me a great deal of invaluable vessel imagery from their major corpus of roll-out photographs. I am grateful to Michael D. Coe, Mary Ellen Miller, Andrea Stone, Elizabeth Boone, Linda Schele, David Wade, and an anonymous reviewer for their perceptive comments on earlier versions of this study. Finally, I wish to thank Lee Hyde Steadman for her thoughtful assistance during the preparation of this manuscript.

List of Figures

CHAPTER 1

Introduction

There is no simple, elegant model with which to integrate and organize the many varied deities, demi-gods, and demons of Late Post-Classic Yucatan. Unlike the highland Maya Quiche, there is no detailed *Popol Vuh* epic describing the various gods involved in the cosmogonic acts of creation. Instead, narrative allusions to particular Yucatec gods must be garnered piecemeal from Yucatec and Spanish Colonial sources. Many of the deity names mentioned in these early accounts cannot even be identified in the pre-Hispanic corpus of Maya art. In part, the confusion derives from the eclectic nature of Post-Classic Yucatec religion. Yucatec religion was strongly polytheistic, with a myriad of divinities with frequently overlapping if not competing attributes and functions. Foreign deities were enthusiastically accepted into the Post-Classic pantheon, often with minimal modification. A number of gods were clearly foreign Post-Classic introductions, although it is becoming increasingly evident that the great majority can be traced to the Classic Maya.

Primary Sources for the Study of Post-Classic Maya Gods

The most important corpus of imagery pertaining to ancient Maya gods is contained in a group of three pre-Hispanic Maya screenfold books, known as the Dresden, Paris, and Madrid codices. A fourth recently reported codex, the Grolier, is but ten painted pages of a once larger screenfold. The Grolier fragment is concerned primarily with gods and calendrics pertaining to Venus and is of comparatively limited use for the broader study of ancient Maya gods. All of the surviving codices are Post-Classic in date, and aside from the Grolier, it is clear that the group derives from the Peninsula of Yucatan. This provenience is indicated primarily by style, calendrical conventions, and the presence of Yucatecan words phonetically written in the hieroglyphic codical texts (see Campbell 1984: 5).

Maya codices are composed of folded bark paper painted on both sides with a thin layer of plaster. The text and figures painted upon the plaster surfaces tend to be in black and red, with particular passages delineated by vertical or horizontal red bands. Remains of Classic Maya codices have been discovered at Uaxactun, San Agustin Acasaguastlan, Nebaj, Altun Ha, and Mirador (Lee 1985: 28). However, all of these examples are in very poor states of preservation and tell us little concerning the appearance and content of Classic Maya screenfold books.

Iconographic research by Michael Coe (1977) has not only identified the presence of folded codices in Classic Maya art, but also particular gods and tools pertaining to the scribal arts. Following a suggestion by Lin Crocker, Coe (1978: 16) subsequently suggested that a certain type of Late Classic black and white vessel was based on the format of codices. In this case, the red bands appearing at the rim and base of the "codex style" vessel would correspond to the horizontal bands delineating distinct passages within a manuscript. Although these ceramic vessels do closely resemble the appearance of codices, it is still highly unlikely that they functioned in a similar context. Codices, and not vases, were surely the primary means of recording detailed religious and historical information during the Classic period. Moreover, it is now known that much of the hieroglyphic writing appearing on Classic codex style vases and bowls pertains specifically to ceramic vessels, not screenfold books (Houston, Stuart, and Taube 1989).

A terse account by Fray Diego de Landa suggests that both historical and ritual matters were recorded in the Maya screenfolds of Post-Classic Yucatan:

> These people also made use of certain characters or letters, with which they wrote in their books their ancient matters and their sciences, and by these and by drawings and by certain signs in these drawings, they understood their affairs and made others understand them and taught them. (in Tozzer 1941: 169)

Although somewhat damaged, the *Relación* of Gaspar Antonio Chi also suggests the presence of historical information: "[They wrote in their books the] outstanding events which had occurred [in their history and prophesies] of their prophets, and the lives, [feasts and conquests] of the nobles" (translation and emendations by J. Thompson 1972: 6). However, the surviving pre-Hispanic codices do not contain detailed accounts of legends and history. They are divinatory almanacs dealing primarily with calendrical and ritual matters. The codices are largely composed of almanacs providing prognostications for particular calendrical cycles, such as the 260-day calendar, the 365-day vague year, the 584-day Venus cycle, and the Tun and Katun periods. Thus, although the surviving screenfolds provide invaluable information on particular gods, rituals, and cosmology, this information is not portrayed in a narrative mode. Each deity tends to appear in isolation, serving as a marker for a particular divinatory prognostication. Moreover, it is often clear that many of the offering and objects appearing in a scene are not specific to the god illustrated, but rather refer to the augury. Thus a whole series of gods may appear holding the same offering or engaged in the same sacrificial act. Even with the background provided by ethnohistoric documents, such as the Yucatec books of Chilam Balam, the Quichean *Popol Vuh,* and the frequently narrative imagery

on Classic Maya vessels, the codices provide little information on Post-Classic Yucatec mythology.

Although the Post-Classic Maya codices contain only tangential allusions to mythic events, they constitute an unsurpassed corpus delineating the physical characteristics and attributes of particular deities. Despite obvious stylistic differences, the Dresden, Paris, and Madrid codices contain many of the same gods, usually with shared complexes of physical attributes and symbolic associations. Thus the situation is analogous to the Late Post-Classic Borgia Group of Mexican codices, where Tezcatlipoca, Ehecatl-Quetzalcoatl, Chalchiuhtlicue, and other major deities can be identified easily in all of the five screenfolds (see Spranz 1973).[1] However, whereas most deities of the Borgia Group cannot be readily seen in earlier Classic iconography, the gods appearing in the Post-Classic Maya codices are generally of great antiquity and can be traced to the beginnings of the Classic Maya era. Thus the Maya gods occurring in the Post-Classic Yucatecan codices are of paramount importance for understanding the Classic as well as the Post-Classic Maya pantheon. The codical series of Post-Classic deities serves as an excellent template on which to categorize the frequently complex divinities appearing in both Classic and Post-Classic Maya iconography.

The Codex Dresden

Of the three Yucatecan codices, the Codex Dresden provides the clearest and most precise information regarding the attributes and names of Maya gods. Although Thompson (1972: 15) argues that the manuscript dates to the Early Post-Classic period, recent iconographic research indicates that this codex is probably Late Post-Classic

---

[1] In the tradition of Seler, Spranz, Nicholson, and others, gods appearing in the Borgia Group of codices will be referred to by Nahuatl terminology. Although it is by no means certain which linguistic groups fashioned the Borgia, Vaticanus B, Cospi, Fejérváry-Mayer, and Laud codices, such Nahuatl names as Mictlantecuhtli, Cinteotl, and Tlaloc serve as convenient and concise means of referring to specific gods. Although they could also be labeled the Death God, Maize God, and Rain God, these general terms obscure the many specific characteristics of these deities, traits also found with their Aztec Nahuatl counterparts.

(Paxton 1986; Taube and Bade 1991). For the study of Maya gods, especially important sections are the series of gods ranging across pages 2 to 23, the Venus pages on pages 24 and 46 to 50, and the new year pages on pages 25 to 28. Purchased in Vienna in 1739, the codex was acquired by the Königlichen Bibliothek zu Dresden in 1740 (Glass and Robertson 1975: 125). Unfortunately the Codex Dresden suffered extensive water damage during the bombing of Dresden in World War II, and for this reason much of my analysis will rely on the 1892 facsimile edition by Förstemann, republished by Thompson (1972).

The Codex Paris

The first report of the Codex Paris was in 1859, when it was discovered in the Paris National Library by Leon de Rosny; how and when the library acquired the document is entirely unknown. Unfortunately the Codex Paris is poorly preserved, and much of the painted stucco surface has worn away, leaving only the central portion of each page. The succession of the roughly twenty-year Katuns on pages 1 to 12 constitutes the most useful passage pertaining to Maya gods, although valuable information can also be gleaned from other of the fragmentary scenes and texts. Sylvanus Morley (1920: 575–576) notes the striking similarity between the Paris Katun pages and Mayapan Stela 9. Morley tentatively dates Stela 9 to 12.4.0.0.0 10 Ahau 18 Uo, the Katun immediately preceding the abandonment of Mayapan in Katun 8 Ahau. Although its precise provenance remains unknown, the Codex Paris may well date to the height of the Mayapan confederacy, that is, during the early half of the fifteenth century.

The Codex Madrid

The Codex Madrid is also known as the Codex Tro-Cortesianus, owing to the fact that it was first considered as two separate screenfolds, the Codex Troano and the Codex Cortesianus. Both fragments appeared at approximately the same time, the Troano in 1866, and the Cortesianus in 1867 (Glass and Robertson 1975: 153). Leon de Rosny (1881) was the first to note that the two parts constituted a single manuscript. Although sloppily executed, the Madrid codex is an especially important source for the study of Late Post-Classic Yucatec gods. In part, its value derives from sheer size. It is the longest of the pre-Hispanic Maya codices, containing fifty-six leaves, in contrast to thirty-nine leaves in the Codex Dresden, eleven leaves in the Paris, and ten leaves in the Grolier. In addition, of the surviving codices, the Madrid is also the most similar to the early Colonial Spanish and Yucatec accounts. For example, Cyrus Thomas (1882) long ago noted the close correspondence between the yearbearer passages on pages 34 to 37 to Landa's sixteenth-century account of the rites heralding the new year.

Of the four Maya screenfolds, the Madrid one seems to be especially late and may well derive from the northwestern portion of Yucatan, the region most extensively documented by Landa and other Colonial sources. Although the content of the Codex Madrid can be often compared to early ethnohistoric accounts, the quality of execution is generally poor. This is not simply a matter of crude draftsmanship. In the case of the structured and repetitive epigraphic texts, one can detect frequent scribal errors, and it is likely that there are also inaccuracies in the portrayal of Maya gods. For this reason, interpretations based on specific texts or iconographic details in the Codex Madrid should be made with caution, particularly if they are based upon only a single scene.

The Codex Grolier

The Codex Grolier was first reported and published by Michael Coe (1973), who identified the manuscript as an authentic pre-Hispanic Maya codex. According to Coe (1973: 150), when the codex was discovered it was accompanied by a mosaic mask, currently in the collections at Dumbarton Oaks (see von Winning 1968: pl. 333). Although plaster covered both sides of the manuscript, only one side was painted with text. Coe numbered the surviving fragmentary pages 1 through 11, and suggested that the manuscript originally would have had at least twenty pages, the number required to complete the illustrated Venus section. John Carlson (1983) subsequently noted that page 11 is actually a fragment of page 10; thus only one half of the original twenty pages is represented. In contrast to the Venus pages in the pre-Hispanic Dresden, Vaticanus B, Borgia, and Cospi codices, the Grolier Venus illustrations do not correspond only to the heliacal rising of Venus as the morning star. Instead, each Grolier page refers successively to one of the four Venus stations of Superior Conjunction, Evening Star, Inferior Conjunction, and Morning Star. Once repeated five times across the twenty pages, the cycle would begin again, eventually making a total of 65 Venus periods, or 104 vague years of 365 days (Coe 1973: 150–151).

Michael Coe (1973: 150) obtained a radiocarbon date of A.D. 1230 ± 130 from the Codex Grolier, placing it squarely in the Post-Classic period. Coe (1973: 151) notes that this date accords well with the style of the manuscript, which recalls the art of the Toltec period of Early Post-Classic Chichen Itza. J. Eric S. Thompson (1975), however, points out that this date may only correspond to the age of the paper not to the painted manuscript. According to Thompson, the codex is probably a forgery fashioned from ancient un-painted pounded bark paper, which is relatively common in dry caves of highland Mexico (e.g., Moser 1975: fig. 10). Thompson (1975) argues that the well-known Venus cycle would be a relatively easy subject for a modern forger to replicate. However, if this be the case, why does the Codex Grolier not conform to the far better-known sequence illustrating only Venus at heliacal rising? As Coe notes, there is nothing in the Codex Grolier that suggests overt copying from other Maya sources—a common clue to forgeries. Recent studies by Carlson (1983) and Mora-Echeverría (1984) provide support that the Codex Grolier is actually authentic.

Other Sources

The Dresden, Paris, Madrid, and Grolier codices are but one body of data pertaining to Post-Classic Maya gods. Aside from these pre-Hispanic Maya screenfolds, there are also the Post-Classic mural paintings, most notable those of Santa Rita, Tancah, and Tulum. In thematic content, the murals are frequently similar to the codices and depict gods in relation to calendrical prognostications. An example would be the murals from Mound 1 at Santa Rita, which represent a series of gods oriented to the succession of the 360-day Tun cycle (J. Thompson 1950: 198). In many cases the mural scenes are as complex as any in the codices. Frequently the mural figures can be identified with particular gods known for the codices. In style, the murals of Tancah and Tulum are strikingly similar to the Paris, Dresden, and especially Madrid codices.

In addition to codices and mural painting, there is also the Late Post-Classic sculpture of the northern lowlands. The complex but little-studied Chen Mul Mayapan style incense burners found widely in Yucatan and Quintana Roo offer a wealth of detailed iconography. These anthropomorphic ceramic censers are especially useful for identifying particular costume elements, since the dress and regalia appear in three-dimensional clarity. Although frequently crude and poorly preserved, the limestone sculptures of Mayapan, Tulum, Santa Rita, and other Late Post-Classic sites are also useful sources, often with valuable contextual information.

The Terminal Classic and Early Post-Classic iconography of Chichen Itza is a crucial corpus that bridges the gap between the gods of the Late Classic and Late Post-Classic Maya. Images at Chichen can be related both to Terminal Classic iconography of the Puuc region and that of Late Post-Classic Yucatan. The art and iconography of Chichen Itza is highly syncretic and incorporates iconography of Central Mexico as well as that of the Maya region. In view of the complex history of contact and exchange between the Maya region and highland Mexico and the Gulf Coast, it is necessary to consider the Maya gods not as isolated phenomena but as integral parts in the greater ideological system of ancient Mesoamerica.

The Study of Post-Classic Maya Gods

In the latter half of the nineteenth century, a number of scholars began the difficult process of identifying the various deities found in the pre-Hispanic Maya screenfolds (e.g., Brasseur de Bourbourg 1869–70; Thomas 1882; Förstemann 1886, 1898, 1901, 1906; Fewkes 1894, 1895; Seler 1886, 1887b). The early work of Charles Brasseur de Bourbourg (1869–70) is substantially flawed, due to misconceptions concerning the nature and content of Maya writing. Nonetheless, Brasseur de Bourbourg made a number of valuable contributions, including the identification of the codical form of Chac, the god of rain and lightning. In these early works, the primary focus was less upon mythology than on the appearance of these gods in the codical almanacs. It was recognized that in the codices, the integration of gods with specific calendrical periods and cycles provides insights into the structural relationship of gods not only to calendrical events but also to cosmology, world directions, colors, and other gods. An excellent example of this approach may be seen in the analysis by Cyrus Thomas (1882) of the Madrid and Dresden codices' new year pages. However, much of the early success in delineating the structural relationships and identity of gods in the codices was due to the work of Ernst Förstemann (1886, 1906), head librarian of the Royal Public Library at Dresden. It was Förstemann who first solved the essential workings of ancient Maya calendrics. Although Förstemann initially focused upon the Codex Dresden, his work eventually encompassed the Madrid and Paris codices and Classic Maya monuments as well.

Along with Förstemann, Eduard Seler clearly ranks as one of the most important scholars in the early era of Maya codical research. Seler possessed a vast encyclopedic knowledge of not only Maya calendrics and belief but also of the complex religious lore and iconography of highland Mexico. Thus Seler can be considered as one of the first great Mesoamericanists, who was able to recognize shared cultural patterns over wide areas of Mexico and Central America. This remarkable breadth had direct bearing on the elucidation of particular gods and scenes appearing in the Maya codices. For example, whereas Förstemann (1886, 1906) discovered the Venus passage on pages 24 and 46 to 50 of the Codex Dresden, it was Seler (1898, 1904c) who first recognized the close correspondence between these pages and the Venus lore of highland Mexico. Thus Seler compares the Dresden Venus pages to similar passages in the Borgia, Vaticanus B, and Cospi codices. In addition, Seler explains these scenes in terms of Colonial Central Mexican texts, most notably the *Anales de Cuauhtitlan*.

The work by Seler (1898, 1904c) on Maya and Mexican Venus Lore is an excellent example of the potential value of Mexican data for the analysis of ancient Maya religion. However, the pan-Mesoamerican approach of Seler is not always successful. A frequent source of error is the assumed degree of similarity between distinct cultures. Thus Seler commonly equates scenes from Mixtec codices with the iconography and gods of Central Mexico. According to Nancy Troike (1978), this assumption has been a major stumbling block in our understanding of Mixtec history and religion. A similar situation can be seen for Seler's studies and Maya religion, which often appears to be perceived and organized through a Central Mexican template. This problem is particularly acute with his studies and Classic Maya iconography (e.g., Seler 1976). Nonetheless, it should be noted that, even during this early period of research, Seler was acknowledged as a "pioneer" (Förstemann 1906: 54). Although certain of his comparisons have not been fruitful, many of Seler's contributions have proven to be fundamental to our understanding of ancient Mesoamerican religion.

Paul Schellhas was one of the first to attempt the systematic identification of gods occurring in the Maya codices. In a work published in 1886, Schellhas identified the name glyphs of eight codical gods. However, as Seler (1887a) quickly pointed out, this by no means exhausts the total number of gods appearing in the Maya codices. Schellhas' (1897, 1904) subsequent publications, describing a total of fifteen gods, were the first major analyses of the deities appearing in the

5

Paris, Madrid, and Dresden codices. As in the previous work of 1886, Schellhas isolated and identified not only particular deities, but also their appellative glyphs. Some of Schellhas' original identifications and interpretations have proved to be incorrect, but the great bulk of his work remains widely accepted today.

Rather than using specific Maya names, Schellhas adopted the noncommittal system of letter designation, in which each deity is labeled with a specific letter, beginning with A. This arbitrary system has proved to be of great value. For one, the label serves as a means of identification independent of the often poorly understood meaning and identity of a given deity. Moreover, many gods have not one but several names; an example is God A, known under such epithets as Yum Cimih, Cisin, or Uac Mitun Ahau in Yucatec. A great many of the codical deities also appear in the Classic period. It is unlikely that Yucatec was the dominant language of the Classic Maya lowlands, and thus the letter designations are usually more appropriate than Post-Classic or Colonial Yucatec terminology.

The Schellhas system of deity classification was quickly adopted by other researchers, and appears in the early works of Seler (1904a), Förstemann (1906), and others. Fewkes (1894, 1895) was among the first to use the Schellhas system, describing the identities of God B and God D. The Schellhas system of deity classification continues to be an essential element in the analysis of Maya deities. In an important discussion of Maya gods, Günter Zimmermann (1956) refers to the Schellhas system, but also proposes a distinct form of deity classification. However, Zimmermann's proposed system has not been widely adopted, and almost all recent studies of pre-Hispanic Maya gods cite the Schellhas letter system. J. Eric S. Thompson (1934, 1939, 1970a, 1970b, 1972) often refers to the Schellhas classification in his many discussions of Maya gods. In the tradition of Eduard Seler, Thompson frequently compares Maya gods to deities of highland Mexico.

Like Thompson, Ferdinand Anders (1963), David Kelley (1965, 1972, 1976), and Michael Coe (1973, 1978, 1982) also make use of the Schellhas classificatory system, and frequently note parallels with iconographic conventions of highland Mexico. *Das Pantheon der Maya* by Anders (1963) is an ambitious study not only of Maya gods, but also of the nature of Maya religion. As in the case of the present study, Anders describes gods of both the Classic and Post-Classic Maya, as well as relevent data from the Colonial and contemporary periods. In his work *Deciphering the Maya Script,* Kelley (1976) devotes an entire chapter to ancient Maya gods and the Schellhas system. This useful analysis summarizes previous research of Maya divinities and provides emendations to Schellhas' letter classification. More recently, Linda Schele and Mary Ellen Miller (1986) describe some of the current knowledge concerning major Classic Maya gods, many of which are referred to by the Schellhas system of letter classification.

In the past two decades, there has been an explosive growth in our understanding of ancient Maya religion. Much of the progress has been not with the Post-Classic codices, but with Classic Maya epigraphy and art. Because of our increased understanding of ancient Maya script, it is now possible to interpret accurately the scenes appearing on Classic Maya monuments. The work of Linda Schele (e.g., 1974, 1976, 1979, 1986) at Palenque is an example of the amount of detailed information now being gleaned from Classic Maya dynastic epigraphy and art.

In addition to recent advances in epigraphic and iconographic research, a great deal of new material has come to light through scientific excavation and, unfortunately, looting. In her unpublished doctoral dissertation, Clemency Coggins (1975) analyzes the vast array of Classic epigraphy and art encountered during the University of Pennsylvania's excavations at Tikal. In 1973 a milestone of Classic Maya iconographic research was published: *The Maya Scribe and His World* by Michael D. Coe. In his analysis of a major corpus of unprovenanced Maya vessels, Coe (1973) calls attention to the complexity and sophistication of Classic Maya vessel scenes. An especially important contribution was the demonstration that a version of the *Popol Vuh* creation epic existed during the Classic era. Although Franz Blom (1950) had previously noted the presence of *Popol Vuh* imagery on a Classic period plate, Coe was the first to note the extent of *Popol Vuh* characters and themes in Classic Maya vessel iconography. In his studies, Coe (1973, 1975, 1977, 1978, 1982, 1989) describes in detail Classic analogues of *Popol Vuh* characters and the nature of the Maya underworld. In a recent publication, Nicholas Hellmuth (1987) elaborates upon a number of Coe's initial insights and, in addition, presents numerous new iconographic identifications and interpretations.

In view of the many epigraphic and iconographic advances that recently have been made, it is clear that a fresh reappraisal of the Post-Classic codical gods and their Classic antecedents is now in order. The recognition of a Classic *Popol Vuh* epic has placed a very different light on ancient Maya mythology. For the first time, Classic Maya ideology and religion can be viewed and ordered in terms of sacred narrative. Many major Classic Maya gods have now been identified with *Popol Vuh* characters. Although a number of the comparisons may be unwarranted, it is becoming increasingly clear that the *Popol Vuh* creation epic is a useful means of interpreting and categorizing Classic Maya religion (see M. Coe 1989). Many of the deities now known to be part of the Classic *Popol Vuh* epic also appear in the Schellhas classification of Post-Classic codical deities.

The Presence of Gods in Ancient Maya Religion

In recent years there has been some debate concerning the fundamental nature of Classic Maya religion, namely, whether the Classic Maya actually had a concept of specific gods or only the personification of natural forces. Essentially, the debate concerns whether Classic Maya religion was animistic—devoted to the worship of specific gods—or animatistic—based on the belief of a *mana*-like impersonal spiritual force residing in the surrounding material world. Tatiana Proskouriakoff (1965, 1978, 1980) was skeptical of the presence of divinities in Classic Maya religion. In a discussion of zoomorphic "grotesques" in Classic Maya art, Proskouriakoff (1965: 470–471)

voices her doubts regarding specific Classic gods:

the elements of which they [grotesques] are composed do not form stable associations but are recombined in such a protean manner that they cannot be conceived as describing definite entities. We are of necessity led to believe that they are not pictorial forms but compositions of ideograms, capable of expressing very complex conceptions and differing from hieroglyphic writing only in their lack of serial arrangement and adherence to syntax.

Joyce Marcus (1978: 180) also argues that the Classic Maya lacked a deity complex: "I feel that we can challenge the notion that the Maya had a pantheon of anthropomorphized gods during the Classic period (A.D. 250–950). Rather, supernatural beings were depicted in Maya art by combining parts from different animals (snake, iguana, crocodile, quetzal, parrot, jaguar, and so on) into fantastic creatures that would never have occurred in nature." In a similar line, Kubler (1969: 32) states that the series of Post-Classic codical gods identified by Schellhas does not appear in Classic Maya iconography: "In general the multiplicity of the deities in the manuscripts is lacking in Classic Maya iconography. There is no body of images of activities accompanied by suitable divine regents, and in place of the gods, we probably see images of spirits, whose attributes and characteristics vary according to place and period."

According to Proskouriakoff (1978: 113; 1980: 9) and Porter (n.d.b), many of the grotesque or strange beings present in Classic Maya art are not gods but costumed performers personifying specific forces of nature and abstract concepts. There are indeed many clear examples of impersonation in Classic Maya art. Thus it is frequently possible to distinguish masks, body suits, and other accouterments of costume. However, it is an entirely different matter to interpret these scenes as impersonations of natural forces or concepts rather than gods. Thus deity impersonation is a widespread phenomena in ritual performances of Mesoamerica and the American Southwest. In the contemporary Pueblo dances of the American Southwest, the Kachina performers simultaneously represent forces of nature and sentient supernatural beings (E. Parsons 1939).

In contrast to the Classic period, which ended

more than 600 years before the Spanish Conquest, Colonial sources are extremely relevant for the interpretation of Post-Classic Maya religion. The Colonial chroniclers make frequent reference to native gods, not only for the Maya region but for highland Mexico as well. According to those who advocate the absence of deities, however, these sources cannot be trusted, because the chroniclers were heavily biased by Classical or Judeo-Christian concepts of divinity (Marcus 1978; Proskouriakoff 1978, 1980). This is an a priori assumption, however, that is difficult to support or disprove. Although the early chroniclers clearly had well-developed conceptions of divinity, there is no reason to assume that these were entirely incompatible with Mesoamerican belief. According to Fray Bernardino de Sahagún (see 1950–71, bk. 2), widely regarded as one of the first ethnographers of the New World, the Aztec did believe in specific gods. Sahagún was well versed in the subtleties of Aztec language and belief, and I find it difficult to dismiss his descriptions of Aztec gods as products of ethnographic bias or naivete.

In a detailed discussion of Aztec conceptions of divinity and ritual impersonation, Arild Hvidtfeldt (1958: 140) states that, while the Aztec had a *mana*-like concept of sacredness, they also had gods, that is, "mythical figures with a life of their own." Hvidtfeldt (1958: 77–78) notes that the Nahuatl term *teotl* can refer both to god or divinity and the concept of sacredness. Similarly, the term *ku* or *ch'u* signifies deity or sacredness in Mayan languages. Recent advances in Classic epigraphy demonstrate that this concept was present among the Classic Maya as well. In our discussion of God C, it will be noted that a particular Maya glyph, T1016, has the phonetic value *ku* or *ch'u* and can qualify the sacredness of certain objects such as regalia, offerings, or temple structures, or introduce particular deity names. In other words, it appears in Classic script that *ku* or *ch'u* can refer both to specific gods and to the general quality of sacredness.

The argument that the Classic and perhaps even Post-Classic Maya lacked gods is a conservative and now outmoded concept that arose during a time when Classic Maya religion was very poorly understood. In 1965, when Proskouriakoff published her description of Maya "grotesques," very few patterns were discerned in Classic Maya iconography. It is not surprising, therefore, that the iconography appeared "protean," with little clear meaning or form. In the following study, it will be noted that many of the Post-Classic figures identified by Schellhas do appear in Classic Maya iconography, frequently with similar or identical name glyphs.

The relative appearance or absence of gods in Maya iconography has much to do with the context and function of particular art forms. Both Proskouriakoff (1965, 1978, 1980) and Marcus (1978) focus their discussions on Classic Maya monuments rather than the elaborate narrative scenes appearing on Classic Maya vessels. Classic Maya monuments are primarily historical and political in nature and clearly function to portray rulers in scenes of self-aggrandizement. Thus, representations of supernatural figures are frequently limited to costume and ornament or the cosmological setting of the ruler. Such is not the case for the small and portable ceramic vessels, which often display narrative scenes that can be related to the mythology of the Quichean *Popol Vuh*. In the present study, I will use the term *god* to refer to supernatural sentient beings that appear in sacred narrative. Aside from God C, who appears to be the embodiment of sacredness, I believe that this definition can apply to all of the entities that will be labeled as gods.

Although I find the argument for a lack of gods among the Classic Maya untenable, it serves as a useful caveat. An uncritical use of such terms as *god* or *deity* can create a plethora of "gods," each distinguished by minute differences in appearance or context. There has, in fact, been an overuse of these terms. Animals in Classic Maya pottery scenes are frequently labeled as the Monkey God, Deer God, and so on, despite the fact there is little evidence these creatures are actually gods. In many instances anthropomorphized animals in Classic Maya art do not depict gods, but ritual clowns (Taube 1989b). But this is not the only significance of animal figures in Classic Maya iconography. In groundbreaking recent research, Stephen Houston and David Stuart (1989) note that many of the creatures appearing in Classic Maya vessel scenes portray supernatural co-essences of actual people, gods, and even polities. Houston and Stuart (1989) note the Classic Maya term for this co-essence was *uay,* a word referring to animal or spirit familiars in Colonial and contemporary Mayan languages. Because of the complexities involved in identifying animal figures as performers, spirit familiars, or gods, I will not consider these figures as distinct gods unless they are associated with a well-known mythic cycle. An example of such a creature would be the Principal Bird Deity, now known to be the Protoclassic and Classic period prototype of Vucub Caquix, the monster bird of the *Popol Vuh.*

According to Proskouriakoff (1978: 113), Classic Maya iconographic study should be less concerned with divinities than with social processes, such as sanctification of lineage and royal descent. Thus the study of Maya gods could be viewed as an epiphenomenal foray into a never-never world that has no basis in anthropological fact. However, it should be stressed that, although divine, the gods should be viewed as models and metaphors of the social and natural worlds. As such, they have everything to do with how the Maya interacted with themselves and their surrounding environment. For example, there are specific gods of subsistence, trade, and rulership. Moreover, through the study of Maya gods and mythology, it is possible to determine some of the underlying motivations of Maya social behavior. For example, Michael Coe (1989) argues that, like the Hindu Ramayana and Mahabharata, the Hero Twins saga of the *Popol Vuh* provided the divine charter for Classic Maya elite behavior. It is hoped that the present discussion of Maya gods will be used for interpreting not only ancient Maya religious belief but other aspects of Maya society as well.

Ancient Maya Writing and Language

The analysis of Maya iconography cannot be divorced from the hieroglyphic writing; both are inextricably combined, not only in terms of text and image but also in the fundamental nature of Maya epigraphy and iconography. Thus Maya writing is strongly pictographic and uses many motifs appearing in Maya art. However, it is now known that Maya writing is also phonetic and as such is linguistically bound to Mayan languages (see Knorozov 1967; Justeson and Campbell 1984; Houston 1988). It is generally agreed that, whereas Yucatec was the language of the Dresden, Paris, and Madrid codices, the Classic Maya of the central and southern lowlands were primarily Cholan speakers (Campbell 1984). Due to the phonetic nature of the script, it is frequently possible to utter the Mayan names or epithets of particular gods. Moreover, the presence of pictorial elements in the script can provide important insights into iconographic conventions, since they are frequently labeled with known phonetic values.

Although Cholan is especially important for deciphering Classic Maya script, Yucatec will be the most-cited language in this study. This is partly because the Paris, Madrid, and Dresden codices are written in Yucatecan—the language family currently comprising Yucatec, Lacandon, Itza, and Mopan. In addition, the majority of cited Colonial information pertains to Yucatec. In most recent studies of contemporary Yucatec, the language is transcribed phonetically. The most popular system is that described by Rober Blair and Refugio Vermont-Salas (1965). However, until recently, Yucatec has been a written language with its own system of orthography based on the Latin alphabet. Because I will be relying heavily on Colonial documents, I will use an orthographic system based on that used for Colonial Yucatec. The system for consonants is as follows:

Present study	Blair and Vermont-Salas
c	k
k	k'
t	t
tt	t'
z	s
x	š
b	b
p	p

Present study	Blair and Vermont-Salas
pp	p'
h	h
tz	ts
dz	ts'
ch	č
ch'	č'
m	m
n	n
l	l
u	w
y	y

Proper names and widely known Colonial words, such as Katun, will be capitalized and retain the original Colonial orthography. Terms from other Mayan languages will not be altered but will keep the original orthography of the cited source.

CHAPTER 2

The Schellhas God List

Introduction

The Schellhas (1897, 1904) god list focuses only upon the Post-Classic gods appearing in the few surviving pre-Hispanic screenfolds. At the time of Schellhas' pioneering investigations, this was a useful strategy: to isolate a series of gods by using a limited universe of highly similar scenes and texts. However, it is now possible to have a more comprehensive view based not only on the codices but also on Post-Classic murals and sculpture and, in addition, Classic Maya epigraphy and art. In the following discussion of the major Post-Classic gods and their Classic antecedents, I will follow the letter designations proposed by Schellhas, although emendations and corrections to the Schellhas system will be noted frequently.

Following the tradition of Schellhas, Seler, Thompson, Coe, and others, I believe that the Maya gods can be identified by specific visual attributes. These attributes can be corporeal, as costume, or as particular items held or associated with a given god. In the following discussion, I focus on attributes that I consider to be diagnostic of a particular god. The approach is similar to that adopted by Seler; that is, the Maya gods will be considered in the broader context of Mesoamerica. Thus, when relevant, particular gods and iconographic conventions of Veracruz or highland Mexico will be mentioned. When possible, specific Maya gods will be traced back to Classic prototypes. This is not simply to document continuity but also to provide important insights into the identity and significance of particular gods.

Of course, the Schellhas system has its limitations, and it is by no means comprehensive of all Post-Classic Maya gods, much less those of the Classic period. Revisions and additions to the Schellhas system will be mentioned, among the more important of these corrections to be noted are the separation of God F into Gods Q and R, the name designations of Goddess O and Goddess I, and the addition of God A', God CH, and God S. After the discussion of Post-Classic codical gods, I review other Post-Classic deities of the northern Maya lowlands, in particular, those of Central Mexican origin.

Gods A and A'

The most readily discernable attribute of God A is his skeletal appearance, as he usually occurs with protruding ribs, rickety limbs, and a fleshless grinning skull (Fig. 1). In both the Classic and Post-Classic periods, portrayals of this deity are studies in decay. Thus God A often has large black spots, which are probably putrification, and a large, grossly bloated belly. During the Classic period, his abdomen may be replaced with outpouring swirls of blood or rotting matter (Fig. 1g). A hairlike ruff with globular elements—aptly termed "death eyes" by Beyer (1937: 151–152) and others (e.g., J. Thompson 1950: 45; M. Coe 1973: 16)—frequently fringes his head, collar, and other elements of costume (Figs. 1f, g). Schellhas (1904: 11) identifies these devices as "globular bells or rattles." Many of the elements do resem-

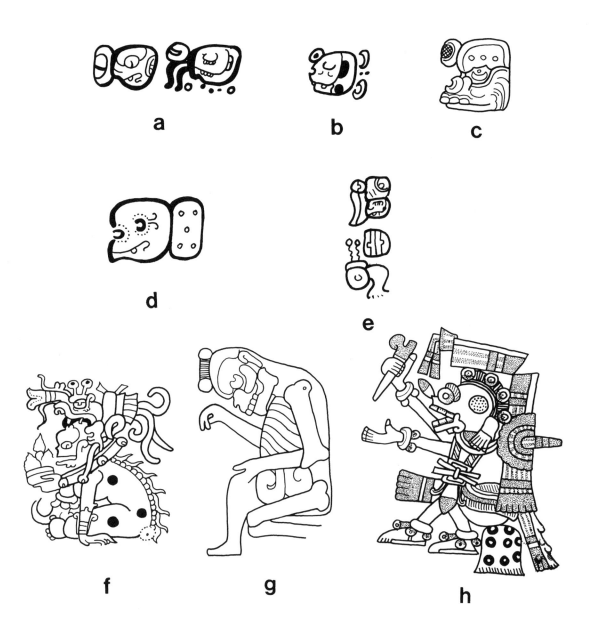

a   b   c

d

e

f   g   h

Fig. 1   God A in ancient Maya epigraphy and art.

(a) Post-Classic appellative phrase of God A, Dresden page 12b

(b) Late Classic appellative of God A, detail of codex style vessel (drawn after Robicsek and Hales 1981: vessel 138)

(c) God A as the head variant of the numeral ten, Copan Stela I (redrawn after Thompson 1950: figs. 24, 58)

(d) Glyphic compound accompanying God A, read *xib(i)*, or "fright," Dresden page 22c

(e) God A phonetically labeled as *cisin(i)*, Codex Madrid page 87c.

(f) Post-Classic example of God A, note *mo* sign delineating sphincter, *molo,* Dresden page 13a

(g) Xunantunich Altar 1, Classic period depiction of death god with death eye ruff on forehead and putrescence pouring out of belly (redrawn after I. Graham 1978, 2: 127)

(h) Mictlantecuhtli, the skeletal death god of Post-Classic Central Mexico, Codex Borgia page 15.

ble hollow copper bells or rattles found on the wrists, ankles, and costume fringes; however, in a thorough study of the God A elements, Rivard (1965) concludes that they represent extruded eyeballs, not bells. Clearly, the Classic examples could not be metal, because metal bells were not common in the Maya region until the Post-Classic period.

Circular elements almost identical to the Maya examples commonly appear in the hair of the Late Post-Classic Central Mexican death god, Mictlantecuhtli (Fig. 1h). In this instance, the circular elements are clearly eyeballs. Thus, in the illustrated example from Borgia page 15, the elements on the wrists, bracelets, and hair appear with a zone of red also found in the actual eye of the seated Mictlantecuhtli. Moreover, it can be seen that the eyes upon the front of the sandals are actually supplied with the red nerve stalk of the extruded eyeball. With the circular eyeballs, the hair of Mictlantecuhtli is virtually identical to the hair crest of God A and the "death collar" eyeball-and-ruff device commonly worn by Maya death gods (e.g., Figs. 1f, g; 2e, f).

Although rarely depicted in scenes on Late Classic stone monuments, God A commonly occurs in texts as the head variant of the number ten (Fig. 1c). He also appears upon Late Classic polychrome vessels, frequently in execution scenes with the Classic Chac, eagerly awaiting the victim with outstretched arms (Fig. 8b; see also Robicsek and Hales 1981: vessels 19–25, 27). The identification with sacrifice continues in the Post-Classic period. Thus in the Codex Madrid, God A is often found with God Q, a god of sacrifice. On Madrid page 76, Gods A and Q sit on either side of a sacrificial victim stretched over an altar.

The Maya God A and Mictlantecuhtli of highland Mexico are much alike in both form and function. Both are skeletal deities of death, the underworld, and sacrifice. In the Codex Borgia, Mictlantecuhtli usually wears a hafted sacrificial flint blade as a pectoral (Fig. 1h). In a narrative scene on Borgia page 42, he greets a sacrificed victim. Thematically, this is quite similar to the Late Classic Maya vessel scenes in which God A receives a victim sacrificed upon a Cauac monster altar (e.g., Fig. 8b). In the Borgia scene, the victim is first slain, then devoured by the caiman earth, only to meet Mictlantecuhtli seated on his netherworld throne. The Central Mexican god was known as a lord, or *tecuhtli,* and similarly, the Yucatec death god was referred to as Uac Mitun Ahau, *ahau* being the Yucatec title for lord or king (see Landa, in Tozzer 1941: 147). However, this may have been a relatively recent borrowing from Central Mexico, since Mitun is suspiciously similar to the Nahuatl Mictlan.

On Dresden page 22c, God A twice appears with a glyphic compound composed of the T1048 skull sign followed by the T585a *bi* glyph (Fig. 1d). The skull glyph is marked with a series of dots around the eye. Stuart (1987b: 31) proposes that this skull sign is to be read *xi*. With this value, the two compounds on Dresden page 22c can be read *xib(i)*. In Yucatec, the root *xib* has such connotations as "death" and "fright," clearly related to the Quichean term for the underworld, Xibalba. Thus, in the Colonial Yucatec dictionaries, *xibalbail* is glossed as "cosa infernal"; *xibalbayen,* "cosa diabolica"; and *xibib,* "temor" (Barrera Vásquez 1980: 941). The compound on Dresden page 22c probably qualifies the death god as a frightful being. The use of the skull for the *xi* phonetic value may well derive from the common deathly and fearsome meanings of *xib* in Mayan languages. In Tzotzil, *ši'* signifies "fright" (Laughlin 1975: 320).

Although a repellent and frightful being, God A does not appear to have enjoyed an especially high status in the Maya pantheon. At times, his grotesque appearance is almost comical, and it seems that he was afforded little respect. In the codices, God A frequently has a ring of dots against his posterior (Fig. 1f). This is the phonetic *mo* sign first described by Floyd Lounsbury (1973). In contemporary Yucatec, a common term for sphincter is *molo,* and it is probable that the *mo* sign serves to delineate the anus, *molo,* of God A. In terms of his widespread association with filth and decomposition, it is not surprising that the sphincter is an important physical trait of God A.

A common Colonial and contemporary Yucatecan name of the death god is Cizin, derived from the root *ciz,* meaning "flatulence." Fox and Justeson (1984: 38–39) note that pages 85c and 87c of the Codex Madrid provide strong phonetic evidence that Cizin was a pre-Hispanic epithet for God A (Fig. 1e). On Madrid page 87c, God A appears with three auguries oriented to the west, east, and north. Each text contains a directional glyph, a form of the God A appellative, a compound composed of T146.102:116, and finally, the augury. The T146.102:116 compound is composed of known phonetic values. Affix T146 is recognized to have the value *zi;* T102, the value *ci;* and T116, the value *ni* (see Justeson 1984: 323, 324, 326). The only ambiguity with this compound is the reading order. Because the T102 *ci* sign appears closest to the preceding compound, it is likely that this sign is to be read before the T146 affix. Given this reading order, Fox and Justeson (1984: 39) note that the entire compound is phonetically transparent as *cizin(i),* the name of the Yucatec death god. On Madrid page 85c, the suggested *cizin* appellative occurs once, here in association with a death deity displaying characteristics of God A and God Q.

Michael Coe (1973: 15) notes that the pre-Hispanic God A may be compared with Cizin of the contemporary Lacandon. Rather than being the paramount lord of the underworld, the Lacandon death deity has the subsidiary role of punishing the dead. Similarly, God A may have been the specific deity of corporal decomposition and the welfare of the deceased.

Although not recognized by Schellhas, there is yet another important Post-Classic death god (Fig. 2). This deity occurs in the Paris (page 22), Madrid (pages 19b, 64c, 72b, 74b), and Dresden codices (pages 5b, 6a, 28b), as well as in Classic Maya inscriptions and art. Zimmermann (1956: 162–163; pl. 6) was the first to isolate this god in the Codex Dresden, and Thompson (1972: 38) subsequently noted his name glyph in Classic epigraphy (T1042). Noting that this entity was distinct from God A, Zimmermann (1956: 162–163) termed this god A', or alternatively, GIa. The face of God A' is characterized by a division sign on his cheek and a blackened region around his eye, usually a broad vertical band. Often above this band is a pair of Akbal eyes, a sign of darkness (Figs. 2a, d–h). Quite frequently a large bone, presumably a human femur, is placed in the hair. Usually supplied with some sort of lashing in midsection, this bone appears with God A' from the Early Classic to the Late Post-Classic (Figs. 2e–f, h).

The name glyph of God A' is usually a portrait glyph of the god, although in the Codex Dresden a jawless head (T1038a) also occurs as the God A' appellative (Fig. 2b). During both the Classic and Post-Classic periods, the God A' portrait glyph may be accompanied by a T23 *na* sign (Figs. 2c, d, g). Although clearly a physically distinct deity, God A' does share roles with the skeletal death god, God A. Thus on the Codex Dresden new year pages 27 and 28, God A' alternates with God A. Michael Coe (1982: 111) notes that God A' is frequently shown in the act of self-decapitation in Classic Maya vessel scenes, and he is clearly a sinister figure of violent death and sacrifice.

During the Late Classic period, God A' seems to have been impersonated during ritual performances. Some of the finest renderings of this being appear to be actual people in the guise of God A'. One example appears on a fragmentary Late Classic polychrome vessel (Fig. 3a). Covered with abundant death signs, the figure has a face painted in the characteristic zones of white and black and also wears the large femur through his headdress. He is flanked by two women in obvious positions of dance and holds a rattle, an excellent indicator of ritual or theatrical performances in Classic Maya art (Taube 1989b).

A similar figure occurs on the renowned Altar de Sacrificios Vase, which also depicts explicitly dancing figures. The vessel scene depicts individuals impersonating supernaturals, and it is readily apparent that they are wearing costumes with headdresses, leggings, mitts, and the like. One of the seated figures bears the facial markings of God A', complete with the white face, a black band through the eyes, and a division sign on the cheek (Fig. 3b). The figure grasps flint weapons in both hands, both a sacrificial blade and an axe. The axe arm is upraised as if the figure has com-

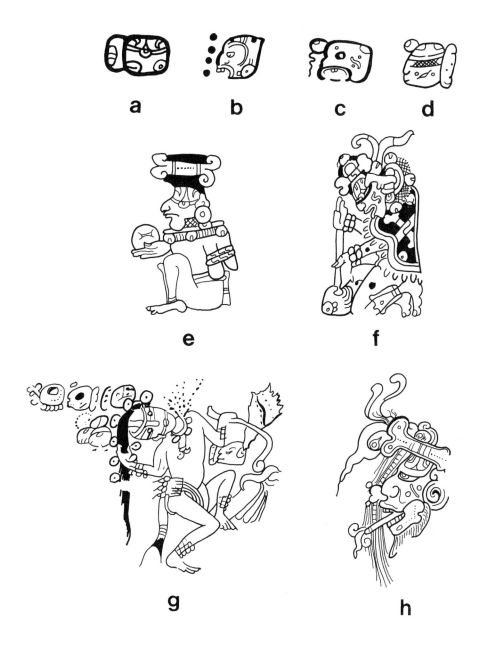

a b c d

e f

g h

Fig. 2 Classic and Post-Classic examples of God A′.

(a–c) God A′ appellative glyphs in Post-Classic codices, Madrid page 64c, Dresden page 28b, Dresden page 5b

(d) Classic example of God A′ appellative with phonetic *na* suffix, Naranjo Altar 1 (redrawn after I. Graham 1978, 2: fig. 103)

(e) Late Post-Classic representation of God A′ as prisoner with death collar, Madrid page 72b

(f) God A′ drilling, Dresden page 5b

(g) God A′ in act of self decapitation, Late Classic vessel (drawn after Robicsek and Hales 1981: vessel 40)

(h) God A′ emerging from jaws of serpent, from lid of Early Classic incised vessel (redrawn after Berjonneau et al. 1985: pl. 354).

mitted self-decapitation—a characteristic of God A'. In seeming confirmation of this act, streams of blood radiate from the neck. However, on close inspection it is clear that these "streams" are actually bloodied paper strips hanging upon a collar or ruff of pendant hair or other material rendered in fugitive gray. The small knot tying this unpleasant device can be seen on the upper chest. It is likely that with the bloodied ruff and the weapons, the figure is dressed as God A' in the act of self-decapitation. Both of these Late Classic vessel scenes appear to be performances portraying God A' and netherworld demons, perhaps analogous to the Late Post-Classic Yucatec *xibalba okot,* "dance of the devil," mentioned by Landa (Tozzer 1941: 147).

Summary

In summary, there are at least two major death gods appearing in the Post-Classic codices, God A and God A'. Both of these gods have obvious Classic antecedents. God A is invariably skeletal, with a prominent fleshless skull. He frequently appears with a hair ruff dotted with disembodied eyeballs; this element can appear both as a hair crest and as a collar worn around the neck. In both the Classic and Post-Classic periods, God A frequently appears with elements suggestive of putrescence and filth, and, in the codices, he often occurs with a prominent and exaggerated anus. Closely identified with human sacrifice, God A appears to be the preeminent god of death presid-

a

b

Fig. 3 Representations of God A' impersonators on Late Classic pottery.

(a) God A' impersonator holding rattle; compare femur in headdress with Figs. 2e, f, and h (redrawn after Coe 1973: 9)

(b) God A' impersonator engaged in mock self-execution; note knotted collar with hanging, bloodied paper pennants, detail of Altar de Sacrificios Vase (drawn after G. Stuart 1975: 774).

ing over the afterlife of the unfortunate deceased. God A is very similar to Mictlantecuhtli of Post-Classic Central Mexico, and in view of a number of specific shared traits, it is clear that they are historically related entities. It is quite possible that certain traits found with Mictlantecuhtli, including the death eye and hair ruff, ultimately derive from the Classic Maya.

In contrast to God A, God A' has no obvious analogues in the Gulf Coast or highland Mexico. The most striking characteristic of this death god is the black horizontal band across the eyes, which contrasts sharply with the blanched whiteness of the rest of his face. God A' seems to be primarily a god of violent sacrifice and is identified closely with the act of self-decapitation. During the Late Classic period, God A' seems to be a popular character in ritual performances illustrating gods and demons of the netherworld.

God B

One of the most important deities of the ancient and contemporary Maya, God B permeates Post-Classic Yucatec ritual and cosmology. Because of the frequent association of this deity with serpents, Schellhas (1904: 17–18) considers God B as the Maya version of Quetzalcoatl and noted that Fewkes, Förstemann, Thomas, and Dieseldorff had reached similar conclusions. However, Schellhas also mentions that Brasseur de Bourbourg (1869–70: 117) and Seler (1886) interpret God B as Chac. There is now overwhelming evidence that this god is indeed Chac, the god of rain and lightning. It is now known that Chac and many of his associations are extremely old and may be traced back even to the beginnings of Classic Maya religion.

During the Post-Classic period, God B is characterized by his long pendulous nose (Figs. 4b, 6a). Schellhas (1904: 16) notes that he is the most commonly represented deity in the codices and appears in a wide variety of activities. God B is often found wielding axes or serpents, both of which are widespread symbols of lightning in ancient and contemporary Mesoamerica. A quadripartite god, he is frequently oriented to the four

directions and colors in the Codex Dresden. At times, his name glyph may also be prefixed by a *yax* sign standing for green and the middle place, suggesting that there was a fifth principal Chac at the center. The conventional glyph of God B (T668) is a profile face with a *Tau*-shaped *ik* sign serving as the eye (Fig. 4a). This curious glyph has a small notch at the back of the head, creating the impression of a thumb protruding from a clenched fist. Although less common, the actual portrait head of God B occurs in free variation with the Ik-eye appellative (Fig. 4b). Both versions tend to be postfixed with the T102 *ci* sign, probably to provide the final consonant of *chac(i)*.

The T668:102 *chac* compound is not limited to the Post-Classic period. Jeff Kowalski (1985) notes its presence at Terminal Classic Uxmal and Chichen Itza (Figs. 4e–f). David Stuart (cited in L. Schele and M. E. Miller 1986: 49, note 55) has recently identified the appellative phrase *chac xib chac* on a Late Classic dish (Fig. 4c). A name specifically mentioned by Landa and the Colonial Yucatec Chilam Balam books (Tozzer 1941: 138, note 642), it is also present on Dresden page 30c. A similar phrase appears on another Late Classic vessel, in this case a cylindrical vase depicting an anthropomorphized Chac figure (Fig. 4d). Here the individual is named *chac xib,* with the final sign being the youthful *xib* head found also on the aforementioned dish. In both cases, the *xib* face has a prominent spot upon the cheek. Although this is a diagnostic attribute of the personified day sign Ahau, cheek spots are also found with Codex Dresden examples of *xib* glyphs (e.g., Dresden pages 29c, 30b, 30c).

Although the codex style dish labels the Classic entity as Chac Xib Chac, he is rarely referred to as Chac Xib Chac in the Classic script. It is thus unwarranted to call all images of the Classic deity as Chac Xib Chac. A more appropriate term for the entity would be the "Classic Chac," the name of the Post-Classic Yucatec counterpart supplied with a temporal qualifier. During the Classic period, the Chac appellative is usually not portrayed with the Ik-eye glyph typical of the Post-Classic codices. Instead, the portrait version is far more common (Figs. 4h, 6e).

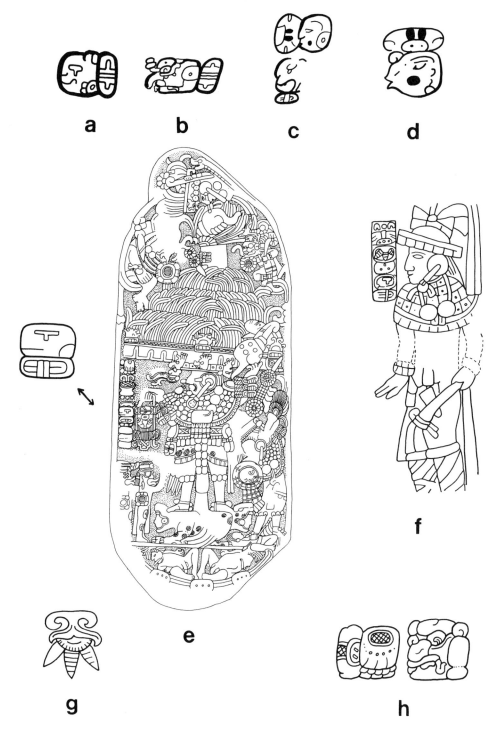

Fig. 4 Classic and Post-Classic examples of Chac appellative phrases.

(a) Late Post-Classic example of Chac name glyph, Paris page 17

(b) Zoomorphic form of Chac appellative with phonetic *ci* complement, Dresden page 32c

(c) Late Classic appellative phrase read as *chac xib chac*, detail of codex style plate (drawn after L. Schele and M. E. Miller 1986: pl. 22)

(d) Late Classic compound read *chac xib* (drawn after Robicsek and Hales 1981: vessel 98)

(e) Chac compound appearing in appellative phrase of Lord Chac of Uxmal, Uxmal Stela 14

(f) Chac impersonator with name phrase probably read *yaxhal chac*, detail of column from Structure 6E1, Chichen Itza (redrawn after Proskouriakoff 1970: fig. 15)

(g) Water lily flower, compare with element in Fig. 4f phrase, from basal register of Lower Temple of the Jaguars, Chichen Itza (redrawn after Maudslay 1889–1902, 3: pl. 48)

(h) Late Classic Chac name phrase containing Imix water lily flower, probably read *yaxha chac*, Lintel 2, Piedras Negras.

Kowalski (1985: note 15) mentions two instances in which an individual glyphically named Chac appears with a large broad-brimmed headdress. The cited examples are Uxmal Stela 14 and a figure from Structure 6E1, Chichen Itza (Figs. 4e–f). In both cases, the Chac appellative is composed of the codical Ik-eye version supplied with the *ci* complement. Dating to approximately the ninth or tenth centuries A.D., these two examples are important transitional forms between the Classic and Post-Classic forms of Chac. The Chichen Itza appellative is preceded by two other compounds constituting part of the same name phrase. The initial compound is composed of the *yax* sign for green superfixed to a T126 *ya* sign, clearly indicating that the first compound is to be read *yax*. The second compound is more unusual and is formed of a curious three-pointed main sign followed by a possible inverted Ahau, providing the phonetic value *la,* and possibly *al.* The same three-pointed glyph also appears in Terminal Classic Cotzumalhualpa epigraphy, here frequently with a coefficient of six (see Parsons 1969, 2: pls. 38a, 41a–b, 52d, 54b, 59a). In the basal relief of the Lower Temple of the Jaguars at Chichen, it can be seen that this sign represents a water lily flower and is thus equivalent to the T501 sign for the day Imix (Fig. 4g). The Chichen phrase appears to be a variant of a common Late Classic Chac appellative composed of a *yax* prefix followed by T501 and ending with the zoomorphic Chac sign (Fig. 4h). David Stuart (personal communication, 1986) notes that the T501 water lily sign can have the phonetic value of *ha,* a Mayan term for water. The "Yax-Imix-Chac" phrase appearing at Chichen Itza and in Late Classic Maya epigraphy is probably to be read *yaxha chac,* or, *yax(h)al chac.*

The broad headdress appearing with the epigraphically named Terminal Classic Chac figures at Uxmal and Chichen Itza is a specific attribute of Chac in the northern Maya lowlands. On Itzimte Stela 12, there is a winged figure with the broad headdress, and in the accompanying text he is named Chac (Fig. 5b). Aside from appearing at Chichen Itza, Uxmal, and Itzimte, this headdress is also present on Oxkintok Stela 12 and in the mural paintings at Mulchic (Figs. 5a, 8a). Although the broad headdress is largely limited to Terminal Classic and Early Post-Classic mural paintings and sculpture, the curious paper or cloth cap occasionally worn by Chac in the Codex Dresden may well derive from this device (see Dresden pages 31a, 31b, 33a). Like many of the cited examples, the Dresden cap is crenelated and topped with one or more horizontal bow knots.

A great many Classic and Early Post-Classic Chac figures have snakes held or dangling from their mouths (Figs. 5a, 5c–d, 6c–e, 8a). One example, from the Lower Temple of the Jaguars at Chichen Itza, bites the snake in midsection, with the head and tail hanging from the front and side of the face (Fig. 5d). In placement, this is quite similar to the two devices frequently curling out of the mouths of the Dresden Chacs (Fig. 6a). Although the mouth elements depicted in the Codex Dresden may no longer represent serpents, Chac is frequently depicted with snakes in the Dresden and Madrid codices (Fig. 6a). Fewkes (1894: 266) long ago suggested that snakes appearing with God B may represent lightning. However, due to an admitted lack of supportive evidence, Fewkes preferred to consider the snake as a generalized symbol of moisture, thus siding with the Kukulcan identification of God B proposed by Schellhas.

In his tentative identification of Maya serpents with lightning, Fewkes relied principally upon ethnographic data of the American Southwest. However, there is widespread evidence that snakes are widely identified with lightning in the Maya region both in the pre-Hispanic era and the ethnographic present. Citing Lenkersdorf (1979) and Montejo (1984), Joanne Spero (1987: 172) states that among the contemporary Jacaltec and Tojolabal Maya, lightning is considered as a fire serpent. Similarly, the serpents appearing with the Classic Chac frequently have a pair of smoke or flame volutes emerging from their mouths (Figs. 5c, 6d–e). Although these volutes may at times resemble serpent tongues, they are identical to the fiery volutes emerging from the forehead of God K (Figs. 32a–b, 34a, 37a). This is an icono-

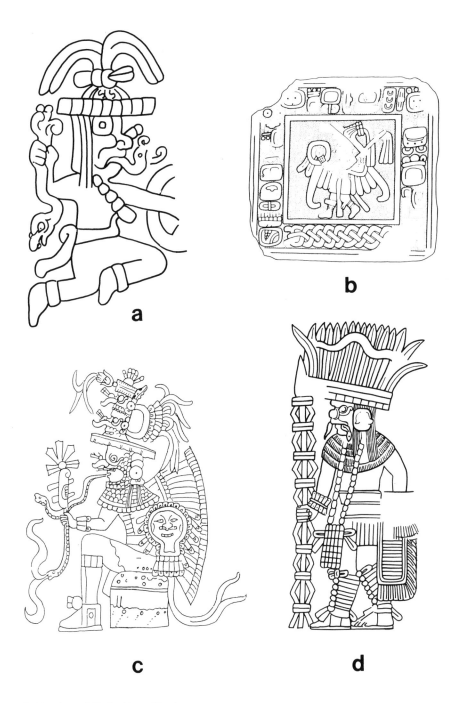

Fig. 5   Terminal Classic and Early Post-Classic representations of Chac with broad headdress.

(a) Chac with shield and burning serpent; note snake in mouth, Stela 12, Oxkintok (redrawn after Mayer 1984: pl. 1)

(b) Figure with wings and Chac headdress, name glyph of Chac at lower left, Itzimte Stela 12 (after von Euw 1977, 4: 29; courtesy of the Peabody Museum of Archaeology and Ethnology)

(c) Chac impersonator holding shield and burning serpent axe; note snake emerging from mouth; Temple of Chac Mool, Chichen Itza (redrawn after Morris, Charlot, and Morris 1931: fig. 305)

(d) Armed Chac grasping snake in mouth, Lower Temple of the Jaguars, Chichen Itza (redrawn after Maudslay 1889–1902, 3: pl. 48, and photographs by author).

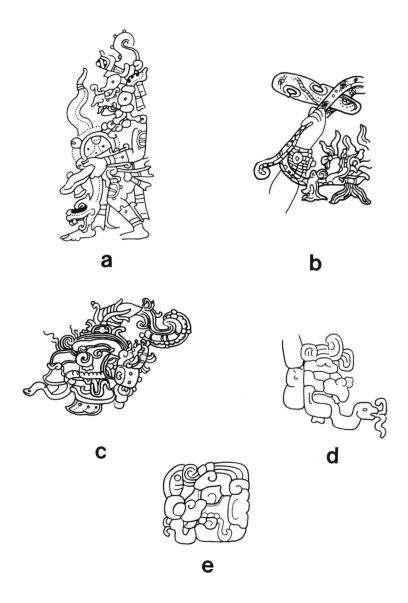

a

b

c

d

e

Fig. 6 Representations of Chac with lightning serpents.

(a) Chac as warrior with spear, shield, and lightning serpent, Dresden page 66a
(b) Detail of Chac impersonator wielding serpent lightning axe; note flame emerging from mouth of snake; Dumbarton Oaks Tablet
(c) Detail of Classic Chac from Early Classic modeled and incised vessel, note serpent in mouth (drawn after Coe 1982: 71)
(d) Classic Chac with burning serpent in mouth, detail of belt assemblage of Early Classic ruler, Yaxha Stela 4 (drawn after Maler 1908–10, pl. 16.1)
(e) Classic Chac with serpent in mouth, Lintel 35, Yaxchilan (redrawn after Graham 1979, 3: 79).

graphic form of the T122 affix, regarded as a sign for smoke or flame (e.g., Stuart 1987b: 10). In Central Mexican codices, Tlaloc is frequently found with lightning serpents (e.g., Borgia pages 27, 28; Vaticanus B pages 43–48). Esther Pasztory (1974: 7) mentions that the identification of Tlaloc with lightning serpents was also present at Classic Teotihuacan. Seler (1963, 2: 34) and others (e.g., Anders 1963: 141; Bernal 1965: 2), have noted that the Central Mexican Xiuhcoatl fire serpent can refer to lightning as well as fire.

As with Tlaloc of Central Mexico, the axe was and continues to be another lightning symbol of Chac (see J. Thompson 1970b: 253). In the Codex Dresden, God B may be found wielding both serpents and axes (e.g., Fig. 6a). At times, the flaming serpent and the Chac lightning axe are conflated into a single object (Figs. 5c, 6b, 35a). In the following discussion of God K, it will be seen that this composite object is actually the manikin scepter commonly wielded by Classic Maya rulers.

The Classic and Post-Classic identification of Chac with lightning is entirely consistent with lightning terminology appearing in Colonial and contemporary Mayan languages. A common contemporary Yucatec statement for lightning is *tun lelem chaac,* or "Chac is flashing" (Taube 1983 fieldnotes). In the seventeenth-century Moran dictionary of Manche Chol, *uleem chahac* is glossed as "resplandor de rayo." J. Eric S. Thompson (1970b: 251) notes that among the contemporary Chol in the region of Palenque, Chac is identical to lightning. Thus in contemporary Chol, *xojob chajc* is the term for the flash of lightning (Aulie and Aulie 1978: 176). In the sixteenth-century de Ara dictionary of Tzeltal, *chahuc* is translated as "rayo o trueno" (Humberto Ruz 1986: 265). Similarly, in Tzotzil, thunder and lightning are referred to as *čauk* (Laughlin 1975: 463).

Michael Coe (1978: 76) is the first to provide a detailed argument that one long-snouted Classic entity, frequently appearing with a long top-knot and a spondylus shell earpiece, is an ancestral form of the Post-Classic Yucatec Chac. Although Coe suggested that the Classic deity was a prototype of the Post-Classic god, he proposed the more non-committal term of *Rain Beast.* Due to the *chac-xib-chac* reading, David Stuart has established that this Classic deity was actually named Chac.

Possibly by the beginnings of the Early Classic period, the Classic entity was phonetically known as *chac.* Stuart (1987a) has pointed out an interesting allograph of the T109 *chac* sign, an inverted bone jaw crossed with a series of parallel lines. In his study, Stuart is primarily concerned with historical names appearing in hieroglyphic texts. However, this jaw device also occurs in Early Classic iconography. It appears as part of the back belt assemblage worn by an especially early representation of Chac (Fig. 35a). Directly below the inverted jaw *chac* sign there is a peccary head marked with a trefoil element in the eye. A similar Early Classic peccary—again with the trefoil eye element—may be seen on Tikal Stela 26. In both Yucatec and Cakchiquel, *ak* (*ac*) is the term for peccary (Barrera Vásquez 1980: 4; Coto 1983: 446, LXXXIV). Similarly, *aq* in Quiche refers to "pig" (Edmonson 1965: 1). The Kekchi term for peccary is *chacou* or *chacuo* (Sedat 1955: 227). As either *chac* or more probably *ac,* the Early Classic peccary head serves as a phonetic complement to reinforce the *chac* reading. Together, the inverted bone jaw and peccary head beltpiece form the name of Chac, the god of rain and lightning.

Chac is one of the oldest known gods in the Maya pantheon and can be traced back to the beginnings of Classic Maya civilization. Rafael Girard (1966: 40) notes that Chac is prominently displayed in Izapa Stela 1, a monument dating to the Late Preclassic period (ca. 100 B.C.–A.D. 100). The figure appears with a thick, downward curving snout and a large top knot of hair, features commonly found with later Classic examples of Chac (Fig. 7a). In addition, he wears a serpent belt. Although not a common feature, serpent belts are also worn by Classic Chacs (see Taube 1986: fig. 4). Some sort of fluid spews in a broad fan out of the mouth of the Stela 1 Chac. In Late Classic vessel scenes, Chac can also be found spewing liquid, or vomiting (e.g., Fig. 37e). In a modern Yucatec *ch'a chaac* rain ceremony recorded by John Sosa (1985: 386), falling rain is metaphorically described as vomit. Izapa Stela 1

a

b

Fig. 7 Late Preclassic and Protoclassic representations of Chac.

(a) Chac engaged in fishing, note serpent belt, Izapa Stela 1 (drawn after Norman 1973: pls. 1, 2)

(b) Chac with lightning axe on flint blade tail of fire serpent, detail of Protoclassic Hauberg Stela (redrawn after L. Schele and M. E. Miller 1986: pl. 66).

suggests that as early as the Late Preclassic era, falling rain may have been considered as the vomit of Chac.

Linda Schele and Mary Ellen Miller (1986: 191) note another early instance of Chac, here upon the Protoclassic Hauberg Stela, dating to approximately the second or third century A.D. (Fig. 7b). This example also possesses the zoomorphic snout and large top knot and, in addition, wears a pointed headpiece, evidently an early form of the shell element cresting the head of the Classic Chac. He also has a beardlike device bracketing the cheek and chin, and it is probable that this is an antecedent of the long, fishlike barbel curling down the cheek of the Classic Chac. The Hauberg Chac wields an axe, an especially important attribute because it reveals that by the

Protoclassic period, the stone axe was the lightning weapon of Chac.

Although possessing a long anthropomorphic nose rather than a thick zoomorphic snout, the codical God B shares many characteristics with the Classic Chac. Michael Coe (1978) notes that along with being quadripartite, both are identified with fishing. In the Codex Dresden, God B may be found fishing or grasping fish (see Dresden pages 44a, 44c). Coe compares the fishing Chac on Izapa Stela 1 to the Late Classic fishing scenes found upon certain of the incised bones of Tikal Burial 116. A contemporary Tzeltal belief provides a rationale for the identification of Chac with fishing. In the town of Quaquitepec, San Angel is the god of fishing as well as lightning. The reason for this association is based on actual observation; when the thunderbolt strikes water, one only has to gather the dead and stunned fish (Maurer-Avalos 1979: 223).

Both the Classic and Post-Classic Chacs are closely identified with war. The lightning axe wielded by these figures is frequently portrayed as a battle weapon. Thus, in the Classic and Post-Classic periods, a shield often accompanies the lightning axe (see mural of South Wall, Mulchic; Dresden pages 65a, 66a, 37c; Madrid page 33a). In the battle scene of Bonampak Lintel 3, the victorious ruler wears the Classic Chac in his headdress (see Mathews 1980: fig. 7). Stela 14 of Uxmal is one of the most graphic representations of Chac as conqueror (Fig. 4e). Here Lord Chac is portrayed as his deity namesake, wearing the broad headdress and grasping an axe and conch, the latter a probable instrument of thunder. Below him are three supine and slain captives undoubtedly taken in conquest.

Sacrifice, frequently the result of war, is yet another trait shared between the Classic and Post-Classic forms of Chac. In a number of Late Classic vessel scenes, the Classic Chac sacrifices a jaguar infant upon a Cauac zoomorph altar (Fig. 8b). Although Lounsbury (1985) and others have interpreted this as the *Popol Vuh* sacrifice of Xbalanque by Hunahpu, the scene actually refers to the role of Chac as executioner. A similar scene is found in the mural painting at Mulchic, where a procession of Chac figures flank Cauac altars (Fig. 8a). A smoking figure, possibly an insect, tops the Mulchic altar, and this figure is probably a version of the smoking insect found in a number of the vessel scenes (e.g., Fig. 8b). However, although the Mulchic scenes depict Chac, the smoking insect, and the Cauac altar, there is no reference to the jaguar infant—an integral part of the *Popol Vuh* interpretation.

A series of Chacs brandishing axes also appears on the circumference of Labna Altar 1 (see Proskouriakoff 1950: fig. 93e). It is likely that these low cylindrical columns, found widely in the Puuc region, served as sacrificial altars. As such, they are probably the actual corollaries of the Cauac zoomorph altars appearing in Late Classic scenes. The identification of Chac with

sacrifice was widespread in Post-Classic times, and it will be recalled that the assistants of human sacrifices were called Chacs (Landa, in Tozzer 1941: 119). According to Landa (Tozzer 1941: 112–113), the principal executioner was the Nacom. J. Eric S. Thompson (1938: 596) notes the similarity of this term to Macon, the Manche Chol god of lightning.

One major question that remains is the relation between the Classic Chac and GI of the Palenque Triad. Although first identified in the texts of Palenque by Heinrich Berlin (1963), GI is widely represented in both Early and Late Classic Maya epigraphy and art. Many of the features described by M. Coe for the Rain Beast are also found with GI, to such a degree that one could consider them as aspects of the same deity. In terms of physical attributes, each may have fish barbels upon the cheek. For the zoomorphic and anthropomorphic Chac figures, these elements tend to be long, like the "whiskers" of catfish (Figs. 7a, 8b). For GI, the barbels tend to be short, broad, and generally finlike (Fig. 9a). Along with similar cheek elements, both gods frequently wear a knotted belt device (e.g., Fig. 8b). When GI appears on Classic polychrome vessels, he is found in contexts similar to that of Chac. Thus in one vessel scene he is portrayed fishing (see M. Coe 1978: vase 12). Another vessel portrays GI seated in a swirl of smoke and flames holding an eccentric flint, possibly an allusion to lightning (see M. Coe 1975: 14). Thus, although the actual mythical role of GI is still poorly understood, this entity does share both physical and thematic traits with the Classic Chac.

Several Late Preclassic masks suggest that GI is also identified with rain and lightning and indicate that GI and Cocijo, the Zapotec god of lightning, derive from a single source. A stone mask attributed to Late Preclassic Veracruz displays attributes of both Cocijo and GI (Fig. 9b). Thus the mask possesses the brow piece of Cocijo—Zapotec Glyph C—along with the barbel cheek markings of GI. In fact, many of the early Monte Alban II depictions of Cocijo exhibit GI barbels (Fig. 9c). An Early Classic greenstone mask attributed to the Peten site of Rio Azul seems to reveal

a

b

Fig. 8 Chac as sacrificer.

(a) Chac with axe and shield above smoking insect and Cauac altar, detail of Late Classic mural, Mulchic (redrawn after Piña Chan 1964: fig. 2)

(b) Anthropomorphic Chac sacrificing jaguar infant on Cauac altar; note insect with cigar at far right (after Coe 1973: 99).

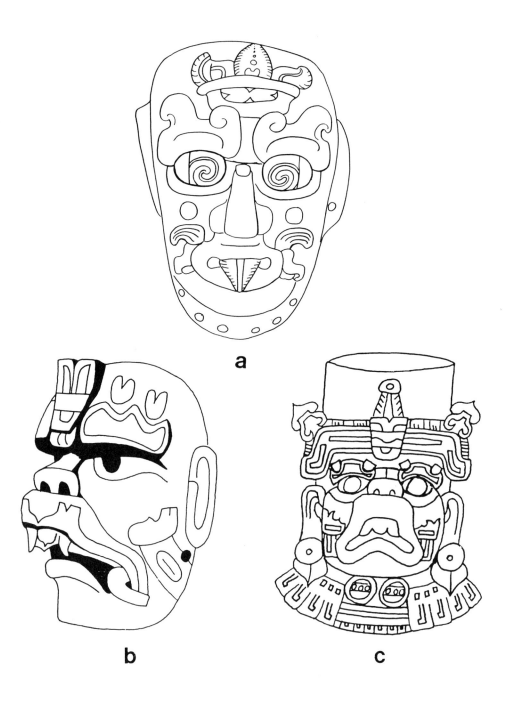

a

b

c

Fig. 9 Comparison of fish barbels found on GI and early representations of Cocijo.

(a) Early Classic greenstone mask reportedly from Rio Azul (redrawn after Berjonneau et al. 1985: pl. 326)

(b) Stone mask of Cocijo reportedly from Veracruz (after Joralemon 1971: fig. 180)

(c) Monte Alban II urn representing Cocijo; note cheek elements (after Joralemon 1971: fig. 179).

an interesting stage in the divergent evolution of the Maya and Zapotec gods (Fig. 9a). Here the brow is marked not with the bowl-like form of Zapotec Glyph C, but the Maya Quadripartite Badge, three elements placed in a *kin*-marked bowl. In view of the many similarities shared between the Rio Azul and Veracruz masks, it is possible that the Quadripartite Badge and the Zapotec Glyph C derive from a single Late Formative iconographic element.

Summary

One of the oldest known gods in the Maya pantheon, God B can be traced in the Maya region to at least the Late Preclassic period. Representations of this deity are extremely common in Classic Maya iconography. Accompanying Classic epigraphy provides conclusive evidence that the Classic being was known phonetically as Chac, the same name found with the Post-Classic and contemporary Maya god. From the Late Preclassic and Protoclassic to the ethnographic present, Chac has been considered as a lightning god. Among the most common emblems of his lightning powers are serpents and hafted stone axes. Consonant with his association with one of the most violent and powerful forces in nature, Chac was closely identified with war and human sacrifice.

God C

Writing more than eighty years ago, Schellhas (1904: 19, 20) notes that God C is among the least understood deities appearing in the Maya codices:

This is one of the most remarkable and difficult figures in the Maya manuscripts, and shows, at the same time, how imperfect must be the information we have received in regard to the Maya mythology, since from the frequency of his representations he is obviously one of the most important deities and yet can be identified with none of the representations of gods handed down to us.

Despite the ensuing years, this account still holds true today. Even the physical appearance of God C defies clear identification (Fig. 10). Although Fewkes (1894: 272) regards the features of God C

as those of a snake, most have interpreted the face as simian (e.g., Förstemann 1898; Schellhas 1904; Kelley 1976; Ringle 1988). In truth, the slightly anthropomorphic face of God C does not closely resemble any living creature. Moreover, his characteristics do not belie a close relation to any animal or quality of the natural world. It has long been suggested that God C is the deity of the North Star (Schellhas 1904; Morley, Brainerd, and Sharer 1983: 475), but this identification is unwarranted. The primary evidence for an association with the North Star is the reputed presence of the God C glyph in the sign for north. However, in the Codex Dresden, the most carefully painted of the Maya manuscripts, the God C glyph never serves as the main sign for north. Although possessing the same forehead bracket, the head in the compound for north lacks the small round nose and mouth of God C, which resemble two stacked balls. Schellhas (1904: 21) notes that on Dresden pages 29c to 30c the same head serving for north is associated with all four directions. This sign (T1008) has the phonetic value *xib* (see Justeson 1984: 360). In the Dresden text, it forms part of the appellatives *zac-xib-chac*, *ek-xib-chac*, *kan-xib-chac*, and *chac-xib-chac*, these being specific names provided by Landa (Tozzer 1941: note 638).

Epigraphically, God C can be traced back as early as the Protoclassic period, that is, to the second and third centuries A.D. Although William Ringle (1988: fig. 2) mentions a possible Late Preclassic epigraphic example of God C on Kaminaljuyu Stela 10, James Porter (personal communication, 1988) notes that the drawing on which this interpretation is based is inaccurate. According to Porter, who has made a rubbing of the monument, the actual glyph does not represent God C or any other deity portrait, but rather is an abstract sign. Clear examples of God C portrait glyphs appear on the Protoclassic Hauberg Stela and on a roughly contemporaneous bone awl from Kichpanha, Belize (Figs. 11a–b). Although earlier, these examples are quite similar to glyphs of God C appearing on the Early Classic Tikal Stela 31 (Fig. 11c).

Although the earliest epigraphic forms of God

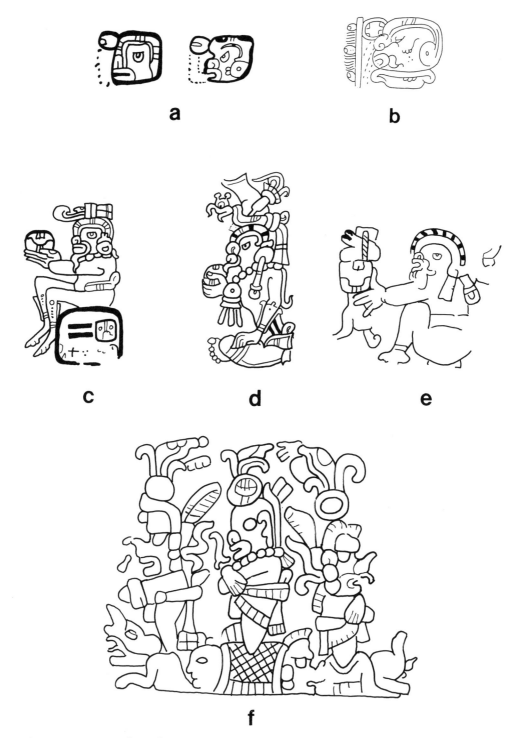

Fig. 10 God C in Maya epigraphy and art.

(a) Codical examples of God C with water group prefix, Madrid page 50c, Dresden page 13b

(b) Classic glyphic compound with head of God C,
probably read *ah ku na* (redrawn after J. A. Graham 1971: pl. 1)

(c) God C holding *kan* sign tamale, Madrid page 50c

(d) God C with *kan* sign tamale, Dresden page 13b

(e) Mural from Tancah Structure 44 (after A. G. Miller
1982: pl. 12)

(f) God C rising out of turtle carapace; bas-relief on
round column from Uxmal (redrawn after Pollock 1980: fig. 468, and rubbing courtesy of Merle
Greene Robertson).

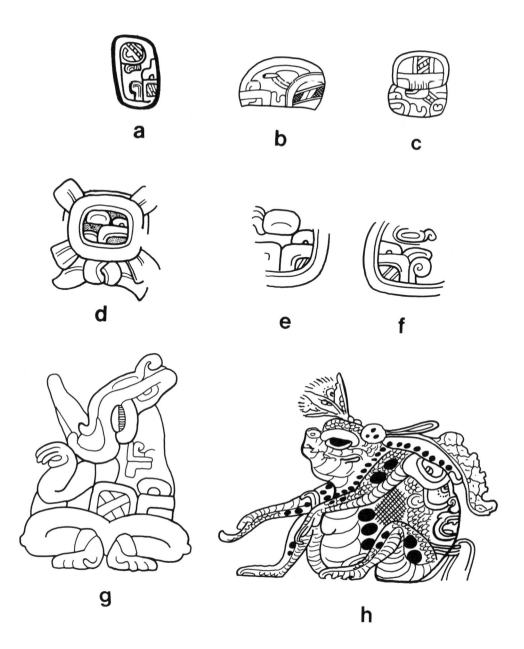

Fig. 11 Representations of God C in Late Preclassic and Classic Maya art.

(a) Protoclassic God C portrait glyph from text on carved bone lancet, Kichpanha, Belize (redrawn after Houston 1989b: 21)

(b) Protoclassic God C portrait glyph from Hauberg Stela (redrawn after L. Schele and M. E. Miller 1986: pl. 66)

(c) Early Classic example of God C glyph, Tikal Stela 31 (redrawn after Jones and Satterthwaite 1982: fig. 52)

(d) Late Preclassic God C face in probable mirror, Kaminaljuyu Altar 9 (redrawn after Parsons 1986: fig. 140)

(e,f) Late Preclassic God C faces on chest of Principal Bird Deity, details from Kaminaljuyu Altars 9 and 10 (redrawn after Parsons 1986: figs. 140, 141)

(g) Late Preclassic squatting toad with God C face on back, Izapa Stela 11 (drawn after Norman 1973: pl. 22)

(h) Late Classic Uinal Toad with God C face on back (drawn after Coe 1978: vessel 3).

C are limited to the Protoclassic period, God C faces are fairly common in earlier Late Preclassic Maya iconography. Several examples can be observed on Kaminaljuyu Altars 9 and 10, which present nearly identical images of the Principal Bird Deity, the Late Preclassic and Classic prototype of Vucub Caquix, the monster bird of the *Popol Vuh* (Figs. 11d–f). The faces appear on the chest of the bird, and in a cartouche on the more intact Altar 9. Supplied with four tab-like elements, the device is notably similar to the Akbal medallion worn on the brow of the Principal Bird Deity occurring on Altar 10. In the discussion of God D, it will be seen that the Akbal medallion represents a mirror, and it is likely that the Kaminaljuyu cartouche is also a mirror.

During the Classic period, God C faces are frequently placed on the bodies of supernaturals; they are especially common on the back of the Uinal Toad, the patron of the period of twenty days (Fig. 11h). Stela 11 of Late Preclassic Izapa displays an especially early example of this convention (Fig. 11g). Here a God C face appears on the back of a squatting toad.

During the Late Preclassic and Classic periods, God C seems to function more as a condensed symbolic sign than a deity with his own personality and mythic cycle. Representations are almost entirely limited to the face, and Classic depictions of God C with a body are extremely rare. Thus, although God C may appear in Late Classic vessel scenes, he is usually attached to a tree or other object. In GI of the Supplementary Series, God C appears as a water group compound held in a hand prefixed by the coefficient of nine. In both Classic inscriptions and the Post-Classic codices, God C is an important component of the water group (Figs. 10a–b). A number of scholars have identified the water group as a sign for blood (Seler 1902–23, 3: 649; Barthel 1968: 168; Stuart 1984). As an entity identified with such varied items as maize offerings, growing trees, stone blades, mirrors, and blood, God C seems to represent an abstract quality or concept, such as preciousness, life, or divinity.

There is a strong possibility that God C represents godliness or divinity. In Classic and Post-

Classic epigraphy, the God C water group often precedes the name of particular gods. On the Vase of the Seven Gods, this compound introduces the appellative of each of the seven deities (M. Coe 1973: no. 49). This pattern also occurs commonly in the Codex Madrid (e.g., Madrid pages 83b–84b, 105a). Thomas Barthel (1952: 94) originally suggested that T1016, the epigraphic form of God C, possesses the phonetic value of *ku* or *ch'u,* terms signifying god or sacredness in Yucatec and Cholan Mayan languages, respectively. This reading was based on the gloss provided by Landa for the month Cumku, in which the month sign is preceded by a complementary phonetic compound composed of T528 and T1016. Together, the glyphs may be read *cuku,* a close gloss for Cumku. With this reading, the T1016 God C sign corresponds to the phonetic value *ku,* the Yucatec term for god. John Carlson (personal communication, 1987) and David Stuart (cited in Ringle 1988) have independently arrived at similar conclusions regarding Landa's gloss of the month Cumku, and there is growing consensus among epigraphers that T1016 has the value of *ku* or *ch'u,* with God C referring to sacredness or divinity. The most thorough published discussion of this argument is to be found in Ringle (1988).

The use of God C as a generalized concept of divinity may explain the presence of this figure on many disparate objects. For example, Stephen Houston (personal communication, 1982) notes that the bowl-like object held by the aged goddess on Dresden page 42a is a mirror (Fig. 52a). In the center of the device, corresponding to the face of the mirror, there is the face of God C. The presence of God C may serve to mark the concept of sacredness, in this case labeling the mirror as an instrument of divination. A more compelling case occurs on Dresden pages 8c and 35a, where diminutive God C figures appear in temple structures. Because God C is not mentioned in either of the accompanying texts, it does not appear that he had a central role in the scenes; rather, he may serve to complement the particular structure depicted. In Yucatec, the common word for temple is *ku* (Barrera Vásquez 1980: 416).

Summary

Rather than being a specific deity with its own mythic cycle, God C appears to embody the ancient Maya concept of godliness. Beginning as early as the Late Preclassic period, he is commonly found as a profile face on inanimate objects and the bodies of supernaturals. During the Classic and Post-Classic periods, there is phonetic evidence that the epigraphic form of God C, T1016, has the phonetic value of *ku* or *ch'u,* Mayan terms for sacredness. Although full-figure forms of God C are relatively common during the Post-Classic period, they do not appear in narrative contexts. Instead, the god frequently presents or receives offerings or appears with temples and other toponyms. In many of these Post-Classic instances, he may function either to express a generalized concept of godliness or to qualify the sacredness of an offering, structure, or place.

God D

God D is one of the most important and perhaps *the* major god of the Classic and Post-Classic Maya pantheon (Fig. 12). Schellhas (1904: 22–23) points out two important attributes of this deity; he is invariably aged and often possesses the T24.533:24 Ahau title of rulership. Although a number of early investigators correctly identify the codical God D as Itzamna (e.g., Seler 1887b; Fewkes 1895), Schellhas considers him a god of the moon and night. The moon interpretation was partly based on the conventional name glyph of God D, an aged face prefixed by a device containing the Akbal sign, a symbol of blackness and night (Figs. 12a–b). However, it is probable that this serves as a phonetic device providing the value *itz,* the first portion of the Itzamna appellative.

Although Michael Coe (1978: 46) originally isolated the identifying attributes of God D on Classic Maya ceramics, Nicholas Hellmuth (see 1987: 303–312) was the first to recognize this entity as the Classic form of God D. Like the Post-Classic codical representations, the Classic period deity usually has a tasseled Akbal device upon the brow, the same form occurring as the Akbal pre-

fix (T152) of the Classic and Post-Classic God D appellative (Figs. 12g–h). One of the earliest examples of the forehead element appears in a possible portrait glyph of God D on the Protoclassic Hauberg Stela, although in this case the tasseled device lacks the Akbal infix (Fig. 12e). An Early Classic example of the device appears on Tikal Stela 26, there worn by a figure holding a probable hoofed peccary (Fig. 12d). Although the face of the figure resembles God C as well as God D, the squint eye and the tasseled Akbal device both point to God D. The peccary probably also refers to God D, since Itzamna appears with the creature in other Classic scenes (Fig. 12g; see L. Schele and M. E. Miller 1986: 55; Hellmuth 1987: 235).

In Classic epigraphy, the T152 Akbal device occurs with personal names, such as Ruler 2 of Dos Pilas, and Shield Jaguar of Yaxchilan (Figs. 13a–b). In the case of Shield Jaguar, this element is generally interpreted as a shield. However, the tasseled Akbal is almost identical to T151, which has been interpreted as a belt ornament (see Justeson 1984: 151). The center of T151 contains the *nen* mirror sign, and clearly this affix represents a Maya version of the Central Mexican *tezcacuitlapilli*—back mirrors attached at the belt. Save for the beaded edge and the Akbal center, T152 is identical to T151, and it is likely that this sign also represents a mirror. The beaded or segmented edge is frequently found on Classic Central Mexican mirrors (see Berjonneau et al. 1985: pl. 172).

On La Pasadita Lintel 2, Bird Jaguar wears a belt piece composed of a human head with a jaguar headdress. The beaded medallion appears on the jaguar forehead; in this case, it is the *nen* mirror, here emanating some sort of vegetal smoke (Fig. 13c). Linda Schele and Mary Ellen Miller (1986: pl. 76) equate the medallion with the Akbal "shield" and suggest that the belt assemblage represents Shield Jaguar. The Akbal sign is also worn as a back mirror. An Early Classic shell carving depicts the Akbal device worn at the small of the back, precisely where *tezcacuitlapilli* are placed (Fig. 13d). Bird Jaguar wears an almost identical device on Yaxchilan Lintel 17, although there the

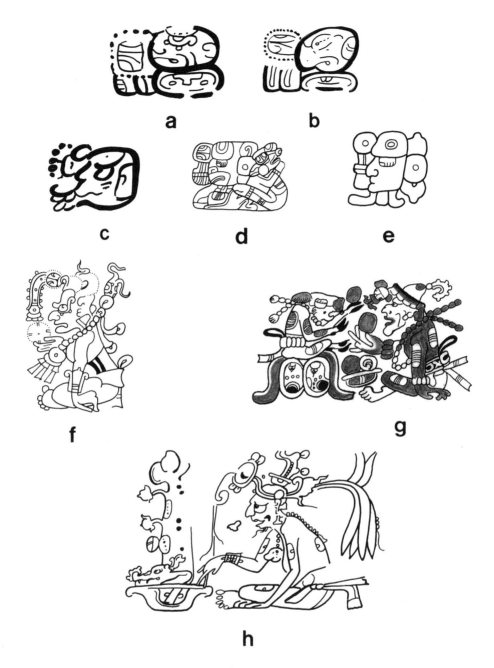

Fig. 12 Classic and Post-Classic representations of God D.

(a,b) Codical versions of God D name glyph; Paris page 11, Dresden page 28c

(c) Classic form of God D appellative (drawn after Robicsek and Hales 1981: vessel 109)

(d) Early Classic face of God D with face of God C holding peccary, Tikal Stela 26 (redrawn after Jones and Satterthwaite 1982: fig. 44)

(e) Possible Protoclassic representation of God D, detail of Hauberg Stela (redrawn after L. Schele and M. E. Miller 1986: pl. 66)

(f) Codical example of God D, Dresden page 15c

(g) Classic representation of God D with peccary, detail of Tepeu 1 vessel (drawn after roll-out photograph courtesy of Justin Kerr)

(h) God D with caiman tree, detail of Late Classic codex style vessel (drawn after Robicsek and Hales 1981: vessel 108).

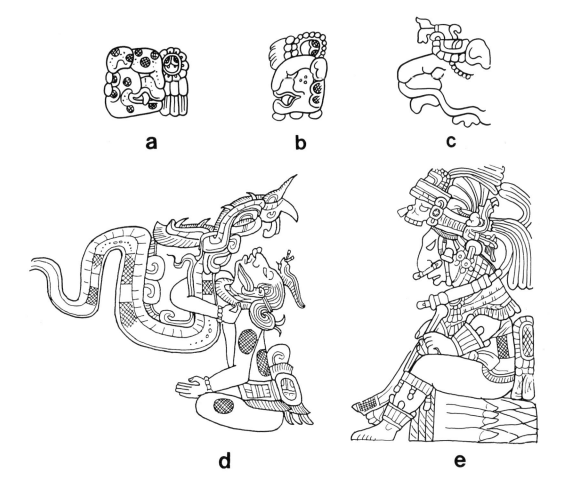

Fig. 13 The God D "shield," an obsidian mirror.

(a) Name glyph of Shield Jaguar of Yaxchilan, Yaxchilan Lintel 25 (redrawn after I. Graham and E. von Euw 1977, 3: 55)

(b) Shield Jaguar appellative, Yaxchilan Lintel 23 (redrawn after I. Graham 1982, 3: 136)

(c) Jaguar with mirror on forehead, possible reference to Shield Jaguar (redrawn after L. Schele and M. E. Miller 1986: pl. 76)

(d) Spotted Headband Twin wearing Akbal back mirror (drawing by L. Schele, after L. Schele and M. E. Miller 1986: pl. 121)

(e) Bird Jaguar wearing back mirror, Yaxchilan Lintel 17 (redrawn after I. Graham and E. von Euw 1977, 3: 43).

Akbal sign is replaced by crosshatching, another means of representing black or darkness (Fig. 13e). Schele (L. Schele and J. Miller 1983: 14) suggests that the *nen* and Akbal signs seem to be in complementary opposition in reference to mirrors, the former representing a bright shining mirror and the latter, a "dark or obsidian mirror." The Akbal medallion (T512) of God D represents an obsidian mirror, a device used for divinatory scrying.

In ancient Mesoamerica, stone mirrors of pyrite, obsidian, hematite, and other materials were widely used in scrying. The term *itz* means divination or witchcraft in Colonial Yucatec (Barrera Vásquez 1980: 271, 272), Cakchiquel (Coto 1983: 268), and Pokomchi (Miles 1957: 751). Barrera Vásquez (1980: 272) tentatively translates *itzam* as "brujo o mago de agua," further noting that the root *na* signifies to contemplate, understand, or divine in a number of Mayan languages. In Mesoamerica, divinatory scrying was often performed with reflective pools of water as well as mirrors (Taube 1983: 112–113). In the *Motul Dictionary*, *nenba* is glossed as "mirarse al espejo, o en agua" (Barrera Vásquez 1980: 565). It is also noteworthy that *nen,* the Yucatec word for mirror, is present in the expression *nen ol,* signifying to "consider" or "contemplate," the same general meaning that Barrera Vásquez (1980: 565) provides for *na.*

The term *itz* present in the name of Itzamna may be a Nahua loan word. In Classical Nahuatl, the root *itz* carries the meaning of both divination and obsidian. Thus, whereas obsidian is referred to as *itztetl* or *itzli, itzpopolhuia* signifies "predecir, anunciar lo por venir," and *itztimotlalia,* "mirar, observar, considerar una cosa, premeditar, reflexionar sobre lo que se debe hacer" (Siméon 1977: 210–211). The Nahuatl meanings of "foretell" or "contemplate" are virtually identical to the cited Mayan meanings of *itz.* In Central Mexico, mirrors were frequently fashioned from obsidian. Thus an important attribute of Tezcatlipoca, the "smoking mirror," was the round obsidian mirror. During the Classic period, Teotihuacan was a major obsidian source for both Central Mexico and the Maya region. The presence of the *itz* obsidian mirror in the headdress and appellative glyph of the Classic God D suggests that this may be an especially early loan.

Although it is a mirror plaque, the headdress device of God D also resembles a flower with a long outpouring stream (Figs. 12f–h). In the iconography of Teotihuacan, mirrors are frequently compared to flowers (Taube n.d.a). However, among the Maya, the identification may be partly phonetic. In Yucatec, *itz* also signifies dew, semen, tears, resin, and other exuding liquids (Barrera Vásquez 1980: 271–272); the dew or nectar of flowers well accords with this meaning of *itz.* In a petition for abundant crops recorded in the *Relación de Kanpocolche y Chochola,* Itzamna is referred to as "señor grande del cielo y que estás puesto en las nubes y en el cielo" (de la Garza et al. 1983, 2: 323). Lizana mentions a similar text regarding Itzamat Ul: "I am the *itz* (dew or substance) of heaven, I am the *itz* of the clouds" (translation by Thompson 1939: 152). The dew

collected from plants was afforded great respect by the Post-Classic Yucatec. The *Relación de Valladolid* states that during the benediction of a temple, the *Ah kin* aspersed dew previously gathered from leaves (de la Garza et al. 1983, 2: 38).

The *Relación de Valladolid* (de la Garza et al. 1983, 2: 38) also mentions that, during a temple benediction, the Yucatec priest wore an alb, chasuble, and miter, and scattered dew (*itz*) with a hyssop. These same elements are mentioned in the following account of fire walking, although here there are important additional details. The "hyssop" is now described as having serpent tails, "un hisopo atadas en el muchas colas de víbora y culebras ponzoñosas" (de la Garza et al. 1983, 2: 39). Landa (in Tozzer 1941: 105) also mentions a serpent aspergillum carried by the priest during baptism; "in his hand he carried an *aspergillum* made of a short stick finely worked, and for the hairs or bristles of the hyssop there were certain tails of serpents which are like rattlesnakes." It is possible that the small, drilled jade rattlesnake-tail pendants from the Sacred Cenote at Chichen Itza were parts of serpent-tailed aspergilla (for examples, see Coggins and Shane 1984: no. 141).

Tozzer (1941: note 480) mentions that the serpent aspergillum is represented on page 100d and 111b of the Codex Madrid. It also appears on Madrid pages 60c and 106a. In these two instances, and on Madrid Page 100d, God D holds the object (Figs. 14a–c). A markedly similar scene occurs at Santa Rita, where God D again appears with the snake aspergillum (Fig. 14d). Whereas *itz* signifies "dew" in Yucatec, *tzitz* signifies "to bless" or "sprinkle." Moreover, the word for hyssop or aspergillum is *tzitzab* (Barrera Vásquez 1980: 862). The Yucatec term *tzab* means "rattlesnake tail," thus *tzitzab,* or *tzitz tzab,* is probably the term for the serpent-tailed aspergillum.

At Santa Rita and in the three Madrid scenes, God D wears a tall cylindrical headdress, probably the priestly "miter" mentioned in the *Relación de Valladolid* (Fig. 14). In the Codex Madrid, God D is represented no less than fourteen times with the miter of the *Ah Kin.* An excellent in-the-round representation of God D wearing the miter can be seen on a Chen Mul effigy censer illus-

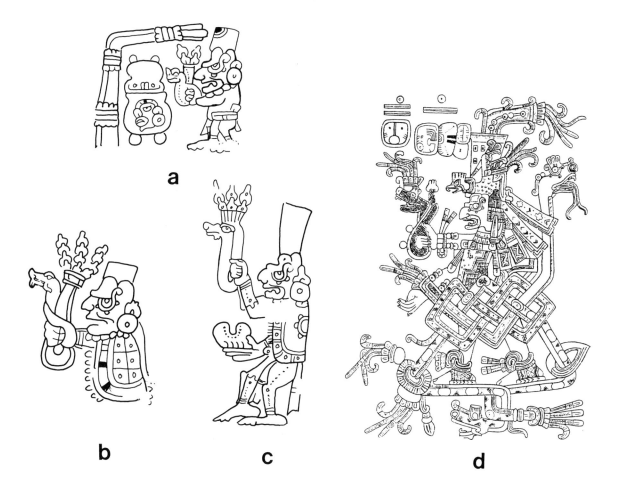

a

b   **c**   **d**

Fig. 14   Late Post-Classic representations of God D in office of priest with "miter," "chasuble," and *tzitzab* snake "hyssop."

(a) God D with miter and aspergillum, God C in *olla* possibly refers to sacred water, Madrid page 100d

(b) God D with aspergillum, miter, and chasuble, Madrid page 60c

(c) God D with aspergillum, miter, and chasuble, *imix* sign in hand may refer to water to be aspersed, Madrid page 106a

(d) God D as priest, detail of mural from Mound 1 of Santa Rita (after Gann 1900: pl. XXX).

trated by Smith (1971: fig. 32k).[2] In the Codex Madrid, God D also frequently wears an ornamented back cape, the probable "chasuble" described in the Colonial texts (Figs. 14b–c). Dressed in the miter and chasuble and brandishing the serpent-tailed hyssop, the Post-Classic

[2] The vast majority of Chen Mul-style *incensarios* wear the upright cloth "miter," and it is quite possible that they are portrayed as surrogate priests, those who make the offerings to the actual gods. Thus the *incensario* figures often hold maize balls and copal bags; rather than being offerings received, these items may actually be goods presented by the *incensario* figures to the gods.

God D was clearly considered as a paramount priest of the Yucatec Maya pantheon.

The significance of Itzamna seems to have differed little in the Classic and Post-Classic periods. In both periods, he was closely identified with wisdom and esoteric knowledge. Colonial accounts describe Itzamna as the high god of the Maya. Thus, in the *Relación de Valladolid,* Itzamna is referred to as the supreme ruler, or *ah tepal,* of the sky. Hernandez (in Saville 1921: 211) compares Itzamna to God the Father of the Christian trinity. According to the *Relación de Ekbalam,*

Itzamna was the paramount god of the Yucatec; "adoraban un solo dios que había por nombre Hunab y Zamna [Itzamna]" (de la Garza et al. 1983, 2: 139). In Classic vessel scenes, Itzamna is frequently seated upon a throne and faces a subsidiary deity, such as God N or God L (e.g., Coggins 1975: fig. 127b). In these scenes, God D is clearly portrayed as a lord receiving a lesser dignitary.

In the Colonial sources, it is also recorded that Itzamna was a god of divination and other esoteric knowledge. In the Pocom ceremony during the month of Uo, the priests, physicians, and sorcerers spread sacred screenfold books on fresh branches in homage to Kinich Ahau Itzamna, who is described as "the first priest" (Landa, in Tozzer 1941: 153). According to Cogolludo, Itzamna was credited with the invention of writing (cited in Thompson 1939: 52). David Stuart (cited in L. Schele and M. E. Miller 1986: 138, note 10) notes that at the Puuc site of Xcalumkin, the name phrase of God D appears in association with the title *ah dzib,* or "he of the writing." Linda Schele and Mary Ellen Miller (1986: 138) mention that God D is often identified with the scribal arts on Classic Maya vessels. In one Late Classic vessel scene, God D appears to be portrayed in the act of teaching writing (Robicsek and Hales 1981: vessel 56). Although the aged figure wears the netted headdress commonly found with God N, his large square eye identifies him as God D.

There are strong indications that during the Classic and Post-Classic periods, God D was considered as an omnipresent god who resided in the heavens as well as on the earth. In Classic iconography, God D commonly appears with sacred world trees, frequently identified with the nadir, zenith, and four quarters in Mesoamerican thought (Fig. 12h; other examples, see W. R. Coe 1967: 100; M. D. Coe 1973: no. 20; 1978: no. 8; 1982: no. 10; Robicsek and Hales 1982: vessel 108). The identification of Itzamna with world trees continues into the Post-Classic period. On Dresden page 41b, the head of God D forms the lower trunk of a tree. Another example appears on the Dresden new year pages. Aside from the red tree of the east, the world directional trees on Dresden pages 26 to 28 are labeled as *yax che* ceiba trees with the *yax* and *che* signs affixed to a portrait glyph of Itzamna. On Madrid page 96a, the head of God D serves as the base of a twisted stone tree or column. This scene recalls the description by Andres de Avendaño of the stone column at the late seventeenth-century town of Tayasal. Termed the *yax cheil cab,* or "first tree of the world," the column was said to have a sculptured face at the base. According to Avendaño, the Itza revered this face as the god Ah Cocah Mut (Means 1917: 135, 136). Also known as Yax Cocah Mut, this entity is an aspect of Itzamna (Tozzer 1941: note 695).

Just as the world trees project into the heavens as well as into the earth, so God D is identified with both regions. Colonial accounts describe Itzamna as the supreme sky god; the celestial aspect of Itzamna was decidedly present during the Classic period as well. Hellmuth (1987: 364–367) notes that the Classic God D merges with a major denizen of the world tree and the heavens, the aforementioned Principal Bird Deity. Thus the figures share particular costume elements, such as the Akbal brow mirror, and in many instances God D has the serpent wings of the Principal Bird Deity (Hellmuth 1987: figs. 555–557). The association of God D and the Principal Bird Deity continues into the Late Post-Classic period. On the Codex Paris page 11, a rare Post-Classic form of the Principal Bird Deity appears in the scene corresponding to Katun 10 Ahau, a Katun concerning God D (Taube 1987). Although there is little direct evidence of a Classic identification of God D with the earth, for the Post-Classic and Colonial periods, it is both explicit and widespread.

According to Thompson (1970b: 210, 218), one Yucatec term for Itzamna was Itzam Cab Ain, or "Itzam Earth Caiman." The great caiman was a widespread symbol of the earth in ancient Mesoamerica, highland Mexico, and the Maya region (Nicholson 1971: 403–404, Thompson 1950: 71). However, in the Colonial Yucatec dictionaries, the term *itzam cab ain* is glossed as "ballena" or whale (Barrera Vásquez 1980: 272), and it could be argued that Itzam Cab Ain simply refers to this beast, not to any cosmological concepts regarding Itzamna and the earth. Nonetheless, it appears that the reference to whales does derive from the concept of an Itzamna caiman floating upon the sea.

In Late Post-Classic iconography, there is strong evidence for the identification of Itzamna with the earth caiman. Thompson (1970b: fig. 4b) illustrates a scene from the Codex Dresden depicting Itzamna peering out of the face of a bicephalic caiman (Fig. 15a). Thompson (1970b: 215) also suggests that a number of cached figurines excavated by Thomas Gann at Santa Rita represent the caiman aspect of Itzamna. Two of the Santa Rita figurines illustrated by Gann (1900: pl. XXXIII) are bicephalic caimans with human faces emerging from the mouths. In at least one case, the figure is clearly aged, and it is likely that these figurines constitute three-dimensional versions of the Dresden scene (Fig. 15b).

A mural within Structure 2 of the Pinturas Group at Coba suggests that the Dresden and Santa Rita caimans represent the earth. Although much damaged, the Late Post-Classic mural represents human figures standing upon the crested and scaly body of a caiman, as if it were the earth (see Lombardo de Ruíz et al. 1987: pl. 52). With its scales and back scutes, the caiman body is extremely similar to the Itzamna caiman represented in the Codex Dresden. A series of day signs runs in consecutive order along the caiman body (Fig. 15c).

Although not mentioned by Thompson, there is another excellent representation of the Itzamna earth caiman at Late Post-Classic Santa Rita. In the famous Mound 1 murals at Santa Rita, the gods of the Tun cycle are positioned above a horizontal band which, in turn, runs above an area containing fish and marine shells. On close inspection, it can be seen that the band is a caiman body, with the same back crest, vertical bands, and scales found on the Dresden example (see Gann 1990: pl. 31). In other words, the human figures are positioned over the caiman earth floating above the sea. The head of the creature appears on both sides of the doorway, with the widely open jaws flanking the door. Although not drawn in full by Gann, the caiman was provided with forelimbs and scaly claws (Fig. 15d).

The headdress of this creature provides an especially pertinent detail. It contains the aforementioned priestly miter pierced with a stingray or bone perforator. A virtually identical miter, again with the same perforator, is worn by God D in the same mural at Santa Rita (Fig. 14d). Clearly, this is no ordinary caiman. Instead, as Itzam Cab Ain, the caiman wears priestly accouterments of Itzamna.

In his initial identification of God D as Itzamna, Seler ([1887b]; 1902–23, 1: 379–381) notes that the Maya god is very similar to Tonacatecuhtli, "Lord of Our Sustenance," the Central Mexican old god of the earth and creation:

> For as the Mexican Tonacatecuhtli, the lord of generation, is supposed to be in the topmost thirteenth heaven, and at the same time also he (or his feminine companion) appears as lord of the earth, so also the ideas of heaven and earth, below and above, seem to me present also in this Yucatec figure [Itzamna]. In the cult this god appears with the distinguishing marks of a fire god, which also among the Mexicans is the old god and coincides to a greater or lesser extent with the lord of generation, the lord of life. (translation from Thompson and Richardson 1939, 1: 68–69)

Seler (1902–23), 1: 379–381) mentions that the Yucatec fire festival of Mac was dedicated to Itzamna (see Tozzer 1941: 162–164). The *Ritual of the Bacabs,* discovered after the early work of Seler, provides further support for the association of Itzamna with fire. In one passage, Itzam Cab is compared to the three-stone *koben* hearth (Roys 1965: 49–50). In another chant, concerning birth and the placenta, the placenta is said to be placed under the "bowels" (*homtan*) of Itzam Cab. Ralph Roys (1965: note 127) suggests that this area corresponds to the hearth, since among the contemporary Yucatec, the placenta is buried under the *koben* hearthstones. In fact, a more literal translation of *uhomtanil itzam cab* would be "the central pit of Itzam Cab," which accords well with the *koben* hearth within the Maya house. In Central Mexico, Tonacatecuhtli is a god of birth and generation and often appears with the primordial copulating human couple, and on Borgia page 61, he is in the squatting position of birth (Fig. 16a). In one remarkable scene on the Aztec Vaticanus A

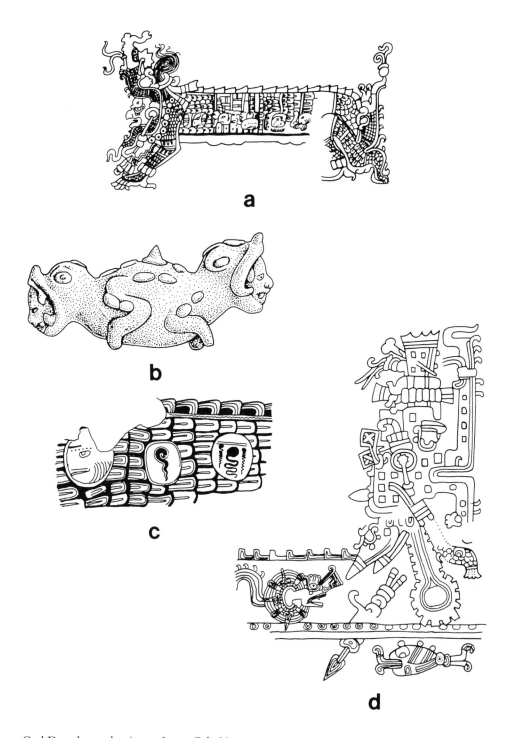

a

b

c

d

Fig. 15 God D as the earth caiman, Itzam Cab Ain.

(a) God D in mouth of bicephalic caiman, Dresden pages 4b–5b
(b) Late Post-Classic representation of bicephalic caiman with two aged faces in mouths, Santa Rita (drawn after Gann 1900: pl. XXXIII)

(c) Detail of fragmentary mural from Structure 2 of Las Pinturas Group, Coba (redrawn after Lombardo de Ruiz 1987: figs. 50–52)
(d) Earth caiman with priestly miter of God D, detail of Mound 1 mural, Santa Rita (redrawn after Gann 1900: pl. XXIX).

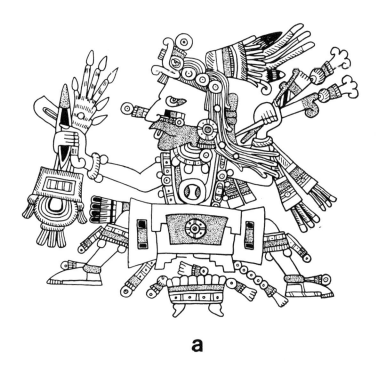

a

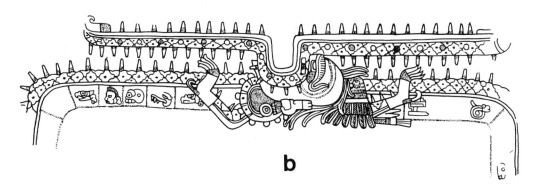

b

Fig. 16 Late Post-Classic representations of Tonacate-cuhtli in the Codex Borgia.

(a) Tonacatecuhtli in birth-giving position, Codex Borgia page 61

(b) Tonacatecuhtli as the caiman earth; note day signs on caiman body; Codex Borgia page 39.

page 12 verso, the primal couple is represented as a pair of fire sticks with a flint blade. Seler (1963, 1: 67) interprets this as an allusion to fire; the making of fire is compared to the act of coitus, the making of life.

Seler (1902–23, 1: 380) also notes that both Tonacatecuhtli and God D are identified with maize. Seler mentions that in the Maya codices,

God D frequently appears with the maize god. One of the Colonial epithets of Itzamna is Itzamna Kauil, *kauil* being a Yucatec term referring to abundance and sustenance. Stuart (1987b: 15) has recently supplied epigraphic evidence that during the Classic period, Kauil was a name for God K. In the following discussion of God E, it will be noted that during the Classic period, Gods

D and K share a particular style of coiffure with an important Classic Maya god of maize.

Both Itzamna and Tonacatecuhtli are aged creator gods associated with earth and heavens, birth, creation, fire, and maize. Like Itzamna, Tonacatecuhtli was also identified with trees. On Borgia page 9 and Vaticanus B page 28, Tonacatecuhtli appears with a flowering tree sprouting from the top of his head (Seler 1963, 1: 64). In the Codex Borgia, the tips of the branches are supplied with round white elements, and it is possible that the scene depicts a silk-cotton tree (ceiba). It has been noted that as the sacred *axis mundi,* the ceiba was closely related to Itzamna.

The concept of Tonacatecuhtli as a sacred tree may well relate to the most striking trait shared between the Mexican and Maya gods: the earth caiman. Tonacatecuhtli is not only the regent of Cipactli, meaning caiman, the first of the twenty day names, but also presides over the trecena 1-Cipactli (Caso 1971: 337–338). On Vaticanus B page 87, a caiman lies underneath the primordial couple appearing with Tonacatecuhtli. Seler (1963, 2: 28, 41) cites a number of instances in the Codex Borgia in which Tonacatecuhtli wears the spiny skin of the caiman. Of course, this immediately recalls the Dresden and Santa Rita representations of God D within the earth caiman. The example on Borgia pages 39 and 40 is one of the developed illustrations of Tonacatecuhtli as the earth caiman (Fig. 16b). Here Tonacatecuhtli appears as a great open-mouthed caiman whose spiny body encloses the entire scene on Borgia page 40. Whereas the head and forelimbs appear on page 39, the remains of the diminutive lower limbs can be seen at the base of the scene on page 40. Seler (1963, 2: 41) notes that Borgia page 40 depicts an underworld event enclosed by the caiman earth. But although the earth creature is supplied with a caiman mouth, the head is that of Tonacatecuhtli, with the pointed chin, white hair, and feathered headdress found with other representations of the aged creator god. Moreover, the colored bar on the cheek of the caiman mouth—an emblem of Xochipilli—is a characteristic also found with Tonacatecuhtli (Fig. 16a).

A series of day signs pass within the body of the Tonacatecuhtli caiman. Seler (1963, 2: 42) points out that to the right side of the caiman head, the mouth of the second day sign, Ehecatl, can be discerned. The day signs then pass in consecutive order, to the third day, Calli; the fourth, Cuetzpalin; the fifth, Coatl; and so on, all the way down the right side of the caiman body to end with Malinalli at the rear of the creature. Another pattern of day signs continues from the rear up the left side of the creature to end near its head. Although Seler does not mention this, it is probable that the great Tonacatecuhtli caiman head serves as the first day sign, Cipactli, with the partially obscured Ehecatl head constituting the second day of the count. In concept, the placement of consecutive day signs along the body of the earth caiman is identical to the Pinturas Group mural at Coba.

Summary

Along with other Maya scenes, the Coba and Santa Rita murals reveal that the Post-Classic Yucatec conception of the earth caiman was very similar to that of highland Mexico. In both regions, the caiman was identified with an aged god of creation and sustenance. In both regions, the aged god also appears as a personified tree, quite probably the *axis mundi.* Because of the many specific parallels, the Maya Itzamna and the Mexican Tonacatecuhtli should be regarded as historically related entities. It is possible that the caiman attributes of Itzamna derive from the iconography of Post-Classic Central Mexico. However, the immediate origins of Tonacatecuhtli are obscure, and this figure cannot be readily identified prior to the Late Post-Classic codices. This is not so for the Maya Itzamna. Representations of Itzamna are widespread during the Classic period and may be traced as early as the Protoclassic Hauberg Stela. However, during the Classic period, the zoomorphic counterpart of God D is not a caiman but rather the Principal Bird Deity. During both the Classic and Post-Classic periods, Itzamna is closely identified with writing, divination, and other esoteric lore. In many Post-Classic scenes, he is depicted as a priest, complete with the priestly regalia and accouterments described by the sixteenth-century Spanish chroniclers. In summary, Itzamna is an extremely powerful and aged god, with a strength based on esoteric knowledge rather than physical prowess.

God E

Schellhas (1897, 1904), the first to isolate the attributes and name glyph of God E, correctly identifies this figure as the maize god (Fig. 17). Schellhas notes that the large element curling off the top of the head is also found growing out of the Kan sign, and for this reason, he identifies it as a maize cob. Cyrus Thomas (1882: 80) had previously identified the Kan sign as maize grain. Although it has been found that this device actually refers to the tamale (Love 1989; Taube 1989a), it nevertheless is a maize sign. According to Schellhas (1904: 24), God E is the Maya counterpart of Centeotl, the Central Mexican god of maize. The correspondence with Centeotl is corroborated by the vertical jogged line passing down the face of the Post-Classic God E (Figs. 17b–e, g). Seler (1963, 1: 167) notes that the same facial marking is found with contemporaneous representations of Centeotl.

The Post-Classic appellative glyph of God E is the foliated head of the maize god supplied with the T24 prefix (Fig. 17a). The maize growth sprouts from the brow and curls back around the head to end over the cheek. Appearing with a series of black rectangular markings, the foliation is notably similar to the forehead bracket of the Post-Classic God C (Fig. 10). In fact, the conventional glyph of God E in the Codex Madrid is the head of God C with the T24 prefix (Fig. 17a, right). The curious conflation of corn with God C may be due to the extreme sacredness the Mayas ascribe to maize. Thus a common contemporary Yucatec reverential term for corn is *santo ixim,* or "holy maize seed." Stephen Houston (personal communication, 1983) has pointed out an interesting version of the Classic period "resurrection scene," which has been identified as a repre-

sentation of maize sprouting out of the earth (Taube 1985, 1986, 1988). In the Classic scenes, the Tonsured Maize God appears rising out of a tortoise shell. However, Houston notes that on a carved cylindrical column from Uxmal, God C is the protagonist emerging from the tortoise shell (Fig. 10f). The reference to corn is still explicit, for a clear maize sign is placed on the head of the God C figure.

God E is extremely common in the iconography of Post-Classic Yucatan, appearing widely in the codices and in Late Post-Classic monumental sculpture and mural paintings. Depictions of God E are frequent in the murals of Tulum and Tancah. In Mural 1 of Tancah Structure 12, God E is seated directly on a sloping grinding stone (Fig. 17d). The vast majority of Late Post-Classic Maya diving gods—erroneously identified as "bee gods" by Roys (1933: 63)—are actually representations of the maize god (Fig. 18). Representations of the diving god usually bear prominent maize foliation at the tops of their heads. In a number of examples, the diving figure has some sort of feather-like elements projecting from the arms (Figs. 18c). These elements are also found with an explicit God E on Madrid page 68a (Fig. 18e). In the scene corresponding to the yearbearer Kan on Madrid page 35, God E appears as a diving god with the same device projecting from the arms (Fig. 18d). The prominent jogged line passing through the face explicitly identifies this figure as God E. On the central column of Tulum Structure 1, there is a partially eroded representation of a diving maize god rendered in profile (see A. G. Miller 1982: pl. 40). Victoria Bricker (1986: 147) notes that the foliated descending figures seen in profile on Dresden pages 15a and 15b are accompanied by a verbal compound to be read *upakah,* or "he planted it," a reading that accords well with the suggested agricultural significance of the diving god (Fig. 18f).

The stucco diving god from Tulum Structure 16 is depicted with flowers rising behind his arms and feet (Fig. 18a). In the *Chilam Balam of Chumayel* description of Katun 11 Ahau, the descent of Bolon Mayel is mentioned in terms of flowers and agricultural fertility:

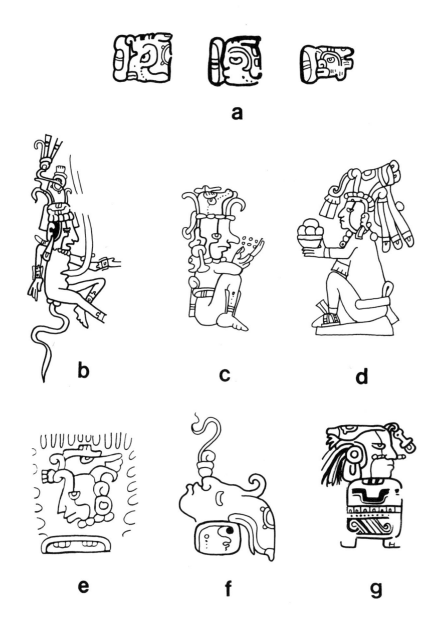

Fig. 17 Representations of God E in Post-Classic
Maya epigraphy and art.

(a) Codical examples of the God E appellative,
    Dresden page 6b, Paris page 6, Madrid page 105a
(b) God E disemboweled, Paris page 19
(c) Seated God E scattering material from hand, Madrid page 51b
(d) God E seated on *metate,* detail of Mural 1, Tancah
    Structure 12 (redrawn after A. G. Miller 1982: pl. 6)
(e) Head of God E surrounded by blood, Madrid page 34b
(f) Lifeless head of God E placed above sign for earth,
    Dresden page 34a
(g) Head of God E in bowl containing *kan* sign for
    tamale, detail of mural in Las Pinturas Group,
    Coba (redrawn after Lombardo de Ruiz 1987: pls.
    35, 37).

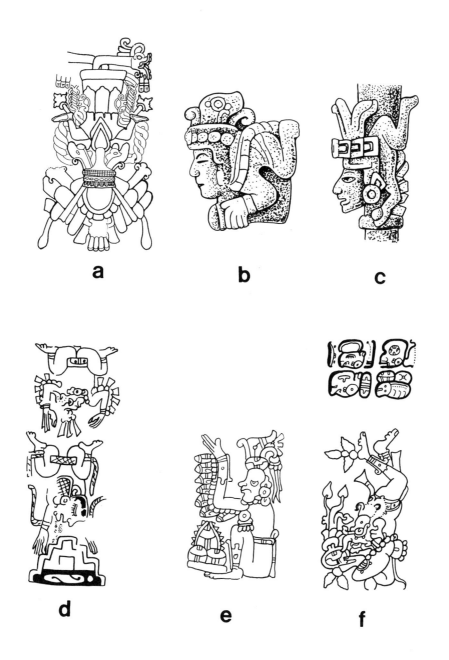

Fig. 18 Post-Classic representations of the diving god as God E.

(a) Stucco diving god with maize headdress of God E, note flowers above rear feet, Tulum Structure 25 (after Roys 1933: fig. 1a)
(b) Diving God E, stone sculpture from Mayapan
(c) Diving God E with winged arms, detail of wooden staff from Sacred Well, Chichen Itza (drawn after Coggins and Shane 1984: no. 126)

(d) Diving God E above bound sacrificial victim, Madrid page 35
(e) Winged God E, Madrid page 68
(f) Diving foliated Chac, Dresden page 15b.

Then the water descended, it came from the heart of the sky for the baptism of the House of Nine Bushes. With it descended Bolon Mayel; sweet was his mouth and the tip of his tongue. Sweet were his brains. Then descended the four mighty supernatural jars, this was the honey of the flowers. (Roys 1933: 104)

In the Colonial Yucatec dictionaries, *bolon mayel* is glossed as either "fragrancia" or "agua bendita" (Barrera Vásquez 1980: 63). In the Motul Dictionary, this term also glossed as *tzitzabil haa* (Barrera Vásquez 1980: 63), that is, water thrown from the serpent-tailed aspergillum, or *tzitzab*. Although this detailed description of perfumed falling water recalls the aged god of sustenance, Itzamna, it is also suggestive of the maize god, who is widely identified with flowers in ancient Mesoamerica. The Central Mexican Xochipilli, or "flower prince," was also a god of corn. Nicholson (1971: 416) discusses Xochipilli and Centeotl under a single complex: "the cult which revolved around the cultivation of the staple food plant, maize." The diving god may be an embodiment of Bolon Mayel, a fragrant god of moisture and fertility.

According to Schellhas (1904: 25) God E was solely a god of life and fertility and lacked any direct association with death and the underworld:

god E has nothing to do with the powers of the underworld; he is a god of life, of prosperity and fruitfulness; symbols of death are never found in connection with him.

However, God E is often affiliated with death and sacrifice in Post-Classic Yucatan. This may be partly due to the agricultural cycle of maize, the planting in the earth equivalent to death and burial, and the harvest, the severing of the maize cob head. On Dresden page 34a and Madrid page 34b, God E is represented as a severed head (Figs. 17e–f). In the Las Pinturas group at Coba, there is a Post-Classic mural depicting the head of God E placed upon a Kan sign (Fig. 17g). God E may even be found disemboweled. Dresden page 42c represents Chac pulling bowels out of the slashed abdomen of God E. On Paris page 19, entrails are also seen pulled from the slit belly of God E (Fig. 17b).[3] Here and with many other examples of the codical God E, he is depicted with closed eyes, clearly denoting death (see Dresden page 34a, Paris page 8, Madrid pages 24c, 25c).

In many cases the death of maize may concern auguries of the yearly harvest, but the association with death appears to be more pervasive. In the *Ritual of the Bacabs* (Roys 1965: 9) the entrance to the underworld is identified with Ix Hun Ahau and Uaxac Yol Kauil. According to Landa (Tozzer 1941: 132), Hun Ahau was the lord of the underworld: "They maintained that there was in this place [Metnal] a devil, the prince of all the devils, whom all obeyed, and they call him in their language Hunhau." The second entity, Uaxac Yol Kauil, has been interpreted as the maize god by Roys (1965) and J. Thompson (1970b: 289).

The Foliated Maize God, or God E, is not limited to the Post-Classic Period; this deity is well represented in Late Classic Maya epigraphy and art (Fig. 19a). Seler (1902–23, 3: 593) was the first to note that the portrait appellative glyph of the Post-Classic codical God E is virtually identical to the Classic numeral eight head variant previously identified by Goodman (1897: 46). Herbert Spinden (1913: fig. 123) describes a number of foliated maize gods on Classic Maya monuments. One of the figures, from the side of Quirigua Stela H, displays a long, flattened brow topped by a growth of hair (Fig. 19c). An almost identical coiffure appears on an unprovenanced Late Classic monument (Fig. 19b). In this case, Foliated Maize God heads replace the conventional *uah* maize curls placed over the ear spools. Like the Quirigua example, each head has an elongated and bare forehead, with a segmented headband across the brow (see also Fig. 21e).

---

[3] On Dresden page 42c, Chac is in the act of pulling bowels out of the slashed abdomen of God E. The identification of maize with disembowelment appears in other regions of ancient Mesoamerica. At the Temple of the Building Columns at El Tajin, there is a late Classic scene of growing maize flanking the strung bowels of a sacrificial victim (see Wilkerson 1980: 220–221). In addition, a curious Aztec phrase describes the disembowelment of maize: "Am I perchance an ear of green maize that one will break open my entrails?" (Sahagún 1950–71, bk. 6: 228). It appears that for the Aztec, some process in the harvesting of green corn was compared to disembowelment.

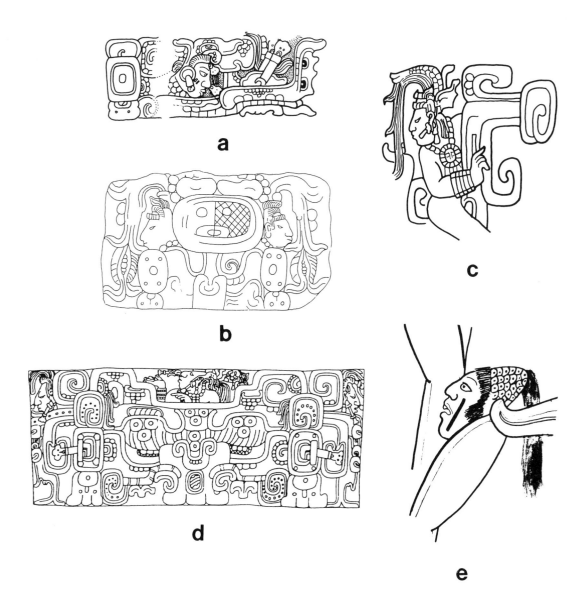

Fig. 19 Classic representations of the Tonsured Maize
God and Foliated Maize God.

(a) Foliated Maize God emerging from eye of Cauac
Monster head, detail of Lintel 3, Tikal Temple IV
(redrawn after Jones and Satterthwaite 1982: fig.
74)

(b) Foliated Tonsured Maize Gods replace maize curls
topping earspool assemblage of central zoomorphic head (drawn from photo courtesy of
Flora Clancy)

(c) Foliated Tonsured Maize god in foliation growing
out of maize curl earspool assemblage, detail of
Quirigua Stela H (drawn after Maudslay 1889–
1902, 2: pl. 45)

(d) Cauac head at base of Bonampak Stela 1, Tonsured
Maize God at center of cleft skull, two maize god
heads in foliation emanating from curls at side of
Cauac head (after Mathews 1980: fig. 3)

(e) Tonsured Maize God as mature corn cob, detail of
mural from Cacaxtla, Tlaxcala (drawn after photograph courtesy of John Carlson).

The two Late Classic monuments display an important link between two aspects of the maize god, the foliated deity and a closely related entity, which I (Taube 1985) identify and label as the Tonsured Maize God. In contrast to the foliated god, the Tonsured Maize God lacks cranial maize growth. Instead, his elongated head is shaved to resemble a mature maize cob (Figs. 19d, 21). At times, a horizontal band of hair is left on the lower brow, creating two distinct zones of hair separated by a shaved region (Fig. 21a). The capping hair crest of the Tonsured Maize God mimics the pollen tassel appearing at the top of the cob. Among the Yucatec Maya, maize silk is identified with human hair. Thus in Yucatec, *tzuc* signifies a crest of hair or the "silk" tassel at the top of the cob (Barrera Vásquez 1980: 866). In one of the Colonial *Chilam Balam of Chumayel* riddles, *pibil nal,* or baked green corn, is alluded to as a woman with twisted hair: "her hair is twisted into a tuft" (Roys 1933: 130). Although virtually absent in Post-Classic Maya iconography, the Tonsured Maize God is widely depicted in Classic Maya art, appearing on stone monuments and especially, Late Classic ceramic vessels.[4]

Recent discoveries at the site of Cacaxtla, Tlaxcala, directly support my initial identification of the tonsured figure as a god of maize. Cacaxtla is perhaps best known for the remarkable polychrome murals from Stuctures A and B, paintings that exhibit clear elements of Maya costume and iconography (Foncerrada de Molina 1980). However, in 1987 and 1988, additional murals were discovered south of Structures A and B (Santana Sandoval et al. 1990). In one area, a pair of murals flanked a stairway. On both sides, there are depictions of growing maize with mature cobs portrayed as the head of the Tonsured Maize God (Fig. 19e). Thus the elongated head has a lower horizontal crest of hair and a capping tuft,

clearly serving as the maize silk. In addition, yellow maize kernels are carefully delineated on the brow. The Cacaxtla depictions of the Tonsured Maize God indicate that this figure probably represents mature yellow maize, in contrast to the Foliated Maize God, who seems to embody the still green and tender growing corn.

Both the foliated and tonsured forms of the maize god are present in the Early Classic period. An excellent example of the Tonsured Maize God can be found in the "Realistic Paintings" mural fragments from the Tetitla compound of Teotihuacan. Foncerrada de Molina (1980: 189–191) notes that the "Realistic Paintings" are not wholly Teotihuacano, but rather, display explicit Maya conventions. One of the fragments depicts a figure with a clear Maya profile and an especially elongated cranium marked with a single tuft of hair (Fig. 20a). Affixed to the side of his head are two ball-like devices, with the uppermost supplied with a sprout of maize growth. These balls are early forms of the corn curl element of Maya iconography, which I (Taube 1989a) consider to be a representation of the maize tamale, or *uah*. With his elongated tonsured head and the maize signs, the Tetitla figure can be safely identified as an Early Classic form of the Tonsured Maize God.

Most Early Classic Maya representations of the maize god are similar to the Tetitla example in one special way—maize foliation does not sprout directly out of the cranium but rather emerges from a discrete maize device placed at the top of the head (e.g., Figs. 20a, d, f–g). Thus, on one Tikal carved vessel, the maize foliation is not an organic part of the head, but sprouts out of a maize seed cartouche (Fig. 20f). Another carved vessel depicts maize growth emerging out of a Kan sign in the zoomorphic headdress of the maize god (Fig. 20g).

Maize sprouting out of a cranial Kan sign is also found on Post-Classic examples of God E (Figs. 17b, 18e). However, the foliation usually sprouts directly out of the head in Post-Classic representations. Although rare, this convention also appears in one Early Classic example (Fig. 20c). Like the conventional Late Classic head vari-

---

[4] It has recently been suggested that the conventional name glyph of the Tonsured Maize God is to be read *nal,* a common Mayan term for "maize ear" (Schele, Mathews, and Lounsbury 1990: 3–5). The authors note that among contemporary Chol, *ña'al* is the term for "el dios de abundancia" (see Aulie and Aulie 1978: 85). According to Schele, Mathews, and Lounsbury, the Classic Maya term for the Tonsured Maize God was *hun nal*.

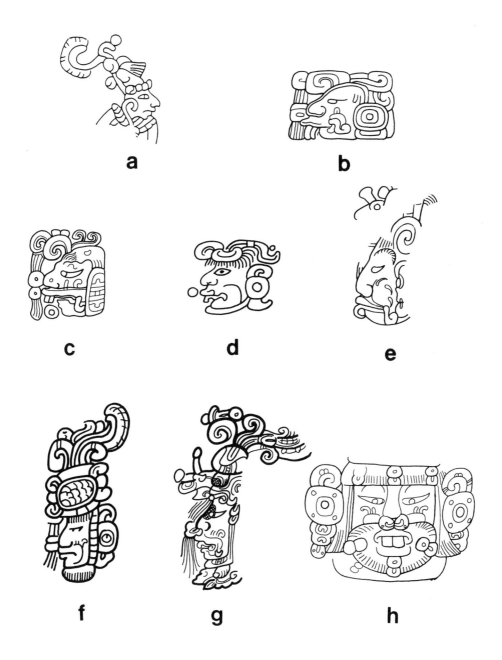

Fig. 20 Early Classic representations of the maize god.

(a) Maya maize god from Pinturas Group, Teotihuacan (after Taube 1985: fig. 2a)

(b) Epigraphic example of maize god, detail of Early Classic alabaster vessel from Santa Rita, Belize (after drawing courtesy of Stephen Houston)

(c) Maize god glyph from Early Classic ceramic vessel (redrawn after Hellmuth 1987: fig. 634g)

(d) Maize god as head variant of the numeral eight on Pomona Flare (redrawn after Justeson, Norman, and Hammond 1988: fig. 3.1)

(e) Maize god as numeral eight head variant, Yaxchilan Lintel 48 (redrawn after I. Graham, 1979, 3: fig. 107)

(f) Detail of maize god from Early Classic Tikal vessel (after Taube 1985: Fig. 10a)

(g) Face of maize god from Early Classic carved vessel (redrawn after L. Schele and M. E. Miller 1986: pl. 75)

(h) Frontal view of Early Classic maize god from carved vessel (drawn after Bolz 1975: no. 49).

ant of the number eight and the Post-Classic God E appellative, a stylized maize cob curls down the back of the head. Both this example and other Early Classic maize gods display a T86 *nal* maize sign affixed to the top of the head (e.g., Fig. 20b). It is possible that the slightly effaced numeral eight head variant from Yaxchilan Lintel 48 represents another Early Classic example of the foliated maize god (Fig. 20e). However, the Pomona Flare numeral eight head variant identified by Justeson, Norman, and Hammond (1988) has maize growing out of a U-shaped element rather than the head itself (Fig. 20d).

The Pomona Flare and other early examples of the maize god have a long, almost "Olmecoid" upper lip with downwardly projecting incisors (Figs. 20b–e, g). On one Early Classic modeled vessel, the maize god's incisors are so large and protruding as to be termed buck teeth (Fig. 20h). This example and many Early Classic maize god representations are supplied with whiskers, quite possibly alluding to the silk growing on the sides of the cob (e.g., Figs. 20d–f, h).

It appears that both the tonsured and foliated Classic forms of the maize god are quadripartite. A set of four foliated maize deities appears on the sides of Copan Stela H and on Lintel 3 of Tikal Temple IV (Fig. 19a). The Holmul Dancer, a red-painted form of the Tonsured Maize God, often occurs in pairs on Late Classic vessels. However, Michael Coe (1978: no. 14) illustrates one vessel depicting three of these figures, each identified with a particular emblem glyph. I suspect that the Holmul Dancer is actually quadripartite, but that the elaborate costumes prevent four from being easily depicted on a single cylindrical vessel. A vessel excavated at Seacal, in the Coban drainage of central Alta Verapaz, depicts four distinct Tonsured Maize Gods, all of them apparently dancing (see Smith 1952: fig. 25a). In addition, a fine Late Classic incised vase from Copan depicts four Tonsured Maize Gods, evidently in the role of court artisans (see L. Schele and M. E. Miller 1986: pl. 44a).

In Classic vessel scenes, the Tonsured Maize God is closely identified with the Howler Monkey artisans and the Headband Twins, Classic counterparts of the *Popol Vuh* Hero Twins,

Xbalanque and Hunahpu. It is now clear that this figure is the Classic version of Hun Hunahpu, the father of the Hero Twins. In many Late Classic dishes, or *lac,* he appears as a severed head, recalling both the fate of the decapitated Hun Hunahpu and the aforementioned heads of the Post-Classic maize god. Although it is not mentioned explicitly in the *Popol Vuh,* I (Taube 1986) have argued that the descent to the underworld for the remains of Hun Hunahpu is a version of the widespread emergence myth describing the origin of mankind. In the form of maize, the remains of Hun Hunahpu supply the substance from which people are made.

One interesting Late Classic form of the maize god may represent corn as the idealized ancestor. In this case the deity is supplied with the conventional torch of God K, although at times, the outcurling elements more resemble vegetation than smoke (Fig. 21). Aside from the cranial torch element, the figure bears no overt characteristics of God K. Thus, rather than possessing saurian body scutes or a serpent foot, he is entirely human. On one carved bone from Copan, he is bearded and appears with a more feminine form of the Tonsured Maize God, as if the somewhat androgenous deity had split into a male and female pair (Fig. 21c). Copan Stela 11 depicts the same bearded form, here standing upon a bony jaw-like device forming the upper portion of the Uayeb sign (Fig. 21d). Quite likely this lunate death element serves to denote the entrance to the underworld, if not the netherworld itself. Linda Schele and Mary Ellen Miller (1986: 152) note that both of the bearded figures appear to depict the Copan lord Yax Pac, with Stela 11 being a posthumous monument.

Virtually the same situation occurs at Palenque. The sarcophagus lid of Pacal depicts the same God K form of the Tonsured Maize God (Fig. 21e). Thus, while lacking the serpent foot, he has the forehead torch and a coiffure almost identical to the aforementioned maize god on the side of Quirigua Stela H. Moreover, the beaded belt and skirt are also attributes of the Tonsured Maize God and are worn by Chan Bahlum upon the Tablet of the Foliated Cross as he impersonates

a   b   c

d   e

Fig. 21   Tonsured Maize God with cranial torch of God K.

(a) One of four maize gods incised on Late Classic vessel from Chipoc (redrawn after Smith 1952: fig. 25a)

(b) Unprovenanced Late Classic Vase (drawn from photograph courtesy of Michael D. Coe)

(c) Incised bone from Copan (drawing by L. Schele, after L. Schele and M. E. Miller 1986: pl. 20)

(d) Roll-out drawing of Stela 11, Copan; Yax Pac standing atop skeletal element (redrawn after Proyecto Arqueológico Copan 1983, 2: fig. M-27)

(e) Pacal in skeletal element, sarcophagus lid from Temple of the Inscriptions, Palenque (redrawn after drawing by Merle Greene Robertson).

the Tonsured Maize God (Taube 1985: 174). On a painted Chenes capstone, the more conventional form of the Tonsured Maize God appears in association with the same skeletal device (Mayer 1980: pl. 70). Much as Ruz Lhuillier (1973: 225) originally suggested, the sarcophagus scene portrays the deceased ruler as the maize god.

Summary

During the Post-Classic period, representations of God E are many. The Late Post-Classic diving god motif clearly represents the descending maize god, not a diving bee deity. In Post-Classic iconography, God E is commonly found in scenes of death as well as of life and abundance. Although some of the codical death associations are surely concerned with specific auguries of crop abundance and failure, other scenes allude to the agricultural cycle of maize. A clear example is the decapitation of God E, which surely alludes to the harvested maize cob.

Many of the underworld and death associations of the Post-Classic God E are also present in classic iconography. One important Classic form of the corn deity, the Tonsured Maize God, is an ancestral form of the sixteenth-century Quichean Hun Hunahpu, the father of the Hero Twins who was decapitated in the underworld. The two Late Classic forms of the maize deity—the Tonsured Maize God and the Foliated Maize God—share many traits, and it appears that they derive from a single Early Classic form. During the Early Classic Period, the cranial maize growth does not usually sprout directly out of the head, but rather out of a maize sign placed on the head. Whereas this maize element is frequently fixed into the cranium of the Late Classic Tonsured Maize God, Late Classic and Post-Classic forms of the Foliated Maize God usually lack the discrete maize sign. Instead, the maize vegetation tends to sprout as a natural and integral extension of the head.

God F (see Gods Q and R)

In his discussion of God F, Schellhas (1904: 25–27) seriously confuses three distinct gods. For Schellhas (1904: 26), the major distinguishing criterion for God F is a particular form of facial marking: "The characteristic mark of God F is a single black line usually running perpendicularly down the face in the vicinity of the eye." However, although Schellhas correctly distinguishes this line from facial lines of Gods C and E, he fails to distinguish between the facial markings of three other deities. Thus one of his cited examples (fig. 34) is actually the face of God A'. The two other gods also display distinct facial markings. Whereas one deity has a prominent Caban curl sign upon the cheek (Schellhas 1904: figs. 30, 33), the other is supplied with a curving black or dotted band that passes down from the forehead through the eye to the back of the cheek. In his discussion of God F, Schellhas actually describes this last god, which he correctly considers to be a deity of war and human sacrifice.

J. Eric S. Thompson (1950: 131–132) is the first to describe in detail the differences between these two gods. In this important discussion, Thompson suggests that the Schellhas God F designation should be entirely abandoned. According to Thompson, the two gods require entirely new letter designations. Thus Thompson labels the god of sacrifice as God Q, and the deity with the Caban facial curl, God R. To avoid any further confusion, I will follow the letter designation proposed by Thompson. Detailed discussion of these two gods will appear below under the headings of God Q and God R.

God G

Due to the prominent solar *kin* sign in the name glyph of God G, Schellhas (1904: 27) correctly identifies this deity as the Sun God (Fig. 22). Floyd Lounsbury (1973: 138–139) states that the entire compound is to be read *ahau kin* and possibly, *kinich ahau,* the latter being a name often mentioned in the Colonial literature (Fig. 22a). Among the diagnostic attributes of the codical God G is the face, featuring a "Roman nose" and a large square eye. The Post-Classic God G tends to wear a beard, possibly an allusion to the

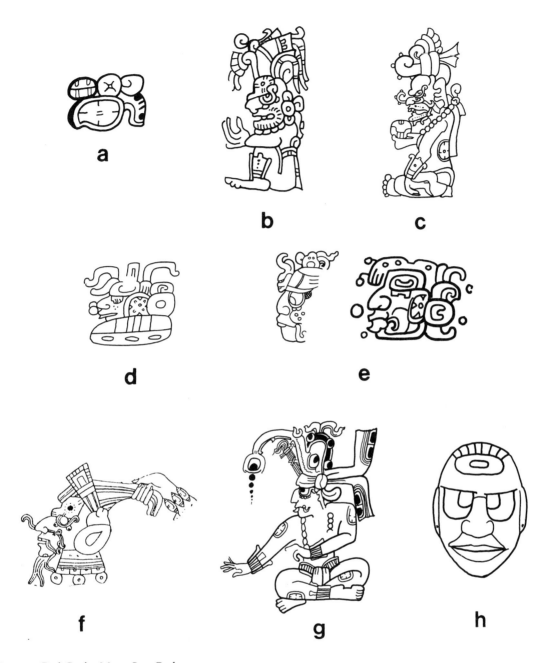

Fig. 22   God G, the Maya Sun God.

(a) Codical God G appellative, probably read *ahau kin,* Dresden page 5a

(b) Late Post-Classic representation of God G, note beard and *kin* sign in forehead, Madrid page 108b

(c) Bearded God G with *kin* sign on back, Dresden page 22b

(d) Early Classic representation of God G serving as patron of month Yaxkin in Initial Series introductory glyph, Leiden Plaque (redrawn after L. Schele and M. E. Miller 1986: pl. 33a)

(e) Early Classic examples of Sun God serving as head variant for the numeral four, Yaxchilan Lintel 49, Pomona Flare

(f) Severed head of bearded God G, detail of mural from Mound 1, Santa Rita (after Gann 1900: pl. XXXI)

(g) Late Classic representation of God G, detail of polychrome vessel (drawn after roll-out photograph courtesy of Justin Kerr)

(h) Late Classic jade carving of Sun God (drawn after Carlson 1981: fig. 33).

bewhiskered jaguar. However, Seler (1904b: 659) notes that the Yucatec referred to solar rays as *u mex kin,* or "beard of the sun." Although the Codex Dresden examples of God G depict him as no more than middle-aged, God G is invariably rendered as an old man in the Codex Madrid. Thus he displays the same chapfallen and snaggletoothed mouth found with God D and other aged gods (Fig. 22b).

In general, Post-Classic representations of God G differ little from their Classic period prototypes. The epigraphic head variants of the number four are among the clearest and most consistent representations of the Classic Sun God (Fig. 22e). Although J. Thompson (1950: 133) states that the Classic head variant of the number four is aged, he is actually shown as a mature man at his peak of strength. If aged, his face would be almost identical to God D, who also possesses a large square eye and Roman nose.

The same portrait glyph (T1010) found with the head variant of the number four occurs as the *kin* glyph in Long Count texts and as the patron of the month Yaxkin (Fig. 22d; see J. Thompson 1950: figs. 22, 27). Thompson (1950: 110) notes that the month Yaxkin carries the same name in Tzeltal and Tzotzil as well as Yucatec. In both Classic and Post-Classic texts, the month is written phonetically as Yaxkin, and at times, the *kin* sign is replaced with the face of the sun god (Thompson 1950: fig. 17, nos. 5, 8).

The Classic sun deity appears with a large square eye, and, in frontal views, it is clear that he is cross-eyed (Fig. 22h). Other important traits are his filed incisors, resembling the Greek *tau* when viewed face on, and rope-like elements curling out of the corners of his mouth. This same mouth device can be found with Dresden representations of God G (Fig. 22c). Quite frequently, the Sun God will have the quatrefoil solar *kin* sign fixed in the cheek, brow, or other part of the body (e.g., Figs. 22b–e, g).

The mature Sun God is widely depicted on Early and Late Classic Maya monuments. In his discussion of the Palenque Triad, Heinrich Berlin (1963: fig. 7) illustrates one form of the GIII appellative identical to the head variant of the number

four. David Kelley (1965) notes that the Palenque Tablet of the Sun records the birth of this god. However, Kelly (1965) identifies GIII as the aged God L rather than the Classic form of God G. Floyd Lounsbury (1985: 50) claims that GIII is the Sun God and suggests that the portrait glyph is to be read *Ahau Kin.* At Palenque, GIII is specifically identified with the T184 prefix, a paramount title of Maya kings. According to Lounsbury (1985: 48–50), this title is to be read *mah kinah.* However, recent epigraphic research indicates that the T184 title is actually to be read *kinich* (Stephen Houston, personal communication, 1990). Lounsbury also notes that GIII has strong jaguar attributes and compares him to the *Popol Vuh* Xbalanque, which he translates as "jaguar sun." Taking this interpretation one step further, Lounsbury (1985: 53–56) identifies GI as Hunahpu and suggests that the mock execution of the *Popol Vuh* Hero Twins is depicted on the Primitive Art Vase (Fig. 8b). Although it is now evident that the Classic versions of the Hero Twins are the Headband Twins, not GI and GIII, the infant jaguar victim present on the Primitive Art Vase and other vessel scenes does appear to represent the sun.

The identification of the Sun God with decapitation is common in Late Preclassic, Classic, and Post-Classic Maya iconography. The head of the Sun God frequently occurs on Classic belt assemblages, as if it were a trophy head (Fig. 23c). On Tikal Stelae 1 and 31, a recumbent figure appears with the back belt assemblage (Fig. 23d). This figure is none other than the jaguar baby commonly found in Classic scenes of decapitation (e.g., Fig. 8b). On Monument 1 of Chalchuapa, El Salvador, a seated figure holds a probable severed jaguar head out before him (Fig. 23e). The bearded figure bears the *kin* sign on the cheek, identifying him as a Late Preclassic form of the Sun God. In the illustrated drawing by William Coe, it appears that the figure has a curious snout. However, in a photograph of a cast, it can be seen that the tip is actually a pair of beads placed at the tip of an entirely human nose (Fig. 23f). Such nose beads are common in Late Preclassic and Early Classic Maya iconography (e.g., Fig. 22d).

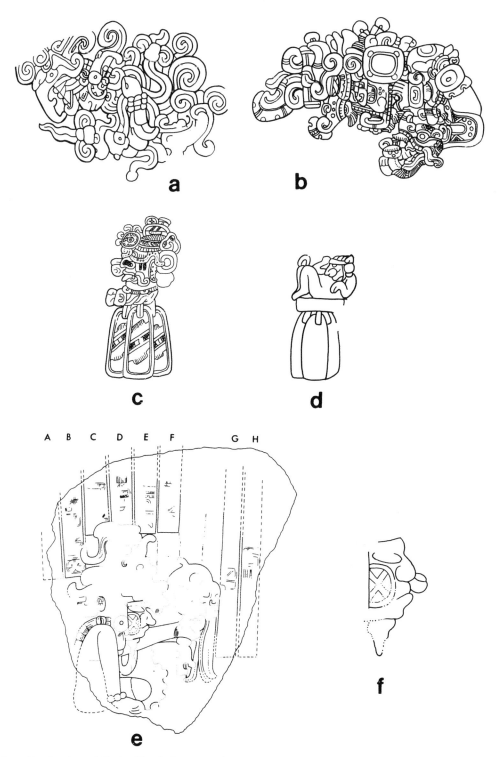

Fig. 23 Late Preclassic and Early Classic iconography pertaining to the Sun God.

(a) Late Preclassic Sun God with burning serpent in crook of arm, note *kin* sign on cheek, detail from upper portion of Abaj Takelik Stela 2 (redrawn after drawing by James Porter)

(b) Curl Nose apotheosized as Sun God with serpent in crook of arm, detail from upper portion of Tikal Stela 31 (redrawn after Jones and Satterthwaite 1982: fig. 51)

(c) Head of Sun God serving as belt-piece, detail of Tikal Stela 31 (redrawn after Jones and Satterthwaite 1982: fig. 51)

(d) Recumbent Jaguar Baby serving as belt-piece, detail of Tikal Stela 1 (redrawn after Jones and Satterthwaite 1982: fig. 1)

(e) Late Preclassic Sun God holding severed jaguar head, Chalchuapa Monument 1 (from a drawing by W. R. Coe, courtesy of the University Museum, University of Pennsylvania; after Sharer 1978, 1: fig. 2a)

(f) Detail of Sun God face of Chalchuapa Monument 1 (redrawn after Sharer 1978, 1: figs. 2a, 3).

During the Late Post-Classic period, the Sun God also appears in the context of decapitation. An example can be seen in the mural paintings at Santa Rita, where the bearded jaguar Sun God occurs as a severed head (Fig. 22f). However, although the decapitation of the jaguar Sun God is common in Maya art, the significance of this event is entirely unknown.

Aside from GIII, a number of other Classic jaguar entities are also identified with the sun. Floyd Lounsbury (1985: 55) considers GIII to be entirely distinct from the deity serving as the head variant of the number seven, lord of the day Akbal and patron of the month Uo. Rather than having the squint or crossed eyes of GIII, the eyes of this deity are spiraled and surrounded by the figure-eight "cruller" device passing over the bridge of the nose. Widely referred to as the Jaguar God of the Underworld, or JGU, this entity seems to depict the night sun. Linda Schele and Mary Ellen Miller (1986: fig. 35) illustrate several examples that appear to be conflations of GIII and the JGU and thus display the cruller along with a *kin* marking and squint eye (e.g., Fig. 23c). The night sun, or JGU, is more commonly represented than GIII and is often found displayed on shields, decorating *incensarios,* and emerging from bicephalic serpent bars.

Schele and Miller (1986: 51) also consider the Water Lily Jaguar to be an aspect of GIII, noting that this figure can substitute for the infant GIII in scenes of decapitation. The Water Lily Jaguar, named for the water lily topping the jaguar head, appears not only in Classic imagery but also on Dresden page 8a, where he appears with the "good" glyph of Zimmermann (T61.507:24), recently read as *utzil* by David Stuart (1987b).

Although still little understood, it appears that the Water Lily Jaguar is identified with fire and lineage through the male line. David Stuart (1987a) notes that a jaguar tail may substitute for the conventional smoking-capped Ahau (T535) occurring in parentage statements, a device interpreted as "child of father" (Figs. 24a–b). The identification of the jaguar with the male line goes further, because the head or tail of the Water Lily Jaguar is frequently capped by the same T535

smoking Ahau sign (Fig. 24e). This may be traced to Late Preclassic times; on Izapa Stela 12, there is a jaguar capped with a smoking Ahau (Fig. 24c). Flames appear to be emanating from his mouth, a convention seen with later Classic depictions of the Water Lily Jaguar (Fig. 24e). Another Late Preclassic monument, Abaj Takelik Stela 1, depicts a probable jaguar with flames curling from its head (Fig. 24d).

The Maya identification of the jaguar with fire continued even into the Colonial period. In the *Chilam Balam of Chumayel,* fire is referred to as "the beckoning tongue of the jaguar" (Roys 1933: 97). In Late Post-Classic Central Mexico, jaguars are also identified with fire. Thus in the Codex Borgia, jaguar tails are used to designate smoke or flames (Fig. 24f). Similarly, a jaguar tail appears as one of the flames depicted in the initial scene of the Vase of the Thirty-one Gods, a Late Classic Maya vessel (see M. Coe 1973: 82). Although it is difficult to explain why the jaguar is related to fire, the Classic Maya identification of this creature with male descent may be due to the widespread association of the jaguar sun with dynastic male power.

Among both the Classic and Post-Classic Maya, the sun god was closely identified with elite rulership. It has been noted that an important title of Maya lords was *kinich,* or sun face. A title recorded for the sixteenth-century highland Maya, it is found widely in Classic Maya inscriptions (Lounsbury 1985: 48–49). Floyd Lounsbury (1985: 48–49) also mentions that terms derived from the word *kin* or "sun" are used to denote rulership and wealth in Yucatec (*kinil*) and Quiche (*q'uinom, q'uinomal*). In the codices, the "ben-ich" *ahau* compound, denoting "lord," appears as a specific title of God G (Fig. 22a). Lounsbury (1973: 117) cites two instances in which the codical appellative is prefixed by Landa's *ca.* This is probably to be read *c(a)ahau kin* (our lord sun). An almost identical phrase for lordship appears in the Cakchiquel Saenz Dictionary: *kajawal* (*cahaual*), "nuestro Señor, Dios" (cited in Lounsbury 1973: 135).

Tikal Stela 31 contains one of the clearest expressions of the Maya identification of the sun god with male dynastic rulership. Above the

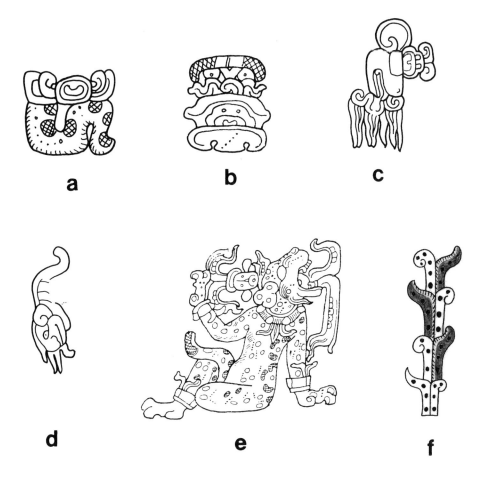

a   b   c

d   e   f

Fig. 24 The identification of the jaguar with fire, smoking *ahau* signs, and male parentage statements.

(a,b) Jaguar tail substituting with smoking Ahau male parentage glyph, Tikal Stela 31 (redrawn after Stuart 1985: fig. 1)

(c) Late Preclassic representation of jaguar with smoking Ahau on head, note probable flames pouring out of mouth, Izapa Stela 12 (redrawn after drawing by James Porter)

(d) Late Preclassic jaguar with probable flames on head, detail of Abaj Takelik Stela 1 (redrawn after drawing by James Porter)

(e) Water Lily Jaguar with fire breath and smoking Ahau on head (drawing by L. Schele, after L. Schele and M. E. Miller 1986: fig. 37)

(f) Post-Classic Mexican convention of jaguar tails serving as smoke or flames, Codex Borgia page 20.

Early Classic ruler Stormy Sky, in the region corresponding to the heavens, there is a representation of his father, Curl Snout, apotheosized as the sun god (Fig. 23b). Although wearing the name of Curl Snout as a headdress, the figure has the Roman nose, squint eyes, and jaguar spot cheek markings found with the Sun God. In addition, the figure wears a sharply upcurving nose bar commonly appearing with Classic and Post-Classic representations of the sun god (e.g., Fig. 22c).

The celestial sun god motif is also found on Stela 2 of Abaj Takalik, a Cycle 7 monument dating to the first century B.C. (Fig. 23a). The position of the figure is almost identical to the apotheosized Curl Snout on Stela 31; he faces downward and holds a serpent in the crook of his right arm. However, in this case, the figure also wears a prominent *kin* solar sign on the cheek. The two individuals below the Late Preclassic sun god have every appearance of being actual historic rulers. As in the case of Tikal Stela 31, the floating solar figure probably serves as a dynastic expression, with an ancestral ruler apotheosized as the sun.

Summary

The Post-Classic form of the Maya Sun God, God G displays many conservative traits that can be traced to even before the beginnings of the Classic era. These traits are represented by specific iconographic devices, such as the *kin* sign, and also by complex ideological concepts. For example, during the Late Preclassic, Classic, and Post-Classic eras, the Sun God was identified with jaguars, decapitation, fire, rulership, and dynastic descent. Of course, such a list of traits is a somewhat artificial construct caused by our limited knowledge of pre-Hispanic Maya religion. To the ancient Maya, these various traits were synthesized into a meaningful and dynamic whole. For example, the identification of the sun with fire and dynastic descent may have been expressed in fire offerings of blood, copal, and other sacred material to honored male rulers apotheosized as the sun. To be sure, the sixteenth-century Maya of Izamal made fire offerings to one of the mythical founders of Izamal, Kinich Kakmo, the Sun-Faced Macaw. This being was said to receive the burning offerings in the form of a macaw, or *kakmo* (Tozzer 1941: notes 689, 902). Although it is beyond the scope of this study, precisely how the Sun God was integrated into the dynastic cult will be an important topic of future investigations.

Gods H and CH

In his discussion of the "Chicchan-God" Schellhas (1904: 28–31) confuses and thus conflates two similarly appearing but distinct gods. Although each of the deity glyphs has a specific prefix and an infix at the back of the skull, Schellhas considers the signs to be equivalent. One of the appellative signs, that of the god

termed "der junger Gott" by Seler (1902–23, 1: 698–700), is a youthful face with a beadlike prefix at the front of the face (Figs. 25a, 26f). This prefix may actually be part of the headdress of the god. In the Codex Madrid, God H frequently wears this device as a vertical element projecting from the top of the headdress (e.g., Madrid page 101b). In the parietal region of the God H portrait glyph, there is a cartouche resembling the T534 inverted Ahau sign. This infixed device tends to be rimmed by a beaded band that is also found curving across the temple region of the face (Figs. 25a, d). This band probably denotes textile edging, such as is commonly found on examples in the Codex Dresden of cloth wrapped around the hips (e.g., Figs. 25c, e). Quite frequently, the figure wears the cylindrical headdress or "miter" found with God D, and it is possible that, like the Post-Classic God D, God H is portrayed as a priest (Fig. 25b).

In the codices, God H is closely identified with God D, the paramount priest of the Post-Classic Yucatec pantheon. On Dresden page 12c, the God H appellative glyph serves as the name of an aspect of God D wearing a Chac headdress (Fig. 25e). Moreover, the God H name glyph also appears in a name phrase of God D on Dresden page 15c. In the Codex Madrid, God H can be labeled with the God D appellative glyph. An example occurs on Madrid page 88b, where the youthful God H is named God D in association with the Kan-Imix augury of "plenty."

An unusual example of God H appears on Dresden page 35b, where the God H appellative glyph serves to name a water serpent with the face of Chac (Fig. 26a). The name glyph is the conventional head of God H, although in this case it is also supplied with the wrapped-cloth turban affair commonly found worn by Dresden examples of God H. The aquatic serpent of the accompanying scene wears what appears to be a headdress of a bound water lily pad. The front of the headdress displays the same beaded knot found in the name glyph of God H. In Classic period examples of this headdress, this frontal element corresponds to a water lily flower (Fig. 26b). The water lily pad headdress is a diagnostic trait of an

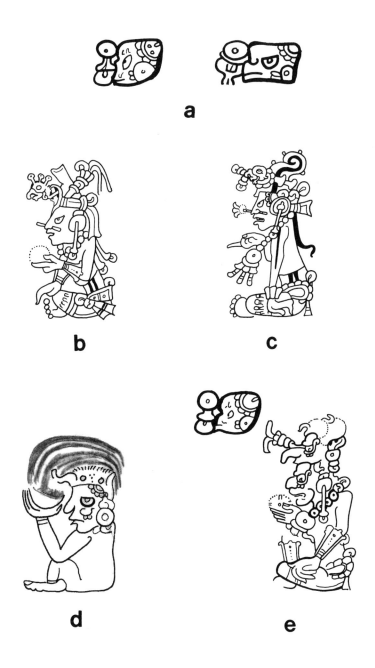

Fig. 25   God H in the Post-Classic codices.

(a) God H appellative, Dresden page 12b
(b) God H with "miter" headdress associated with Late Post-Classic Yucatec priests, Dresden page 7c
(c) God H with beaded device at side of head, Dresden page 12b

(d) God H with beaded device at side of head, Madrid page 63a
(e) God D with headdress of God B, figure named as God H, Dresden page 12c.

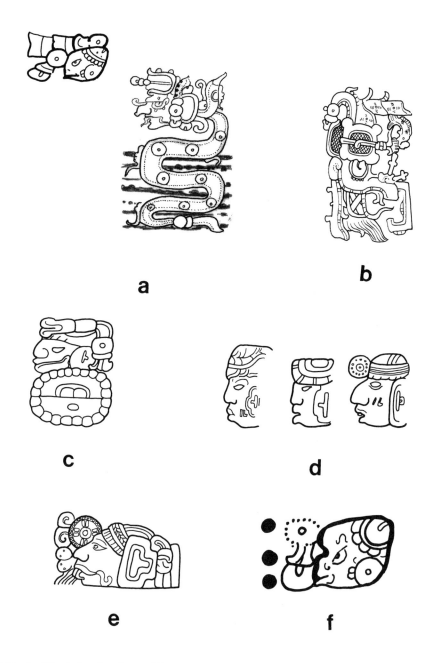

Fig. 26   God H, the Classic head variants of the numerals three and thirteen, and the Classic patron of the month Mac.

(a) Chac serpent with headdress of Classic numeral thirteen head variant, entity named as God H in accompanying text, Dresden page 35b

(b) Example of head variant of the numeral thirteen, detail from Late Classic vessel (redrawn after Parsons 1980: no. 314)

(c) Conflation of head variants of numerals three and thirteen appearing in calendrical expression 13 Mol, Step V, Hieroglyphic Stairway 3, Yaxchilan (redrawn after Graham 1982, 3: 171)

(d) Classic examples of the numeral three head variant (redrawn after Thompson 1950: fig. 24)

(e) Patron of the month Mac, detail of Early Classic stone panel, Bonampak (drawn after Mayer 1984: pl. 26)

(f) Codical example of God H appellative with dotted bead element; note numeral three prefix; Dresden page 6a.

important but little understood Classic entity appearing as a personified head variant of the number thirteen. For this reason, Hellmuth (1987: 301) suggests that the Dresden serpent is a Post-Classic form of the Classic entity. In support of this identification, it should be noted that the wrapped turban worn by the God H appellative glyph on Dresden page 35a is also frequently found on Classic period examples of the serpent deity (Fig. 26b).

The Water Lily Serpent is not the only head variant of the number thirteen. The god of the number three also appears in this context, although here with the bone jaw of the death god, the head variant of the number ten. Of course, it is not surprising that three and thirteen are related. In Yucatec, the numerals thirteen to nineteen are simply the numerals three to nine followed by the term for ten. Thus the Yucatec term for three is *ox,* and thirteen, *oxlahun.* Although there is no known instance of the Water Lily Serpent serving for the number three, there is a case where this serpent and the head variant of the numeral three are conflated into a single being. Thus, in the text of Stairway 3 at Yaxchilan, the numerical glyph for 13 Mol is the head variant of the numeral three with not only the bone jaw, but also the headdress of the serpent entity (Fig. 26c). It thus appears that the two gods are related, possibly as zoomorphic and human aspects of the same being.

Since the work of Herman Beyer (1931: 105, 108), it has been recognized that the Classic entity appearing as the head variant of three also occurs as the patron of the month Mac (Fig. 26e). Thus the figure has the same segmented headband and the circular brow element. In the illustrated Early Classic example, it can be seen that the round element clearly represents a flower. Another especially important identifying element is the prominent *tau*-shaped Ik element, the Maya sign for wind. In certain examples of the Mac patron, the *ik* sign can directly substitute for the youthful head (e.g., Thompson 1950: 8, fig. 23). Stephen Houston (personal communication, 1989) notes that substitution between the youthful Classic entity and the *ik* sign is not limited to the Mac

patron but is relatively common in the Classic script (e.g., Houston 1989a: fig. 5b, B7; fig. 5c, D1).

The Classic Water Lily Serpent is also identified with the Ik wind sign. Thus, in one Late Classic vessel scene, two aged males with the headdress of the Water Lily Serpent wear large *ik* sign plaques on their chests (see Robicsek and Hales 1981: fig. 23a). A stucco relief in the Palace at Palenque depicts common elements of the Water Lily Serpent affixed to *ik* signs accompanied by a T23 *na* sign (see Maudslay 1889–1902, 4: pl. 18). Together, the *ik* and *na* signs may be read *ik na,* or "House of Wind." Both Hellmuth (1986, 1987) and I (Taube 1986) have independently noted that Dzibilchaltun Structure 1-sub appears to be devoted to the Water Lily Serpent. During Late Post-Classic reuse of this temple, an interior altar displayed a consecutive series of painted *ik* signs (see Andrews and Andrews 1980: figs. 125, 128). This structure may have been regarded as a house of wind, or wind temple, during the Late Post-Classic period.

On close inspection, it is evident that the Post-Classic God H and the Classic entity appearing as the patron of Mac and the numeral three head variant share a number of traits. Thus the segmented rim headband of the Classic god—found also on the Classic Howler Monkey scribes—is quite similar to the beaded rim headpiece of God H (Fig. 26d). Moreover, the flower brow element appearing with the Classic entity compares closely to the beadlike device on the brow of the God H portrait glyph. In the Codex Dresden, the brow device can also be supplied with a beaded rim, as if it were a flower (Fig. 26f). It has been noted that on Dresden page 35b, this beaded device corresponds to the flower worn in the center of the Classic water lily pad headdress (Figs. 26a–b). It is intriguing that both the illustrated example from Dresden page 6 and the God H portrait glyph on Dresden page 34c are prefixed by the numeral three. However, this may be simply coincidental, since on Dresden page 11a, the God H name glyph is prefixed by the coefficient of six. Nonetheless, due to the similarities shared between God H and the Classic head variants of the numbers three and thirteen, I suspect that the numeral three head variant is the Classic antecedent of God H.

Seler (1902–23, 1: 698–700) contrasts the youthful God H with the individual found on Dresden page 4a, despite the fact that this figure has the identical name phrase (Fig. 27a). According to Seler, this individual is old, but actually he is of undetermined age. Because of the hand-held serpent, shell jewelry, and especially the probable quetzal on the back, Seler (1902–23, 1: 698) suggests that the figure on Dresden page 4a is Kukulcan, the Yucatec version of Quetzalcoatl. This identification is surely correct. Although Seler does not mention it, the specific headdress element this figure wears is identical to that of the Late Post-Classic Ehecatl-Quetzalcoatl: a disk flanked by two knots, one partially obscured behind the bird head. This particular disk, the Aztec symbol of turquoise, is virtually identical to Xochicalco Glyph A, save that here the bow is infixed in the sign. Aztec representations of Quetzalcoatl are frequently found with precisely the same elements, the turquoise disk and the flanking knots (Figs. 27b–c). Of course, Ehecatl-Quetzalcoatl was the Mexican god of wind, which immediately recalls the Classic Maya youthful being appearing as the patron of Mac and the head variant of the numeral three. Because of the explicit accompanying God H name glyphs, it is clear that on Dresden page 4a, Quetzalcoatl is described as an aspect of God H.

Whereas "der junger Gott" continues to be referred to as God H, Zimmermann (1956) termed the other figure God CH (Fig. 28).[5] Although God CH is also youthful, he can be readily identified by his jaguar skin markings around the mouth and in patches on his body. In contrast to the beadlike affix of the God H portrait glyph, the God CH appellative is prefixed by the Yax sign (Fig. 28a). In addition, the back of the head is marked not with an inverted Ahau, but with a

curious cross-hatched patterning, interpreted as serpent markings by Seler (1902–23, 1: 699).

On Dresden page 3a, there is a variant of the God CH glyph depicting the deity with the jaguar skin facial markings. In this case, the portrait glyph is prefixed with the coefficient of one rather than the Yax sign (Fig. 28b). In the subsequent discussion of God R, it will be noted that in the Codex Dresden, the twin counterpart of God CH—the spotted Hunahpu—also has the numeral one prefix. Hermann Beyer (1933: 678) was the first to recognize that God CH occurs in Classic period monumental inscriptions as the head variants of the numbers nine and nineteen. Thus the Classic glyphs are prefixed with forms of the Yax sign and are supplied with jaguar spots around the mouth (Fig. 28d). Beyer also noted that in the Post-Classic Codex Dresden, the God CH appellative also serves as the coefficient for nine and nineteen (Fig. 28c).

It is now known that the Classic God CH is one of the Headband Twins, Classic forms of the *Popol Vuh* Hero Twins commonly found on Late Classic ceramic vessels (see M. Coe 1978: no. 8; Robicsek and Hales 1981: 94; Coe 1982: 123; Taube 1985; L. Schele and M. E. Miller 1986: 51). Although both twins wear the Ahau headband, one is marked with large black spots and the other with patches of jaguar pelt. Peter Mathews (cited in Coe 1978: 58, 60) is the first to suggest that the black-spotted figure is Hunahpu, and the individual with jaguar markings, Xbalanque. In the Classic vessel scenes, they frequently assist the Tonsured Maize God, whom I identify as their father. The close association of maize with God CH continues into the Late Post-Classic period. On Madrid page 28d, God CH is merged with God E, the god of corn (Fig. 28e). Thus although the appellative glyph has the Yax prefix and jaguar skin facial markings of God CH, the figure has the cranial maize foliation of God E, along with a *kan* sign placed on the forehead. Nonetheless, the composite deity still retains the jaguar skin markings, which appear as spots around the cheek.

Following an earlier identification by Zimmermann (1956: 164), Fox and Justeson (1984: 39)

<hr>

[5] Kelly (1976: 65, 67) attributes the God CH designation to Eduard Seler. However, no precise citation is provided, and I have found no mention of God CH in the voluminous work of Seler. Thompson (1972: 32) credits the God CH term to Günter Zimmermann, and this attribution appears to be correct.

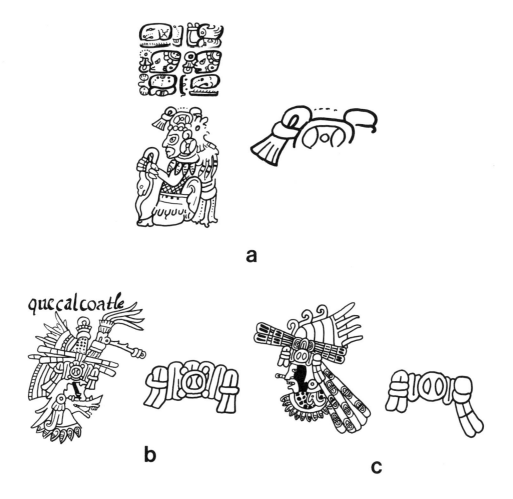

Fig. 27 Depictions of Quetzalcoatl in the Codex Dresden and Aztec manuscripts.

(a) Quetzalcoatl holding snake and wearing quetzal bird upon back; note disk and flanking knots in headdress. Pair of appellative glyphs identify figure as form of God H; Dresden page 4a

(b) Aztec representation of Ehecatl-Quetzalcoatl with disk and flanking knots in headdress, Telleriano-Remensis page 9
(c) Quetzalcoatl with headdress element, Codex Borbonicus page 3.

state that the standing figure on Paris page 10 is phonetically named as *uuc zip* (Fig. 28h). Zip, also known as Ek Zip or Uuc (*wuc*) Yol Zip, is a well-known Yucatec god of the hunt (J. Thompson 1970b: 308–309). In support of his association with hunting, the Paris figure wears a deer headdress and stands before an *atl-atl* and javelins, but of more interest are the unusual markings around the mouth. A crenated edge filled in with spots, the device is identical to the jaguar pelt "patch" frequently placed around the mouth of the Classic Xbalanque. Certain of the hunters in the Codex Madrid deer pages also seem to display jaguar skin markings about the face (Figs. 28i–j). The text accompanying one of the figures on Madrid page 40b contains the phrase *ah ceh uinic,* or "deer hunter" (Fig. 28i). But although the Paris and Madrid hunting gods may refer to God CH as Zip, the representation of Uuc Zip on Dresden page 13c in no way resembles God CH. How-

Fig. 28 God CH in Maya epigraphy and art.

(a) Appellative glyph of God CH, Madrid page 104b
(b) Variant God CH appellative; note jaguar skin marking around mouth; Dresden page 3a
(c) God CH serving as head variant of the numeral nineteen, Dresden page 69
(d) Classic God CH portrait as head variant for the numeral nine, stucco glyph from Olvidado Temple, Palenque
(e) God CH with maize elements on forehead, Madrid page 28d

(f) God CH with jaguar skin markings on face and body, Dresden page 7b
(g) Late Classic representation of God CH, detail of Tepeu 1 polychrome vessel (redrawn after Hellmuth 1987: fig. 444)
(h) Possible God CH labeled *uuc zip* in accompanying text, Paris page 10
(i) Possible God CH labeled as *ah ceh uinic* in accompanying text, Madrid page 40b
(j) Possible example of God CH, Madrid page 40c.

ever, the appearance of this figure is also entirely different from the Paris example of Uuc Zip. It is thus likely that there were several forms of Uuc Zip in Post-Classic Yucatan, one in the form of God CH.

Pre-Hispanic, ethnohistorical, and contemporary Maya lore suggests that Xbalanque was closely identified with hunting. In Classic vessel scenes, the Headband Twins are frequently found shooting down the Principal Bird Deity. Many have noted that this represents the destruction of the monster bird Vucub Caquix as described in the *Popol Vuh* (Blom 1950; Coe 1978: 58–60; Robicsek and Hales 1981: 147; Stone 1983; Cortez 1986; Taube 1987). In the *Popol Vuh,* the defeat of Vucub Caquix is not the only episode in which the Hero Twins are portrayed as hunters. The *Popol Vuh* describes the twins as great blow-gunners who frequently shoot birds in their forest travels (Recinos 1950: 105, 127–128). The *Popol Vuh* stresses their predilection for hunting in no uncertain terms: "These two [the Hero Twins] did nothing all day long but shoot their blow-guns" (Recinos 1950: 126). Then there is also the episode where Xbalanque and Hunahpu attempt to capture all the wild forest creatures endangering their *milpa* (Recinos 1950: 131–133).

In an important contemporary Mopan version of the *Popol Vuh* Hero Twins cycle, Lord Kin and Lord Xulab are great hunters who turn their brother, T'up, into a monkey (J. Thompson 1930). The principal hero and avatar of the sun, Lord Kin probably corresponds to the *Popol Vuh* Hunahpu. Lord Xulab is identified with the morning star and is principally a god of hunting and fishing (J. Thompson 1930: 63). In the myth, Lord Xulab is described as a sort of master of animals: "Lord Xulab is owner of all the animals in the world" (J. Thompson 1930: 124). In the same passage, he is said to be bearded. One of the striking traits of the Classic God CH is that he frequently has a long, flowing beard. In view of descriptions in the contemporary Mopan myth, the *Popol Vuh,* and pre-Hispanic Maya epigraphy and art, it appears that Xbalanque, also known as God CH, the jaguar pelt Headband Twin, and the personified form of the number nine, was an important god of the hunt.

Summary

Under the classification of God H, Schellhas conflates two distinct gods sharing a number of overt characteristics. Both are youthful males with portrait glyphs containing cartouches at the back of the head. However, on close inspection, the similarities quickly fade. Thus the infixed elements in the portrait glyphs are quite distinct: in the case of God H, it is usually a form resembling an inverted Ahau; for God CH, it is a cross-hatched device also found in Classic and codical examples of the day Chicchan. God H appears to be closely identified with the paramount Post-Classic god of priests, God D, and gods of water, such as Chac and the Post-Classic form of the Water Lily Serpent. It is possible that the entity appearing as the patron of Mac and the head variant of the number three is the Classic counterpart of God H. The Classic entity is closely identified with the *ik* sign and may function as a wind god. During the Classic period, the *ik* sign also appears with the Water Lily Serpent. On Dresden page 4a, God H is compared to Quetzalcoatl, the Mexican serpent god of wind. The identification with Ehecatl-Quetzalcoatl evokes both the youthful Classic god and the Water Lily Serpent. However, the correlations of God H with Classic gods is still uncertain, and God H remains one of the poorest known of the codical gods. At present, God H cannot be identified securely in the earlier Classic iconography nor with any named god of the Contact period and Colonial texts.

In contrast to God H, God CH can be easily identified not only with a Contact period god, but also a major deity of the Classic period. It is clear that God CH is none other than a Yucatec form of Xbalanque, one of the Hero Twins described in the Quichean *Popol Vuh*. Scenes in Classic Maya iconography reveal that this figure was fully present during the Classic period, and he frequently appears with his twin brother, Hunahpu, and his father, the Tonsured Maize God, the Classic form of Hun Hunahpu. In both Classic text and the Dresden codex, God CH serves as the head variant of the numbers nine and nineteen. Like the Classic examples of Xbalanque, the codical God CH tends to display patches of jaguar skin upon his body, especially around the mouth. Without the rich Classic imagery pertaining to Xbalanque, it would be extremely difficult to compare the codical God CH to Xbalanque of the early Colonial Quichean *Popol Vuh*. Codical portrayals of God CH are sparse and tell little of the significance and complex lore surrounding this divinity. A possible exception are the scenes in the Paris and Madrid codices, which seem to depict God CH as a deity of the hunt. A Post-Classic Yucatec identification of God CH with hunting accords well with both the Classic and early Colonial forms of Xbalanque.

Goddess I

In comparison with Gods H and CH, Schellhas' description of Goddess I is more seriously muddled and has been a source of much confusion in subsequent studies (Fig. 29). According to Schellhas, Goddess I is an aged and frequently clawed water goddess who wears a serpent as a headdress. Oddly, Schellhas does not provide the appellative glyph corresponding to the goddess described. The suggested glyph, a youthful female head prefixed with the *zac* white sign, is almost identical to the glyph assigned for Goddess O (see Schellhas 1904: figs. 41, 52). Schellhas (1904: 32) compares the aged deity to other female figures with serpent headdresses, but suggests that these women are distinct and lack any direct allusion to water. Although not mentioned by Schellhas, these latter figures are not aged but young (Fig. 29e). The portrait glyph of this young goddess is composed of a main sign with a caban curl usually placed on the temple and the brow (Figs. 29a–c). The sign tends to carry one of two affixes, either the *zac* prefix or a T102 *ci* postfix. Zimmermann (1956: 167, pl. 7) labels the youthful entity as Goddess I and places the aged water goddess under the title of Goddess O. J. Eric S. Thompson (1972) generally agrees with this terminology, although he had previously noted that the Schellhas Goddess O and Goddess I seemed to be old and young aspects of the same being (1950: 83). Because it has become widely accepted in the literature, I will follow the same

nomenclature. Whereas Goddess I seems to have both youthful and aged aspects, Goddess O is invariably aged and is accompanied by a particular appellative phrase.

The young and beautiful aspect of Goddess I has been generally interpreted as the moon goddess. Seler (1904: 50–52) was the first to suggest that the youthful head of Goddess I represents the moon deity. Due to the work of J. Eric S. Thompson (1939, 1950, 1970b, 1972: 47–48) this interpretation has received wide acceptance and popularity. Thompson (1950: 86) also notes that the Caban curl, an important identifying trait of the portrait glyph, is also present in Landa's alphabet. Here it corresponds to the phonetic value *u*, the Yucatec term for "moon." But although the young Goddess I is widely termed Ix Chel in the literature, there is no evidence that this was actually her name. In fact, it will be seen that the term *chel* is associated primarily with the aged Goddess O.

In the Post-Classic codices and other scenes, there is little explicit evidence for an identification of the young Goddess I with the moon. The only explicit example of the moon goddess in the Post-Classic codices occurs on Dresden page 49, here as one of the gods presiding over the heliacal appearance of Venus as Morning Star (Fig. 30c). In this case, she appears with a lunar crescent projecting from her back. It is noteworthy that neither the depicted moon goddess nor her appellative glyph appears with the Caban curl *u* sign.

The clearest representations of the young moon goddess are to be found in Late Classic Maya epigraphy and art. However, not every Classic female deity is the moon goddess, and care must be taken in identifying this entity. The most important identifying features are the lunar crescent and the rabbit, a well-known moon symbol (Figs. 30a–b, d–e). In many Classic examples, the moon goddess also appears with a beaklike appendage projecting out from the upper lip (Figs. 30a–b, e).

Almost invariably, the Classic moon deity is female, but a number of possible male or dually sexed examples do exist (Fig. 31). A full-figure glyph from Quirigua, Zoomorph P, depicts the

Fig. 29   Post-Classic glyphs and portrayals of Goddess I.

(a) Goddess I portrait glyph with *zac* prefix, Dresden page 22b
(b) Goddess I appellative with T102 *ci* postfix, Dresden page 16c
(c) Goddess I appellative with eroded *zac* prefix, Madrid page 95a
(d) Aged Goddess I appellative with *zac* prefix, Madrid page 107b

(e) Seated Goddess I with bound serpent in hair, Dresden page 22b
(f) Seated Goddess I, Dresden page 16c
(g) Goddess I letting blood from ear, Madrid page 95a
(h) Aged Goddess I with offerings, Madrid page 107b
(i) Aged Goddess I weaving, Madrid page 102c

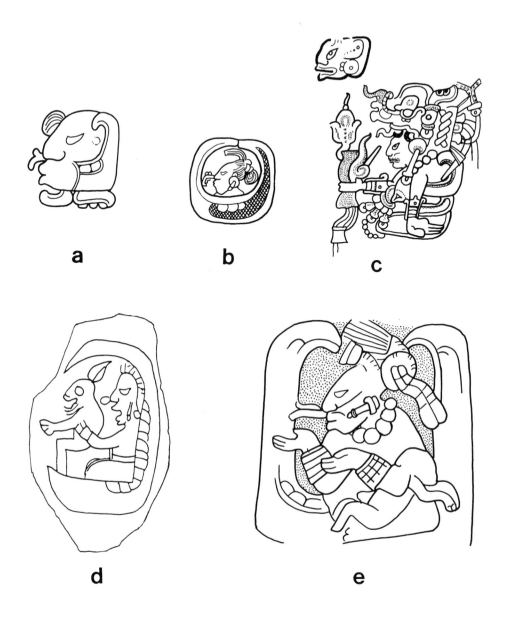

a   b   c

d   e

Fig. 30 Classic and Post-Classic representations of the moon goddess; note beak-like nose element in a, b, and e.

(a) Late Classic moon goddess portrait glyph with in-fixed lunar sign, Yaxchilan Lintel 23 (redrawn after I. Graham 1982, 3: 136)

(b) Moon goddess within lunate element, Piedras Negras Stela 19 (redrawn after L. Schele and J. H. Miller 1983: fig. 17k)

(c) Moon goddess and appellative glyph from Dresden Venus pages, Dresden page 49

(d) Moon goddess in moon sign with rabbit, incised obsidian flake (redrawn after L. Schele and J. H. Miller 1983: fig. 18e)

(e) Moon Goddess with lunate sign and rabbit, compare nose element with that of Figs. 23b and 24c, Lintel 2 Chicazapote (drawn after Maler 1903: pl. XXXVII, 2).

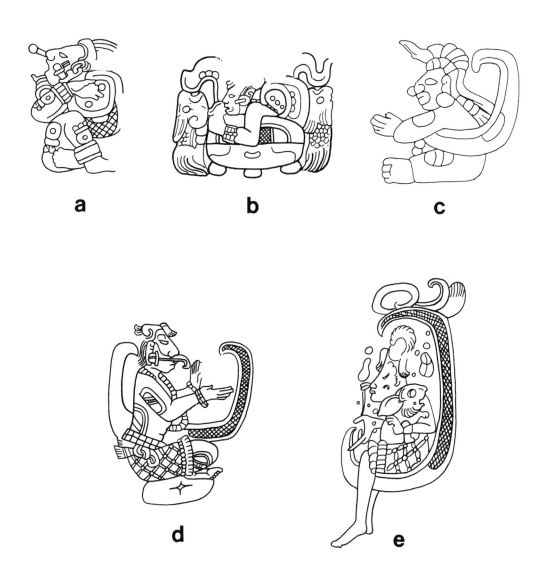

Fig. 31 Classic depictions of figures exhibiting traits of moon goddess and Tonsured Maize God.

(a) Bearded figure with lunar element, note *sac* or "white" signs on limbs, detail of Zoomorph P, Quirigua (redrawn after Maudslay 1889–1902, 2: pl. 64)

(b) Patron of month Ch'en, Copan Stela D (drawn after Thompson 1950: fig. 60)

(c) Tonsured Maize God with lunate sign, detail of Late Classic bas-relief (drawn after Mayer 1984: pl. 174)

(d) Composite form of Tonsured Maize God and moon goddess, detail of incised Early Classic conch trumpet (redrawn after L. Schele and M. E. Miller 1986: pl. 121)

(e) Composite Tonsured Maize God and moon goddess sitting within moon with rabbit; note maize element at top of lunar sign (redrawn after L. Schele and M. E. Miller 1986: pl. 120).

moon deity with a beard along with *zac* markings and the moon sign (Fig. 31a). In the Initial Series introductory glyph on Copan Stela D, the sign corresponding to the month Ch'en is composed of a human figure accompanied by a moon crescent. Although the figure is somewhat eroded, it ap-

pears to be male, with the spiral maize cranial infix found on the Tonsured Maize God (Fig. 31b).

On an Early Classic incised conch trumpet, there is a young individual seated upon a phonetic *po* sign seat (Fig. 31d). Due to the large U-shaped moon sign placed behind the individual, Michael

Coe (1982: 122) tentatively suggests that the figure represents the moon goddess. However, Linda Schele and Mary Ellen Miller (1986: 309) consider the figure to be male and suggest that he is the *Popol Vuh* Hero Twin who becomes the moon. That the figure is identified with the moon is undebatable, all the more so because of the *po* sign seat; in Kekchi, Pokomchi, and Pokoman, *po* signifies "moon" (Thompson 1970b: 241).

The Early Classic conch figure also possesses attributes of the Tonsured Maize God. Thus the elongated head and tuft of brow hair is identical to Early Classic examples of this entity (Fig. 20a). The beaded skirt worn by the conch figure frequently appears with individuals dressed as the Tonsured Maize God (see Taube 1985: 174). The same skirt is worn by the moon goddess on an incised vessel in the American Museum of Natural History, New York (Fig. 31e). There is no doubt that this figure represents the moon; she not only sits in the crescent but also holds a rabbit. Nonetheless, her profile, facial markings, and coiffure are identical to the Tonsured Maize God. Moreover, there is a specific maize sign placed directly atop the lunar crescent.

In contemporary Maya ethnography, the moon and maize are closely associated. Among the highland Mam, the moon, earth, and maize are known collectively as "Our Mother" (Siegel 1941: 66; Valladares 1957: 196). Then there is the *Popol Vuh* Xquic, the wife of Hun Hunahpu and the mother of the Hero Twins. Tedlock (1985: 328) considers Xquic to be an aspect of the moon and notes that her name suggests the Quichean term for "moon." As previously mentioned, the Classic form of Hun Hunahpu is the Tonsured Maize God. Laughlin (1977: 245–246) compares Xquic to Thunderbolt Girl, a Tzotzil variant of the "Maize Girl" found widely in southern Mesoamerica. In part, the identification of the moon with maize may be due to the widespread use of the moon to time the planting of maize and other crops. For example, the Pipil of Izalco, El Salvador, plant during the waxing moon (J. Thompson 1939: 142). The highland Chorti Maya study the moon to learn the advent of the rainy season (Fought 1972: 387), whereas the Yucatec of Chan

Kom plant root crops and fruit trees according to the phases of the moon (Redfield and Villa Rojas 1934: 205). It is intriguing that the Tzeltalan term for the aforementioned month Ch'en is Tzun, or "sowing" (Thompson 1950: 111). However, during the Late Classic period—the time of Copan Stela D—Ch'en was during July and August, too late for sowing at the onset of the spring rains.

During the Post-Classic period, Goddess I is identified with weaving. The T58 *zac* or "white" prefix frequently accompanying her name glyph may refer to weaving as well as the whiteness of the moon (Figs. 29a, c–d).[6] J. Thompson (1972: 47) notes that *zac* is the root for the Yucatec verb "to weave." In the Codex Madrid, T58 occurs with both young and old representations of Goddess I. The aged aspect of Goddess I is identified as a distinct deity by Schellhas (1904: 38), who terms her Goddess O. The portrait glyph of the aged goddess tends to have a series of short vertical lines, aptly interpreted as wrinkles by Schellhas (Fig. 29d). On Madrid page 32b, it can be clearly seen that this convention refers to wrinkles, as it is placed on the stretched and hanging breasts of Goddess O. The name glyph of the aged deity on Madrid page 105a is identical to that of the youthful Goddess I on Dresden pages 15b and 20b. In the Codex Madrid, the aged Goddess I is often found weaving, and in a number of instances she wears a pair of horn-like elements on her head (Fig. 29h). Although Seler (1902–23, 4: 738) interprets these elements as insect antennae, they are more probably spools of cotton. Similar pairs of cotton spindles are found in the headdress of Tlazolteotl and other Mexican goddesses (Figs. 65b–c). It will be seen that weaving is not unique to Goddess I, but is also a basic feature of Goddess O, the great genetrix.

Summary

Although often referred to as the moon goddess Ix Chel, there is little direct evidence that

---

[6] The Huichol also appear to identify the moon with cotton and weaving. Lumholtz (1900: 129–130) describes a Huichol model of the young waxing moon. It is formed of large netted hoop with wads of unspun cotton placed at intervals along the rim. The entire net is termed *wi'ta*, or "cotton thread."

Goddess I was the moon or was named Ix Chel. In the one clear codical representation of the moon goddess on Dresden page 49, the deity lacks both the name glyph and the curling lock of hair of Goddess I. However, it is likely that both the Dresden page 49 example and Goddess I are related to the Classic period moon goddess. In the Post-Classic codices, Goddess I is usually a young woman, although at times, she is also aged. During the Classic period, the moon goddess is also young, and frequently appears with a lunar crescent, the rabbit, and a beaklike nose piece. In a number of instances, the Classic moon goddess merges with the Tonsured Maize God. The Initial Series introductory glyph corresponding to the month Ch'en appears to be a conflation of the moon goddess with the god of corn. The Classic association of maize with the moon suggests that planting cycles based on phases of the moon could well be pre-Hispanic in origin.

God K

Schellhas (1904: 32) terms this deity "the god with the ornamented nose," owing to the strangely irregular form of the long, upturned snout. In the codices and Post-Classic mural painting, this is the principal identifying feature of God K (Fig. 32). Seler (1902–23, 1: 377) interprets the accompanying name glyph as a caiman-like creature with fire running out of the eyes (Figs. 32a–b). Although, at first sight, the deity face and name glyph appear to have little in common, Classic epigraphic and iconographic representations of God K possess a long, upturned snout and the same fire element in the brow region (Figs. 32c, 34a). In Classic depictions, this latter device usually represents a smoking torch or axe blade.

During the Post-Classic period, God K lacks the cranial axe and serpent foot of the Classic deity. The earliest examples of the Post-Classic form of God K appear on X Fine Orange vessels from Chiapas and Yucatan. In Yucatan, these vessels form part of the Sotuta ceramic complex of Early Post-Classic Chichen Itza. An X Fine

Orange vessel from Moxviquil, Chiapas, portrays an important link between the Classic and Post-Classic form of God K (Fig. 33a). Thus, although possessing the lumpy irregular snout of the Post-Classic God K, the figure also displays the smoking cranial element of the Classic form. The snout and curling front tooth of this figure are notably similar to representations of God K in the Grolier Codex, a manuscript attributed to Early Post-Classic Chiapas (Fig. 33d). According to J. Eric S. Thompson (1975: 7), the human-like teeth found in the Grolier examples do not appear with other known images of God K. Partly for this reason, Thompson (1975: 7) declared the Grolier a forgery. However, an X Fine Orange vessel attributed to Yaxchilan, Chiapas, portrays a crude but identifiable form of God K with similar anthropomorphic teeth (Fig. 33b). Images of God K are especially common on X Fine Orange vases of the Sotuta complex of the northern Maya lowlands (Fig. 33c). A detailed study of God K images appearing on Fine Orange pottery could shed much light on the chronological development of this god during the Terminal Classic and Early Post-Classic periods.

In the Terminal Classic art of Yucatan, God K frequently appears with wings; clearly, this alludes to the celestial aspect of this diety (Fig. 34). In the recently discovered Xt'elhu bas-reliefs, winged God K figures appear floating in the upper portions of the scenes (Fig. 34b). Moreover, representations of the winged God K frequently appear in the uppermost portions of architectural settings, that is, in the region corresponding to the sky. Excellent examples appear upon the lintels of Sayil Structure 4B1 (Fig. 34a). Winged God K figures are also frequently found on Puuc and Chenes capstones (e.g., Mayer 1983: figs. 11, 12, 24, 50, 51).

Although the winged God K is absent in the Post-Classic Maya codices, this concept does continue into the Late Post-Classic period. Thus, in Mural 1 of Tulum Structure 5, two winged God K figures serve as the ends of a sky band (Fig. 34c). Another possible example of a Late Post-Classic winged God K occurs on a stela discovered at Flores, Guatemala (Fig. 34d). The monu-

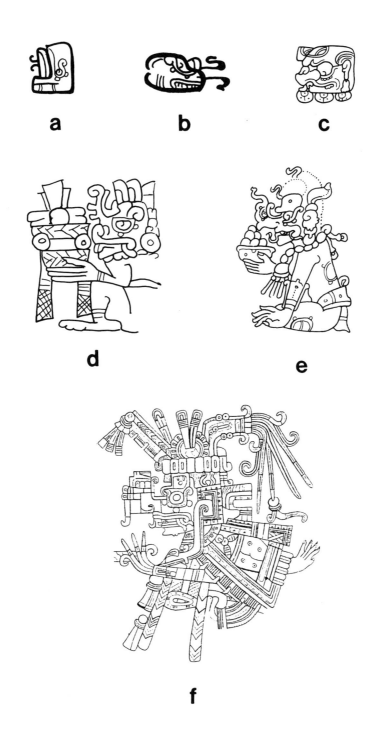

Fig. 32 God K in Maya epigraphy and art.

(a) Late Post-Classic example of God K appellative, Madrid page 77
(b) Late Post-Classic God K appellative, Paris page 24
(c) Late Classic God K appellative with phonetic *la* suffix, Yaxchilan Lintel 25 (redrawn after Graham and von Euw 1977, 3: 57)
(d) God K holding headdress, Madrid page 21c
(e) God K holding bowl of cacao, Dresden page 12a
(f) God K as bound prisoner, Mound 1, Santa Rita (after Gann 1900: pl. XXIX).

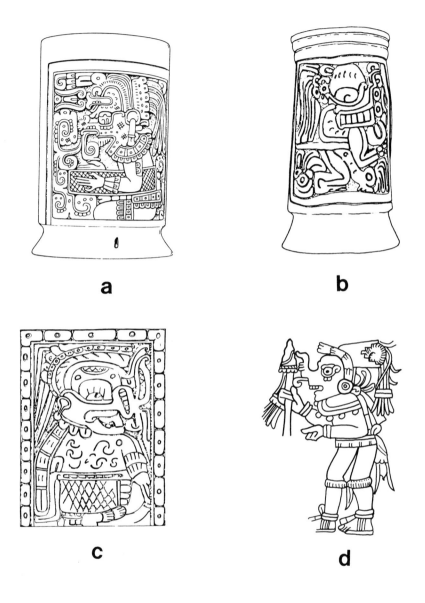

a   **b**

c   **d**

Fig. 33 Early Post-Classic representations of God K from X Fine Orange vessels and the Codex Grolier.

(a) Vessel from Moxviquil, Chiapas (after Smith 1958: fig. 4f)

(b) Vase from Yaxchilan, Chiapas (after Brainerd 1958: fig. 90e)

(c) Detail of vase from Yucatan Peninsula (after Brainerd 1958: fig. 79r)

(d) Representation of God K, Grolier page 4.

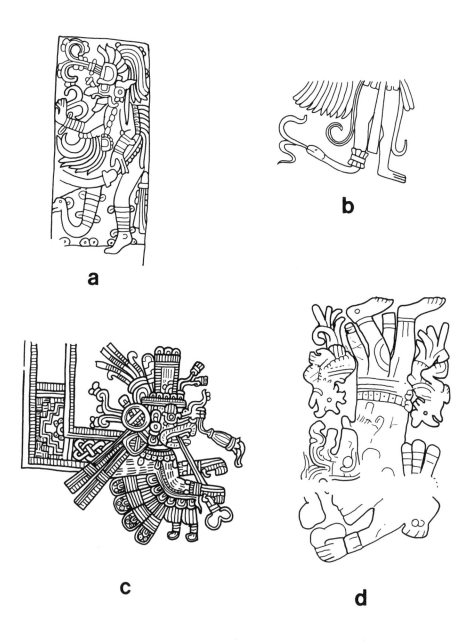

Fig. 34 Winged God K figures in Terminal Classic
and Post-Classic Yucatan.

(a) Winged God K from lintel of Sayil Structure 4B1
   (redrawn after Pollock 1980: fig. 255)
(b) Partially intact winged God K, detail of bas-relief
   from Xt'el Hu, Yucatan (redrawn after Robertson
   1986: fig. 7)

(c) Winged God K as sky band, detail of mural from
   Tulum Structure 5 (redrawn after A. G. Miller
   1982: pl. 28)
(d) Winged diving god with God K headdress, detail
   of Late Post-Classic stela from Flores, Guatemala
   (redrawn after A. F. Chase 1985: fig. 9).

ment depicts a diving anthropomorphic figure flanked by Quetzal birds; the figure is winged and wears a God K headdress quite similar to examples known through the codices. However, because God K only occurs as the headdress and not the actual face, it is unclear whether the figure represents God K or a diving god wearing a God K headdress.

According to Schellhas, God K is a star deity, but this interpretation is based primarily on a reputed association with God C, erroneously identified as the "god of the polar star." Seler (1902–23, 1: 377) provides a far more convincing identification of God K as Ah Bolon Dzacab, equivalent to the Bolon Zacab mentioned by Landa for the year Kan (see Tozzer 1941: 139–141). The identification of Bolon Dzacab, or "he of the nine generations," as a Post-Classic Yucatec form of God K is widely accepted (e.g., Tozzer 1941: note 673; Thompson 1970b: 227; Kelley 1976: 6, 65, 97; L. Schele and J. Miller 1983: 12).

Eduard Seler (1976: 5) states that as a god of water and fertility, Ah Bolon Dzacab was strongly identified with Chac, the Yucatec counterpart of Tlaloc. Although Schellhas (1904: 32) does not recognize the actual symbolic meanings shared between Gods B and K, he notes that they are closely related. As an example, Schellhas (1904: 33) points out Dresden pages 34b and 65a, where God B wears a God K headdress; another instance of Chac wearing a God K headdress may be found in Mural 2 of Tulum Structure 16 (see Miller 1982: pl. 37). Eduard Seler (1902–23, 1: 377) notes that on Madrid page 31b, Chac rides on a serpent with the head of God K; he also mentions Dresden page 25a, where the carried image corresponding to God K of Dresden page 25b is not Bolon Dzacab, but Chac. More recently, it has been noted that Classic period 819-day cycle texts are quite like a passage on Dresden pages 30b and 31b, which contains the same verb and a similar reference to the four colors and directions (Berlin and Kelley 1961). However, whereas God K is the subject of the Classic texts, it is God B in the Dresden passage.

Images of God K abound in the Classic period; unlike the Post-Classic representations, he almost invariably has a serpent foot and the smoking device set in the forehead. Moreover, although long and upturned, the snout lacks the protuberances found with the Post-Classic God K. The Classic period God K is often referred to as GII of the Palenque Triad, owing to his importance in Palenque texts (Berlin 1963; Kelley 1965).

In a number of studies, Coggins (1975; 1979; 1988) states that God K is a god of rain and lightning, a Maya version of Tlaloc. In support of this interpretation, Coggins (1979: fig. 3–2) illustrates a figure from Copan displaying a syncretic merging of Tlaloc and God K traits (Fig. 72a). Thus, although he possesses the large teeth and goggle eyes of Tlaloc, the figure also has the smoking torch and serpent foot. During the Classic period, the most diagnostic representations of God K are to be found in the form of the Manikin Scepter, an object frequently wielded by rulers on stelae and other monuments. Coggins (1979: 49) suggests that the God K Manikin Scepter is the personification of the Mexican atl-atl as the "Lightning Hurler." However, in a more recent study, Coggins (1988) states that the Manikin Scepter is a lightning axe. This later interpretation is surely correct; in many instances God K is depicted explicitly as a zoomorphic axe (Fig. 35a): each of the four stucco-painted wooden images of God K from Tikal Burial 195 are provided with an axe blade set into a backward sweeping head (Fig. 36a). In profile, the head and axe blade mimic a Classic Maya wooden axe, which is frequently tipped with a backwardly curving element (e.g., Figs. 8, 37e). To reinforce the comparison to a hafted axe, the artisan carefully depicted the forehead with wood che markings. A Terminal Classic relief from Santa Rosa Xtampak depicts a God K axe with not only the forehead celt but also a large pointed axe blade transfixed through the chest and shoulders (see Proskouriakoff 1950: fig. 94a).

An explicit lightning weapon, the burning God K axe is frequently wielded by the Maya god of rain and lightning. From the beginnings of the Classic to the Early Post-Classic period, Chac may be found holding a God K lightning axe. Thus one of the earliest known depictions of God

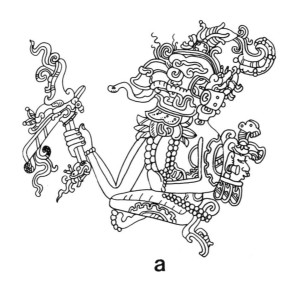

a

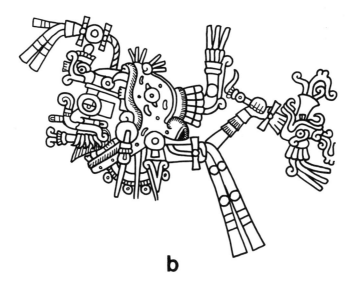

b

Fig. 35 Comparison of the God K scepter with the serpent lightning axe of Tlaloc.

(a) Classic Chac holding burning God K serpent axe, note smoke rising from blade, serpent mouth, and forehead of God K; detail of Early Classic incised and modeled vessel (drawn after M. Coe 1982: 71)

(b) Tlaloc wielding burning serpent lightning axe, Codex Laud page 2.

a

b

Fig. 36 God K holding mirrors.

(a) One of four God K plastered wooden effigies found within Burial 195, Tikal; note mirrors held in front of figures (drawn after W. R. Coe 1967: 57)

(b) Early Classic Maya form of *tezcacuitlapilli* back mirror, Burial 10, Tikal (redrawn after Hellmuth 1987: fig. 497).

K appears as a burning serpent lightning axe held by Chac (Fig. 35a). In concept, this God K lightning axe is virtually identical to the smoking serpent lightning axe wielded by Tlaloc on Codex Laud page 2 (Fig. 35b). Smoke volutes may be seen pouring out of the serpent snout and blade of the axe. At Chichen Itza, Chac figures are frequently found holding burning, serpent-footed axes, clearly an allusion to God K (Fig. 5c). The frequently burning serpent foot of the Classic God K is a fire serpent, in other words, lightning.

The mirror constitutes an important, recently discovered attribute of the Classic God K. The four wood figures from Tikal Burial 195 each portray God K holding a large mirror plaque before himself (Fig. 36a). With their pendant elements, these mirror assemblages are almost identical to the *tezcacuitlapilli* worn on the back of the two-part effigy from Tikal Burial 10 (Fig. 36b). It is now known that the T617a element in the brow piece of God K is a shining mirror (see L. Schele and J. Miller 1983: 9). Linda Schele and Jeffrey Miller (1983: 9) suggest that the *ocote* wood torch frequently found in the center of the brow mirror serves as a phonetic marker for the reading of "obsidian mirror," as the words for "obsidian" and "torch" are generally homophonous in Mayan languages, usually designated as *tah* or *toh*. This dovetails nicely with Tohil, the Quichean god of lightning and storms. Dennis Tedlock (1985: 365)—who considers God K an ancestral form of the Quichean deity—notes that Tohil is an aspect of Hurakan, or "one leg." It has been noted that the Classic God K is essentially one-legged, one leg being human and the other serpentine.

Linda Schele and Jeffrey Miller (1983: 12) interpret the elements infixed to the head of God K as phonetic devices, but all may refer to lightning. The smoking celt, the earliest and probably most important form, is an obvious and widespread lightning symbol. Similarly, lightning is also identified with burning torches and fire. Joanne Spero (1987) cites a number of Jacaltec and Tojolabal tales in which lightning becomes stuck in a pine tree, the material from which the fiercely burning *ocote* is derived.

The smoking cigar may also allude to lightning, in part because the Yucatec Chacs are reported to be great smokers. In one recorded tale, lighting the cigar with flint and steel causes thunder and lightning (Thompson 1970b: 113, 171). The Pedrano Tzotzil closely identify tobacco with lightning. This plant is personified as an *anhel,* a rain and thunder deity, and it is believed that ground tobacco protects one from lightning (Thompson 1970b: 116).

Along with axe blades, torches, and cigars, the forehead mirror also relates to lightning. Because of their bright, flashing quality, mirrors are widely identified with fire and lightning in Mesoamerica (Taube 1983, 1986, n.d.a). Whereas *lem* signifies "mirror" in Quiche, Cakchiquel, and Kekchi, the same term in Yucatec, Chol, and Tzeltal means "to shine" or "lightning" (L. Schele and J. Miller 1983: 13). Yucatec speakers in the region of Chichen Itza and Ignacio Zaragoza have informed me that household mirrors are covered during thunderstorms to prevent Chac from striking the reflective surface. Moreover, in the Early Post-Classic iconography of Tula and Chichen Itza, *xiuhcoatl* fire or lightning serpents frequently appear on mosaic turquoise and pyrite mirrors. A similar concept occurs in the mural paintings at Santa Rita and Tulum, where God B or God K

serpents emerge from mirrors worn at the back of the head (Taube n.d.a). In summary, all of the elements in the head of God K—mirrors, fire, burning axes, torches, and cigars—may allude to lightning.

One of the clearest identifications of the Classic God K with lightning and rain is to be found with composite figures possessing attributes of both Chac and God K. On Naranjo Stela 22, ruler Smoking Squirrel wears a large Chac headdress supplied with the smoking cranial torch of God K (Fig. 37a). Another composite example of Chac and God K appears in the form of Chac with the serpent foot of God K (Figs. 37b–e). A possible Protoclassic example of this being occurs as a beltpiece pendant worn by the lord on Abaj Takelik Stela 1 (Fig. 36b). Worn dangling behind the knees, this particular beltpiece ornament is usually a representation of Chac. Early Classic examples, to name a few, appear on Tikal Stelae 2, 28, 33, 35, Uolantun Stela 1 (Jones and Satterthwaite 1982: figs. 2, 48, 55b, 55d), and Yaxha Stela 4 (Fig. 6d). The Abaj Takelik example differs in one special way: the foot of this figure ends in a device that could well represent the fanged upturned snout of a serpent. In other words, the figure may bear the serpent foot of God K. Unfortunately, erosion prohibits a precise identification of this crucial area. If this is a God K serpent foot, it could constitute the earliest known example in the Maya region.[7]

The composite God K-Chac is fairly common in Maya iconography, and it appears that this being functions as a form of Chac. The serpent-footed figure entity occurs on the Early Classic Tikal Stela 1, where he is paired opposite a conventional God K. Whereas God K has his characteristic cranial axe, the latter seems to have only a

[7] Mary Ellen Miller (1986: 61) notes a possible example of a serpent-footed God K on a still earlier monument, Izapa Stela 3. The scene represents a figure brandishing a weapon over the upper portion of a serpent body. However, the leg region of the standing figure is badly eroded, and it is difficult to determine whether the serpent forms part of the human leg or is separate. In the photograph provided by V. Garth Norman (1973: pl. 5), it appears that the creature is not joined to the leg but rather, constitutes the upper half of a severed snake body. However, this does not necessarily contradict the God K identification, for it is possible that this scene may describe the mythical origin of the God K serpent foot.

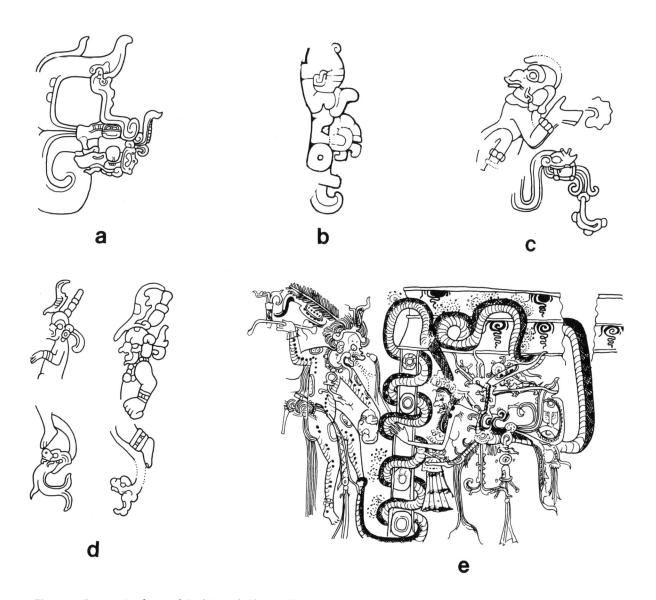

a

b

c

d

e

Fig. 37   Composite form of God K and Classic Chac.

(a) Chac head with smoking cranial torch of God K, detail of Naranjo Stela 22 (redrawn after I. Graham and E. von Euw 1975, 2: 55)

(b) Possible Protoclassic example of serpent-footed Chac, detail of Abaj Takelik Stela 1 (after Porter n.d.a: fig. 2)

(c) Early Classic serpent-footed Chac, detail of Tikal Stela 1 (redrawn after Jones and Satterthwaite 1982: fig. 1)

(d) Classic Chac with serpent foot held in arms of Late Classic rulers, Xultun Stela 3, Stela 10 (after von Euw 1978, 5: 15, 37)

(e) Detail of Late Classic vessel representing Classic Chac with axe and serpent foot penetrating structure marked with mirrors and Caban earth curls (drawn after Kerr 1990: 285).

simple crest of hair (Fig. 37c). On the roughly contemporaneous Tikal Stela 2, the figure occupying the same position as the composite god of Stela 1 is an eroded but conventional axe-wielding Classic Chac. Thus, along with the axe,

he wears a crenelated Spondylus shell earpiece, has the upturning shell brow element, and holds a snake within his mouth (see Jones and Satterthwaite 1982: fig. 2). The composite God K-Chac is also found on Xultun Stelae 3 and 10, where he is held in the left arm of the ruler (Fig. 37d). In each case the figure is paired with a small jaguar held in the opposite hand. Xultun Stela 5 portrays an almost identical pairing. However, as in the case of Tikal Stela 2, a Classic Chac, with no evident attribute of God K, constitutes the left arm figure (see von Euw 1978: 23).

In view of the substitution of the conventional Chac for the composite entity at Tikal and Xultun, it seems that the Chac and composite God K-Chac figures have similar, if not equivalent, meanings. In other words, the composite being functions as a form of Chac. The serpent-footed Chac also appears on a Late Classic vessel, wielding a hafted axe with a burning torch rather than a stone blade (Fig. 37e). His serpent foot penetrates a house marked with Caban curls, quite probably a representation of lightning penetrating the earth (see Taube 1986). In this scene, the composite entity probably also refers to Chac. In related Classic scenes, Chac serves as the lightning figure who splits open the earth (e.g., Taube 1986: figs. 3, 4). The identification of Chac with God K may extend into the ethnographic present. In the Tzeltal community of Amatenango del Valle, one aspect of the lightning god *tatik cha'uk* is San Pedro Martyr, who has a hatchet piercing his head (Nash 1970: 205).

Aside from noting the close correspondence between Gods B and K, Schellhas (1904: 32) also suggests an identification of God K with maize. Thus Schellhas mentions that the texts accompanying the representations of God K on Dresden pages 12a and 26c contain the God K name glyph followed by that of the maize god, God E. In the Chilam Balam books of Chumayel, Tizimin, and Mani, Bolon Dzacab is created from a bundle of edible seeds (Roys 1933: 99; Craine and Reindorp 1979: 118; Edmonson 1982: 46–47). Similarly, the Tizimin mentions *bolon dzacab uah,* the prepared tortilla, or more probably tamale, of the god Bolon Dzacab (Edmonson 1982: 62). In Terminal Classic painted Puuc capstones, God K is frequently found with tamales (Mayer 1983: figs. 11, 19, 36, 53). Moreover, Glyph Y of the lunar series and the 819-day count appears to be a tamale supplied with legs and the smoking head of God

K; in other words, it is a tamale personified as God K (Taube 1989a). One of the most complex representations of Classic maize iconography, the Temple of the Foliated Cross, has as its principal event the birth of GII, or God K (Kelley 1965). Along with the Classic God D, God K tends to have the elongated head and "double-domed" coiffure of the Tonsured Maize God. In the previous discussion of God E, it is noted that the Tonsured Maize God at times wears the smoking headpiece of God K.

A recent phonetic reading at Chichen Itza provides strong support for the identification of God K with maize. David Stuart (1987b) notes that at Chichen, the God K appellative is phonetically written as *kauil*. Stuart further suggests that *kauil* was a widespread Classic name for God K and cites supportive evidence at Yaxchilan and other sites. Stuart also notes that Kauil was a major deity of protohistoric Yucatan. Thompson (1970b: 289) stresses the close identification of this god with maize and translates Kauil as "Surplus of Our Daily Bread."

In view of his direct association with lightning, rain, and maize, it is clear that God K is identified with the fertile forces of life. Linda Schele (1976: 12) considers the Classic God K as a deity of lineages and royal descent. In this light, the Manikin Scepter is interpreted as an "icon of rulership and bloodletting" (L. Schele and M. E. Miller 1986: 73). The Tablet of the Foliated Cross and its flanking jambs clearly associate God K with bloodletting, as three of the figures hold perforators (Schele 1976: fig. 10). Moreover, many of the blades or lancets found in Peten caches and burials contain incised representations of God K (e.g., see Trik 1963: fig. 11; Robicsek 1978: fig. 99). Schele provides strong epigraphic evidence that God K is closely identified with the acquisition of royal power. Thus the "Ahau in hand" and "God K in hand" glyphs usually denote the presentation of God K in dynastic scenes, frequently at the time of heir designation or accession (Schele 1982: 62–63, 118, 169). In support of Schele, I should mention that the head of God K is frequently capped with the smoking Ahau, a sign designating male parentage in Classic texts.

With the abundant epigraphic evidence found on Classic monuments, it is clear that God K is identified with lineage and bloodletting.

Michael Coe (1973: 16; 1981: 163; 1982: 47; cited in Robicsek 1978: 104–106; Carlson 1981: 125–126; L. Schele and J. Miller 1983: 9) notes a striking series of correspondences between God K and the Aztec Tezcatlipoca: each is identified with rulership and royal descent, frequently displays a smoking mirror upon his head, and has a serpent foot. However, although there are many parallels, the two deities are also distinct in a number of important ways. Thus God K is decidedly a scaly reptilian figure, whereas Tezcatlipoca is identified with the jaguar. Recent epigraphic work by Houston and Stuart (1989: 8) indicates that the serpent was considered as the *uay,* or co-essence, of God K. However, the co-essence of Tezcatlipoca was clearly the jaguar (Nicholson 1971: 412). Moreover, whereas God K is strongly identified with agriculture and maize, these traits are weakly displayed by Tezcatlipoca. Although Tezcatlipoca and God K are perhaps cognate in a general sense, there is not a direct one-to-one correspondence between the deities.

Summary

One of the more important gods of the Maya pantheon, God K is a complex figure with a broad range of iconographic and epigraphic associations. Many of these associations appear to revolve around one of his most basic meanings, that of a celestial lightning god. In the Classic period, God K often appears as a lightning axe wielded by Chac, another major god of rain and lightning. The burning torch, smoking celt, cigar, and mirror inset into the forehead of God K are all recognized lightning symbols in contemporary Maya lore. In addition, the burning serpent foot is probably yet another allusion to lightning, for fire serpents are a widespread symbol of thunderbolts in ancient and contemporary Mesoamerica. Along with his lightning and agricultural associations, God K was an important god of Classic Maya lineage and rulership. Although it has been little pursued, the agricultural dimension of God

K pertains directly to elite power and dynastic descent. A deity identified with lightning, rain, and fertile maize, God K epitomizes the vital, engendering force from which life comes.

God L

Schellhas (1904: 34) notes that the primary attributes of God L are agedness and black body coloration. Another important trait mentioned by Schellhas is the bird worn on the head of God L on Dresden page 14c (Fig. 38b). It was subsequently demonstrated that this creature is the Moan screech owl, a bird closely identified with rain as well as the underworld (see J. Thompson 1950: 114–115). In the case of this Dresden scene and many Classic period representations, the Moan owl actually rests in a large-brimmed hat topped with broad, spotted feathers, undoubtedly those of the same bird (Figs. 38b–c; 39a–c; 40c, e; 41a–b; 42a–b; 43a–d). According to Schellhas (1904: 35), God L is found in neither the Paris nor Madrid codices. In fact, he does appear on Paris page 21 and Madrid page 32a. God L is not a major deity of the Late Post-Classic period; instead, the vast majority of known God L representations appear in earlier Classic scenes.

Schellhas (1904: 35) states that the limited scenes of God L in the Codex Dresden provide no obvious clues to the identity of this divinity. However, Schellhas does point to Dresden page 46b, on which God L appears as a warrior supplied with spear-thrower and shield. Due to the important analysis of the Venus pages by Seler (1904c), it is known that God L is here portrayed as one of the Venus gods. The text establishes that he is responsible for spearing God K, who lies directly below the God L scene. During the Classic period, God L also appears with weapons or staffs, but with no clear Venus associations.

Although Günter Zimmermann (1956: 164–165) views God L as a benevolent deity, Michael Coe (1973: 14; 1978: 16) identifies him as one of the principal lords of the underworld. One of the most striking images of his underworld office occurs on the Princeton Vase: God L sits in a

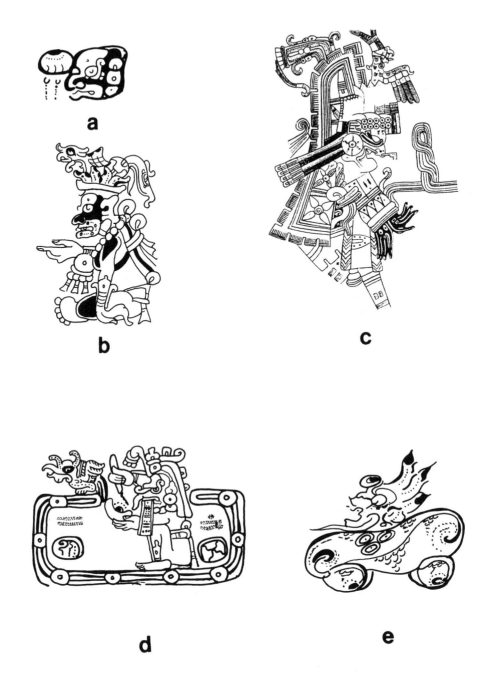

Fig. 38   God L and the Moan Owl.

(a) Portrait glyph of God L, Dresden page 14c
(b) Seated God L with Moan Owl headdress, Dresden page 14c
(c) God L with Moan Owl headdress, Mound 1, Santa Rita (after Gann 1900: pl. xxix)

(d) Chac in cave or sinkhole painting tail feathers of Moan Owl black, possibly with *sabac* soot, Madrid page 73b
(e) Head of Classic Chac with crest of Moan Owl feathers (drawn after Robicsek and Hales 1981: vessel 37a).

curtain-swathed palace topped with jaguars and gleefully observes a rite of human decapitation (Fig. 39c). In another vessel scene, God L sits with a bundle on a jaguar throne as he presides over six subsidiary deities (Fig. 39b). This scene appears to be an event near the beginning of time, because it is associated with the date 4 Ahau 8 Cumku, the Long Count base of the present great cycle (Coe 1973: 108).

In Classic scenes, God L has a large, squared eye, jaguar characteristics, and frequently appears smoking a cigar. He is a complex deity having both mortuary and life-giving attributes. Thus although a god of nether regions, he is also identified with water, agricultural fertility, and riches.

At times, God L appears with a wrapped bundle, evidently a form of the sacred bundle found over much of ancient Mesoamerica. On the aforementioned 4 Ahau 8 Cumku vessel (Fig. 39b), the cloth is marked with a glyphic compound identical to that occasionally carried by the Classic Hero Twins and the Tonsured Maize God (see Taube 1985: fig. 7). The bundle compound is composed of a Spotted Kan main sign prefixed by Landa's *i* and *ca*. David Stuart (1987b) suggests that the Spotted Kan is read *tzi*. Both Stross (1988) and I (Taube 1989a: 42) have noted independently that this compound is to be read *icatz(i)*, a term meaning bundle or burden in Tzeltalan languages.

In many instances, God L appears with another form of bundle, here covered with a network of ropes. In this case, the bundle represents the carrying packs of Mesoamerican merchants, not ceremonial bundles (Figs. 40, 41b). At times, this merchant bundle is accompanied by a quetzal or another long-feathered bird, suggesting that it contains feathers or other rare commodities (Figs. 40c–d). A pyrite mirror discovered in a tomb at Uayma, Yucatan, represents God L and another figure with the merchant bundle, here evidently topped by a bird (Fig. 40b). Although Raymond Thompson (1962: 244) does not identify the principal figure as God L, he notes that the scene appears to depict a pair of merchants or merchant gods with a cargo of precious plumes.

In the case of the Uayma mirror and many other Classic scenes, God L wields a staff of either simple or complex form. In several Terminal Classic examples from Yucatan, the staff appears to be an early form of the *chicahuaztli* rattle staff of Post-Classic Mesoamerica (Fig. 41). Along with the netted cylindrical bundle, staffs are one of the diagnostic attributes of merchants. In many scenes of the Post-Classic Borgia group of Mexican codices, merchants commonly appear with both the staff and the bundle, which may even be topped with a bird (Fig. 40a). It is clear that in the Classic period, God L is frequently portrayed as a merchant lord.

The ambivalent, dual nature of God L—the deadly underworld and fertile riches—is also characterized by the Moan bird frequently appearing in his headdress. Schellhas (1904: 41) notes that the Moan is frequently depicted with the Cimi death sign. But although a messenger or avatar of the underworld, the Moan owl is also identified with maize and rain. Thus in the Classic and Post-Classic periods, the God L Moan bird is frequently accompanied with the *kan* sign or maize foliation (Figs. 38b, 42a–b, 43b). J. Eric S. Thompson (1950: 115) notes that in Yucatec, *moan* signifies "cloudy" or "drizzle." Because the Moan bird is frequently accompanied with a coefficient of thirteen, Seler (1902–23, 4: 615) suggests that it represents the thirteen layers of clouds composing the heavens. Thompson (1950: 115) considers the Moan to be closely related to Chac, as on Dresden page 38c, God B sits upon the head of the Moan. An even more striking scene occurs on Madrid page 73b, on which God B and the Moan are depicted in a cave, sinkhole, or well. Holding an ink pot and quill, God B is depicted painting the black tail feathers of the Moan (Fig. 38d). The identification of the Moan with Chac is also present in the Classic period; for example, there are scenes of the Classic Chac wearing a crest of spotted Moan feathers (Fig. 38e). The convention of Chac appearing with Moan feathers seems to have continued into Post-Classic times. Thus in the Codex Dresden, the long, spotted element rising out above the ear of Chac is probably a Moan feather (Fig. 6a).

a

b

c

Fig. 39   Classic portrayals of God L.

(a) God L facing dwarf with cape, hat, and other rega-
    lia of God L (drawn after Kerr 1989: 98)
(b) God L seated upon jaguar throne, note caiman with
    water signs directly above (after M. Coe 1973:
    109)

(c) God L seated in palace structure (after M. Coe
    1973: 92).

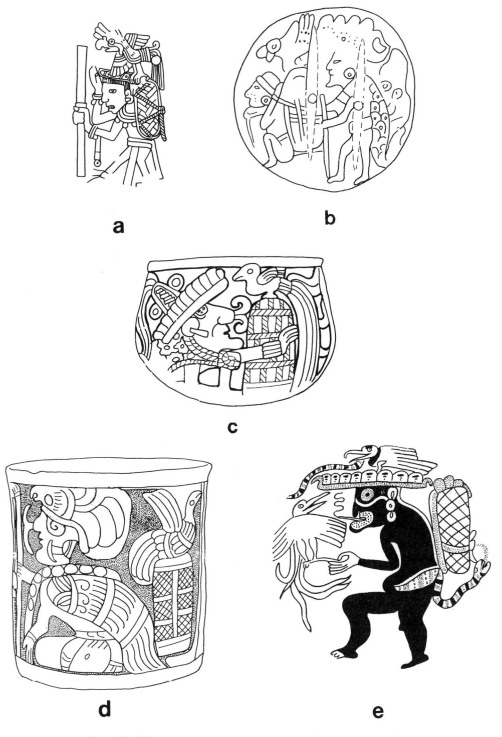

a b

c

d e

Fig. 40 The merchant bundle of God L.

(a) Merchant with staff and bundle topped with Quetzal bird, Codex Borgia page 4
(b) Center of mirror back from Uayma depicting God L with staff behind squatting figure with bundle topped by bird (redrawn after J. Thompson 1962: fig. 3)

(c) God L with merchant bundle topped with long-tailed bird (redrawn after Tate 1985: fig. 10)
(d) Seated God L with staff and merchant bundle topped by bird (drawn after Westheim et al. 1969: pl. 260)
(e) Smoking God L with merchant bundle and long-tailed bird (redrawn after Robicsek 1978: fig. 159).

a

b

Fig. 41 Terminal Classic representations of God L from the Yucatan Peninsula.

(a) God L with early form of *chicahuaztli* rattle staff; note God K carried on back; carving upon cylindrical column, possibly from Santa Rosa Xtampak (drawn after rubbing courtesy of Merle Greene Robinson)

(b) God L with *chicahuaztli* staff standing upon merchant bundle, bas-relief in Hopelchen reportedly from Dzehkatun (drawn after photograph courtesy of Flora Clancy).

Both God L and the Moan are identified with the powers of rain and lightning. For one, the black coloring of God L may allude to rain. Contemporary Maya peoples identify dark smoke as rain clouds, and the Lacandon collect the *sabac* or black soot from copal smoke for its use in the rain ritual or as black paint. The Lacandon god of rain is Mensabac (maker of sabac) (Tozzer 1907: 71). In the Codex Dresden, the sign of God L is a portrait glyph prefixed with an *imix* sign from which fall black beaded elements (Fig. 38a).

These streams of beads, beginning with large dots that gradually diminish as they fall, are identical to the patterning frequently found in the Dresden codex and on Classic period Moan feathers. A representation of a water lily flower, the *imix* sign is a well-known water symbol, and it is probable that the black dots represent falling water or rain.

It is possible that during the Late Classic period God L was identified with the western Maya area, a moist region of great produce and trade. Some of the most elaborate monumental representations of God L derive from the western Maya region of Palenque. In the Cross Group, he not only appears in the Tablet of the Sun, but also as one of the jambs in the Temple of the Cross (Fig. 42b). In addition, a youthful figure wearing a God L headdress appears on a fragmentary tripartite scene panel displaying the Palenque emblem glyph (see Mayer 1989: pl. 75). The figure is backed by a tree sprouting cacao pods from the trunk (Fig. 42a). The deep soils of the western Maya area are well suited for cacao. For example, the region of Comalcalco, Tabasco, is still an important cacao-producing region today.

God L appears not only in the western Maya region but in southern Veracruz as well. God L is one of the few Maya gods appearing in the Classic art of the Gulf coast. On one molded vessel from the Rio Blanco region of southern Veracruz, he appears as an aged man with a walking stick. However, his most striking attribute is the broad headdress topped by the bird head (Fig. 42c). In form and concept, the headdress is entirely comparable to the Moan bird headdress of God L. A figure wearing a markedly similar broad headdress appears on Cerro de las Mesas Monument 2 (Fig. 42d). In this case, the bird displays a thick and curved owl-like beak. Like the Rio Blanco vessel figure, this figure probably represents a form of God L.

It has been noted that the Moan bird appearing in the Classic Maya God L headdress is frequently accompanied by a sky sign. I suspect that together, these two elements may have served as an epithet of God L. In Cholan—the language of the western Maya lowlands—the word for sky is *chan*. The Moan Owl and sky sign may spell out the term *moan chan*, or "misty sky." This immediately brings to mind the legendary Nahuatl place of Tamoanchan. Michael Coe (1984: 62) notes that *tamoanchan* is actually a Mayan phrase signifying "Land of Rain and Mist." A number of researchers have placed Tamoanchan in the Gulf Coast region of Veracruz (e.g., Coe 1984: 62; Davies 1977: 105; Delhalle and Luykx 1986: 121).[8]

A merchant god identified with rain and mist, the Classic God L may have been specifically identified with the western Maya region and neighboring Veracruz.

One of the most striking and revealing appearances of God L derives not from the Maya region or the Gulf Coast but from still farther west, from the site of Cacaxtla, Puebla. During excavations in 1984, a series of murals were discovered in El Templo Rojo, flanking a staircase. One of the scenes depicts an individual impersonating God L (Santana Sandoval et al. 1990; John Carlson, personal communication, 1990). Along with wearing a God L mask and shoulder cape, the Cacaxtla figure also displays a jaguar headdress, along with a jaguar skin kilt, boots, and mittens (see Santana Sandoval et al. 1990: figs. 3, 4). In addition, he wields a walking staff and merchant bundle, with packages containing feathers and other goods. The broad-brimmed Moan bird hat of God L is affixed to the side of the bundle. However, in this instance, the Moan bird is partly serpentine, with a snake-like snout and teeth. In many Mayan languages, the term *chan* refers to snake as well as sky. Quite probably, the serpent traits are substituting for the conventional sky sign of God L, here again to refer to *moan chan*. It is widely recognized that the Olmeca-Xicalanca inhabitants of Cacaxtla had close ties to the western Maya region (e.g., Foncerrada de Molina 1980: 184). The Cacaxtla depiction of God L could well refer to the verdant western Maya area of Chiapas and Tabasco, the probable realm of Tamoanchan.

In one vessel scene, a regal-looking rabbit holds a truncated form of a serpent staff before a nude and craven God L (Fig. 43b). Also in the rabbit's outstretched paw is the Moan bird headdress with a large necklace falling in two beaded streams. This scene is part of a poorly understood Classic myth concerning the theft of the regalia of God L. The rabbit, along with the Classic moon goddess, plays an important part in this event (Figs. 43c–d).

[8] The upper portion of Borgia page 21 provides support for the identification of Tamoanchan with eastern Mexico. In the scene, the Red Tezcatlipoca appears as a merchant facing a prominent cleft tree, a conventional sign for Tamoanchan (e.g., Codex Borbonicus page 15).

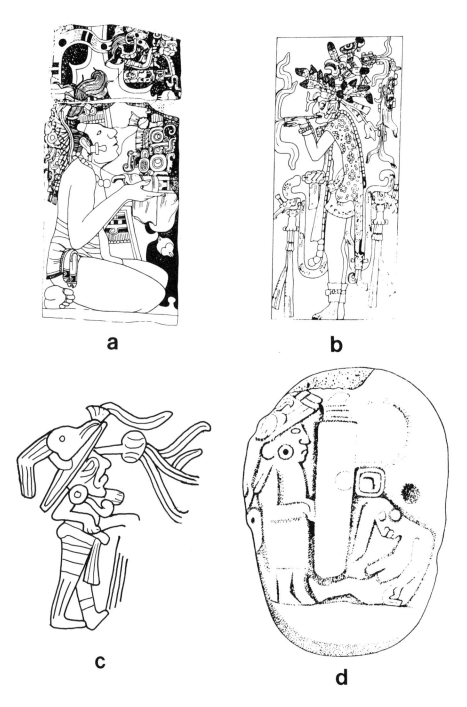

Fig. 42   Depictions of God L from the western Maya region and the neighboring Gulf Coast.

(a) Figure with God L headdress backed by cacao tree (detail of drawing by Donald Hales, after Mayer 1989: pl. 75)
(b) God L smoking, from Temple of the Cross, Palenque (detail of drawing by Linda Schele)

(c) God L on mold-made vessel from Rio Blanco region, Veracruz (redrawn after von Winning 1982: fig. 2b)
(d) Figure with God L headdress, Monument 2, Cerro de las Mesas (after Stirling 1943: fig. 12d).

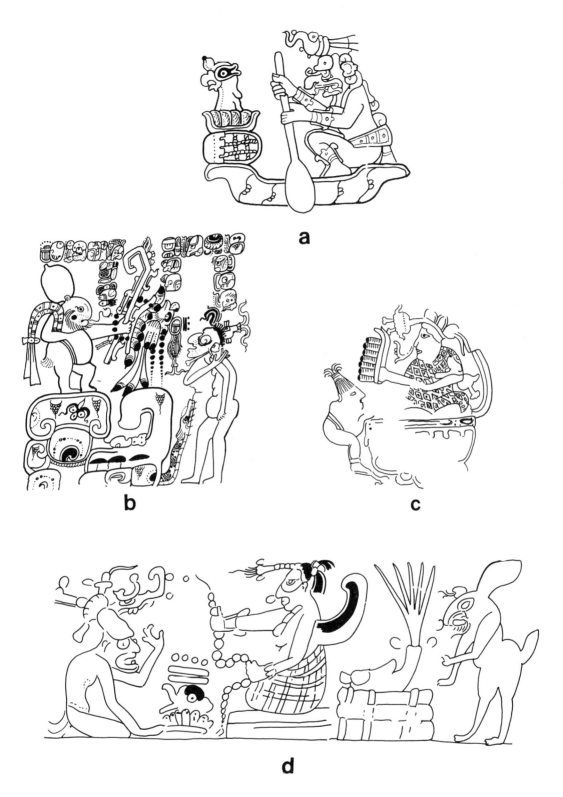

Fig. 43 The taking of the God L regalia.

(a) Chac in canoe with merchant bundle topped with God L headdress, Dresden page 43c
(b) God L facing rabbit holding serpent staff and God L headdress (drawn after Kerr 1989: 81)

(c) Moon goddess holding God L headdress while facing semi-nude supplicant; note lunar crescent and rabbit held in crook of moon goddess' arm (drawn after Joyce 1927: 103)
(d) God L Moan Owl headdress between young moon goddess and probable God D, rabbit at far right (drawn after Robicsek and Hales 1981: fig. 48c).

It appears that in this instance, the rabbit functions as an avatar of the moon. A Late Classic vessel scene represents the feathered Moan Owl head-dress of God L between God D and the moon goddess, who is provided with a crescent moon; an anthropomorphized rabbit stands nearby (Fig. 43d).

A Late Classic tripod bowl represents another scene of the God L headdress episode. Attributed to northern Belize, the vessel depicts a female figure holding the feathered hat of God L before a male. The woman is clearly the Moon Goddess for she appears with both the crescent and a rabbit in the crook of her arm (Fig. 43c). Eroded versions of the same scene also appear on the encircling rim (see Joyce 1927: 103). Hellmuth (1986: 280–281) notes that a Post-Classic form of this episode occurs on Dresden page 43c, although here the principal protagonist is not the rabbit but Chac, who carries the merchant bundle and Moan bird head-dress of God L in his canoe (Fig. 43a). It has been noted that on Dresden page 46, God L appears as a god of the morning star. In view of the combined presence of the Moon Goddess and God L, it may be that the theft of the God L regalia was an epi-sode of cosmic importance.

Summary

God L is an aged black god with close ties to the underworld. This identification is reflected in two of his animal avatars, the jaguar and the Moan Owl, both creatures of caves and the night. In the Codex Dresden, God L also appears as one of the malevolent Venus Gods who appear at dawn after the disappearance of Venus into the underworld during inferior conjunction. However, God L was not simply a deity of death and de-struction. Instead, he is frequently depicted with riches, and often appears with a merchant bundle and a staff or spear. The Moan Owl and sky sign headdress may serve an an epithet of God L, here read *moan chan,* or "misty sky." God L may have been specifically identified with the verdant re-gion of the western Maya area and neighboring Veracruz. It has been suggested that the Nahuatl region of Tamoanchan may correspond to the southern Gulf Coast area, an important region of cacao and trade. It is clear that during the Classic period, God L was considered a merchant lord and should be regarded as a form of merchant god. His obviously regal status suggests that, like the Post-Classic Maya of Yucatan, the Classic Maya saw no contradiction between rulership and mercantilism. The many Classic scenes of the moon goddess taking the regalia of God L reveals that there was a complex body of mythic lore surrounding this being, most of which remains poorly known.

God M

Due to his long, Pinocchio-like nose, God M is one of the most easily recognized gods of the Post-Classic codices (Fig. 44). Schellhas (1904: 35) notes that God M appears but rarely in the Codex Dresden, but is frequently depicted in the Codex Madrid. In addition to the exaggerated nose, God M is usually black with a long, pendulous lower lip accentuated with red. The name glyph of this deity is an eye within a U-shaped element that recalls the device frequently encircling the eye of the god (Fig. 44a). The eye ornamentation resem-bles a broken circle with the two ends curling out at the back of the eye, like the eye piece of a hook-and-eye fastener. In short, God M is a strange and strikingly ugly entity, entirely alien to the canons of Maya beauty. In fact, it appears that he is a foreign deity, probably derived from Yacatecuhtli, the Central Mexican god of mer-chants.

Schellhas (1904: 35–36) suggests that God M corresponds to the Contact period Ek Chuah, the Post-Classic Yucatec merchant god. In the Ma-drid codex, God M appears frequently with a car-rying pack and a spear. Schellhas (1904: 36) inter-prets the military aspect of God M as a reflection of the dangerous life of the merchant, who fre-quently must repel attacks while traveling in for-eign territories. As implied by the name, which contains the term for black (*ek*), Ek Chuah is a black god. He seems to be closely identified with cacao, because in the month of Muan, the owners of cacao groves performed a special festival in

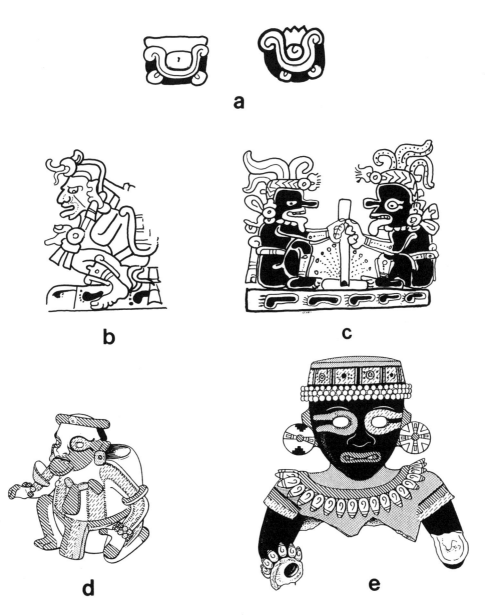

Fig. 44 The Post-Classic God M.

(a) The codical name glyph of God M, Dresden page 16b, Madrid page 54c
(b) God M with merchant bundle on road, Dresden page 43a
(c) Pair of black God M figures making fire upon a road, Madrid page 51a
(d) Effigy vessel, Mayapan (after Thompson 1957: fig. 1g)
(e) Fragmentary effigy censer, Mayapan (after Thompson 1957: fig. 1h).

honor of Ek Chuah, Chac, and Hobnil (Tozzer 1941: 164). In view of the value of cacao, it is not surprising that the god of merchants was associated with this esteemed commodity. In fact, cacao beans were an important form of currency not only in Yucatan but over much of Post-Classic Mesoamerica. But rather than being simply a cacao god, Ek Chuah was a deity presiding over all traveling ventures. Landa (in Tozzer 1941: 107) notes that during a journey, one would offer incense at night to Ek Chuah to ensure a safe return.

The same traits of militarism, cacao, and night fire ceremonies are to be found with the Yacatecuhtli merchant complex of Central Mexico. Although he is not black, Yacatecuhtli has the same elongated nose found on God M. To the Aztec, merchants were considered as front-line warriors or vanguards of the army. One particular type, the *naoaloztomeca,* were disguised merchants, who penetrated enemy territory as spies (Sahagún 1950–71, bk. 9: 21–25). Before a journey, Aztec merchants made a night offering of bloodied paper and copal to Yacatecuhtli and other gods (Sahagún 1950–71, bk. 9: 9–11). Upon their return, the merchants were offered a special drink of cacao (Sahagún 1950–71, bk. 9: 27–28).

The complex ritual lore surrounding merchants was not limited to particular cultures or political boundaries. Instead, it was a symbolic language, a sort of "ritual pidgin" that could be readily shared among many differing groups engaged in trade. Precisely where the long-nosed merchant god originated is unknown, but it probably does not derive from the Maya region.

Although decidedly ugly anthropomorphic gods do exist for the Classic period, representations of the long, pointed merchant nose are virtually absent. A possible exception is the Chama vase. Following Seler (1904b), Michael Coe (1973: 13; 1978: no. 9) interprets the group of individuals with fans as a meeting of merchants. Coe states that one of the figures, depicted with black body paint and a somewhat long bulbous nose, is Ek Chuah. However, all of the figures have features exaggerated to the point of grotesque caricature. For example, although not black, the figure in front of the suggested Ek Chuah has an almost identical profile.

The long-nosed Yacatecuhtli or Ek Chuah figures generally do not appear in the Maya region until the Post-Classic period. Among the earliest examples are the stone masquettes excavated at an Early Post-Classic tomb at Chipal, Guatemala (see Kidder and Samayoa Chinchilla 1959: pl. 89). With the Post-Classic advent of metal working,

representations of the long-nosed merchant god frequently appear on rings, pendants, and other metal jewelry (see Bray 1977: 15, 12, figs. 3, 7). An excellent depiction of God M occurs on an embossed gold disk from the sacred cenote at Chichen Itza (Fig. 45a). Rendered in the style of Santa Rita, Belize, the disk depicts God M with a tumpline, long beard, and the broken eye loop (see Coggins and Shane 1984: pl. 137). One scene in the famous murals of Santa Rita depicts God M three times: as a figure playing music, as a pendant occurring on the same individual, and finally, as a severed head carried by another figure (Fig. 45b). At Mayapan, God M is frequently depicted on ceramic *incensarios,* often with a long flowing beard (see Smith 1971: figs. 32h; 68b, no. 9).

Michael Coe (1973: 14) notes that Gods L and M appear to be closely related entities. Because of the shared black body coloration, God M, God L, and black Chacs have frequently been confused. On Madrid pages 79a to 84, there is such a complex merging of God L with God M that it is difficult to keep them apart. Cyrus Thomas (1888: 358) identifies God L as Ek Chuah, the black merchant god. Thomas may not be far off the mark, God L was in large part the Classic Maya counterpart of God M. It appears that as God M became of increasing importance in the Maya region, he supplanted God L and in doing so, acquired some of his particular characteristics. Thus, although not a characteristic of Yacatecuhtli, God M is often black, the conventional color of God L. Moreover, unlike Yacatecuhtli, God M is often found with aged, chapfallen features. In the Codex Madrid, God M frequently has a snaggle-toothed mouth (e.g., Madrid pages 52a, 53a), quite like the mouth of God L, God D, and other aged gods in the codex. At Mayapan, there is an excellent example of God M represented as an aged black god; here the snaggle-toothed mouth is rendered in the round (Fig. 44e).

Along with agedness and black body coloration, the Post-Classic God M displays another physical aspect of God L: a face with jaguar attributes. Thus, on the aforementioned gold disk in

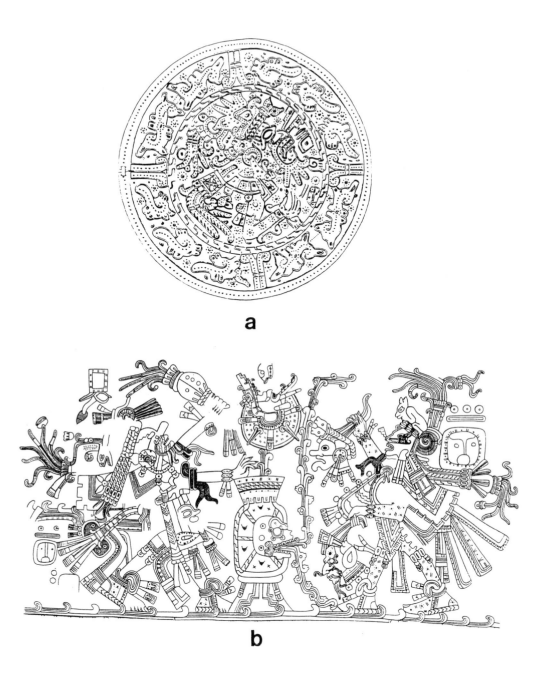

Fig. 45   Depictions of God M rendered in Santa Rita
style.

(a) God M in center of gilt copper disk from Sacred
Well, Chichen Itza (after Coggins and Shane 1984:
120)

(b) God M playing rattle and drum facing another figure with severed heads of God G and God M,
Mound 1, Santa Rita (after Gann 1900: pl. XXXI).

Santa Rita style, he appears with long canines and spots around the mouth, characteristics suggestive of the jaguar (Fig. 45a). In the previously mentioned mural scene at Santa Rita, the full figure God M also appears to have jaguar ears and spots around the mouth (Fig. 45b). The spotted mouth is also found with both Classic and Post-Classic representations of God L, and probably refers to jaguar markings (Figs. 38b, 39b, 40e).

Summary

Aside from physical attributes, Gods M and L have much in common. As a merchant deity, the symbolic domain of God M frequently overlaps with that of God L. It has been noted that the Classic God L is depicted with staffs and merchant bundles topped with long-tailed birds in Classic vessel scenes. The simple staff and cylindrical bundle clearly represent the walking staff and goods of the traveling Pre-Columbian merchant. Tobacco, an important attribute of God L, is also associated with merchants. For example, Aztec merchants received tobacco as well as cacao on their return to Tenochtitlan (Sahagún 1950-71, bk. 9: 28). Moreover, during the feast of the merchants, tobacco was ceremoniously offered to the Aztec lords (Sahagún 1950-71, bk. 9: 34). Like God L, God M is also identified with the Moan Owl. It will be recalled that the cacao ceremony held in the honor of Ek Chuah and other gods was performed during the month of Moan. Moreover, the Moan on Dresden page 43c bears the unmistakable eye marking of God M (Fig. 43a). It is noteworthy that none of these four attributes (the black coloration, agedness, the jaguar, and moan owl) appears in the Yacatecuhtli complex of Central Mexico. Instead, they seem to derive from the earlier God L, who served as a Classic Maya merchant god.

God N

Although God N is one of the major gods of the ancient Maya, his role and identity has been the source of much confusion and debate (Fig. 46). Since the pioneering work of Förstemann

(1901: 189–192) and Schellhas (1904: 37, 38), it has been generally thought that God N was the god of the five-day Uayeb period. In a discussion of the Classic numeral five head variant, J. Eric S. Thompson (1950: 133–134) states that this aged face represents God N as the Mam, god of the Uayeb, and that the contemporary Kekchi and Pokomchi regard the Mam as an aged and powerful earth deity. Thompson also notes a parallel to the Yucatec worhip of the Uayeb Mam in contemporary Kekchi Easter ceremonies, where an image of Mam is buried during an "unlucky" five-day period. In a later recantation, Thompson (1970a: 473) states that God N was not the malevolent god of the dying year but rather the quadripartite Bacab supporting the heavens: "it is abundantly clear that Mam, the dressed up piece of wood with his five day rule and contemptuous end, had nothing in common with the four Bacabs."

Michael Coe's phonetic reading (1973: 15) leaves no doubt that Pauahtun was the principal epithet of God N. Coe notes that the conventional name glyph of God N appears with a phonetic *pa* superfix and a main sign composed of phonetic *tun* allographs (Fig. 46a). Together, these elements give the reading *patun*, quite similar to the term *pauahtun*. However, I (Taube 1989a) have recently noted that the glyphic compound often contains a phonetic *uah* (*wah*), providing a complete reading of *pauahtun*. The *uah* device is a globular element appearing in the center of the *pa* superfix. This is a representation of the maize tamale, read *uah* in the Classic and Post-Classic Maya script (Taube 1989a). Post-Classic examples of God N often wear this maize device in their headdresses, and frequently the element sprouts maize foliage (Figs. 46b–c, e). The Pauahtuns mentioned in Landa's description of the Yucatec new year ceremonies are equated to the Bacabs and the Xib Chacs, all oriented to the four directions with their appropriate color (see Tozzer 1941: 137). Landa may actually be correct; the terms Bacab and Mam are probably aspects or simply epithets of Pauahtun.

In both Classic and Post-Classic Maya iconography, God N is strongly quadripartite. Classic ves-

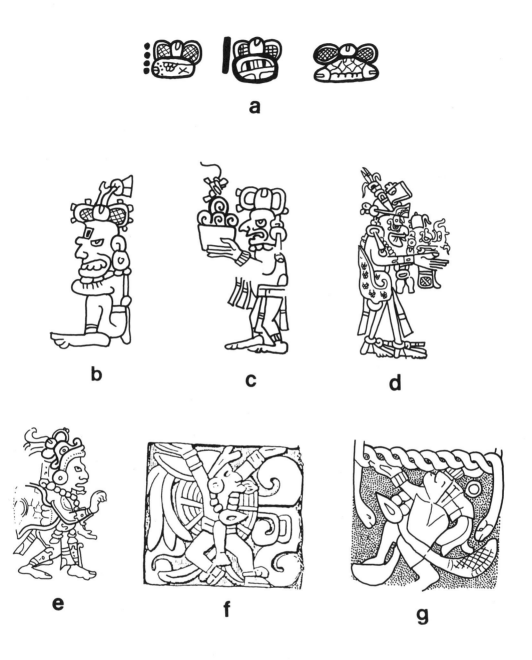

Fig. 46 The Post-Classic God N.

(a) Appellative glyphs of God N; Madrid pages 71a, 104b, Dresden page 60
(b) Seated God N, Madrid page 104b
(c) God N with offerings, Madrid page 96a
(d) God N holding head of God K, Paris page 6
(e) God N with turtle carapace, Dresden page 60

(f) God N with spider web on back, Chichen Itza (after Seler 1902–23, 5: 301)
(g) God N with costume elements commonly found with God N figures from Chichen Itza, Yaxcopoil Stela 2 (redrawn after Proskouriakoff 1950: fig. 88e).

sels and stone monuments frequently depict the four-part nature of God N (e.g., Tikal Altar 4; Coe 1978: vase 11). At Late Post-Classic Mayapan, Structure H-17 contained four sculptures of God N wearing a tortoise carapace (D. E. Thompson 1955: 282). Paris page 22 depicts four God N figures seated upon a sky band. Similarly, the upper "sky" register of a round column from Structure 6E1 at Chichen Itza contains four God N figures interspersed with star signs (see Proskouriakoff 1970: fig. 15). The remains of four God N figures can also be discerned in the uppermost register of Jaina Stela 1 (see Proskouriakoff 1950: fig. 45c).

According to Landa (in Tozzer 1941: 135), the Bacabs support the sky. However, the only pre-Hispanic deity who assumes such a role is God N, named phonetically as Pauahtun. Whereas J. Eric S. Thompson views God N as the Bacab sky bearer, Michael Coe (1973, 1978) considers him to be the supporter of the earth, not the heavens. Coe interprets God N as a preeminently underworld god. But although God N does possess strong cthonic attributes, he is also closely identified with the heavens. In Maya iconography, God N frequently appears as a denizen of the sky. The celestial scenes on Paris page 22 and at Chichen Itza have been mentioned, and there are many others. I know of no explicit example of God N sustaining the earth, and in a number of instances, he clearly holds up the sky. Thus, on a Late Classic vessel, a pair of aged Pauahtun figures serve as the supporters of a sky band throne (Fig. 47a). The Pauahtun figures on Temples 11 and 22 at Copan are interpreted as sky bearers (L. Schele and M. E. Miller 1986: 122).

According to Schele and Miller (ibid.), the Bacabs are simply young aspects of the Pauahtuns. Although I agree that both the Bacabs and Pauahtuns are sky bearers, I see little reason for distinguishing them by age. Instead, I suspect that Bacab is but a variant epithet for Pauahtun. Rather than making a sharp distinction between earth and sky bearers, it may be more appropriate to consider the Pauahtuns as sustainers of the world. This would be entirely in accord with contemporary Tzotzil belief. Among the Zinacantecos, there

are the *vasak men* who, as the gods of the four corners, hold up the earth and apparently the sky as well (Vogt 1976: 15–16). Similarly, the Chamula earth bearers are supporters of the "universe" (Gossen 1974: 22). At San Andres Larrainzar, there are the Cuch Uinahel Balumil, or "sky-earth bearers" (Holland 1963: 92).

At Early Post-Classic Chichen Itza, God N often appears wearing a cut shell pendant and hanging crosshatched belt elements (Fig. 46f). This form of God N costume has been previously recognized only at Chichen Itza. However, God N also appears wearing the shell pendant and hanging belt pieces on Yaxcopoil Stela 2 (Fig. 46g). In this Terminal Classic scene, God N supports a band of twisted serpents that probably refer to the sky; in Yucatec, *ca'an* is "sky" and *can,* serpent.

In the North Colonnade at Chichen Itza, there is a group of fragmentary cylindrical columns bearing representations of four God N figures in the upper and lower registers (Fig. 48a). Each of the figures stands in the world-bearer posture while rising out of a cleft zoomorphic head. Quite similar split zoomorphic heads appear on a Terminal Classic vessel from Seibal, here marked with explicit *cauac* signs (Fig. 48b). The Chichen and Seibal examples are probably examples of the frequently cleft-headed Cauac Monster, an entity that David Stuart (1987b: 17–18) identifies as a mountain. Quite likely, the Chichen registers depict god N oriented to the four cosmic mountains of the Maya world.

The identification of God N with mountains also occurs at the Classic site of Copan. On the sculptured doorway of Temple 22 and the hieroglyphic bench from the House of the Bacabs there are seated God N figures marked with Cauac signs. In both cases, God N appears holding up the serpent sky. Like the Chichen columns, God N is here rendered as a personified mountain supporting the sky. The role of God N as a sacred mountain was probably widespread in the Classic Maya region. It will be subsequently noted that the contemporary form of God N, the Mam, is widely identified with mountains in the Maya region and Veracruz.

Many of the God N figures at Chichen wear a

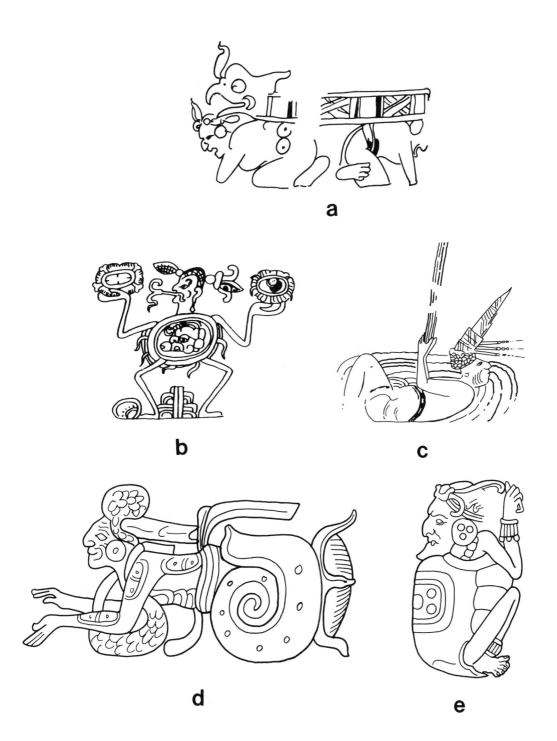

Fig. 47   Classic representations of God N.

(a) Pair of God N figures serving as supports for sky band throne, detail of Late Classic polychrome vessel (drawn after Robicsek and Hales 1981: fig. 9b)

(b) God N as a spider holding sun and moon, detail of Tepeu 1 vessel (drawn after Robicsek 1978: pl. 138)

(c) God N in center of possible web (drawn after Robicsek and Hales 1981: vessel 110)

(d) God N in conch (drawn after M. Coe 1973: no. 70)

(e) God N in turtle shell, Quirigua Zoomorph P (redrawn after Maudslay 1889–1902, 2: pl. 63).

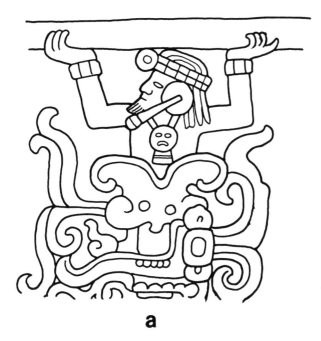

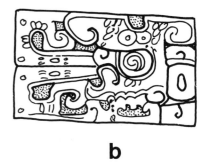

a

b

Fig. 48 God N as a mountain.

(a) God N emerging from cleft zoomorphic head. Composite drawing by author from two sections of cylindrical columns, North Colonnade, Chichen Itza

(b) Smoking cleft head with Cauac signs. Detail of incised vessel, Seibal (redrawn after Sabloff 1970: fig. 48).

large spider web upon the back (Fig. 46f). God N spider figures also appear in Classic Maya iconography. The earliest known example occurs on a Tepeu 1 polychrome vessel depicting God N holding the sun in one hand and the moon in the other (Fig. 47b). In another Late Classic scene, God N lies on his back in a spider web while holding a filament strand in each hand (Fig. 47c). In the aforementioned scene on Paris page 22, the celestial God N figures sit among twisted cords, quite possibly an allusion to spider thread. In Post-Classic Central Mexico, the spider was an important symbol of the *tzitzimime,* sky bearers who descended at eclipses and calendrical period endings to menace the world (Thompson 1934). According to J. Eric S. Thompson (1934), God N is a Maya version of the *tzitzimitl.*

Many of the overt characteristics of God N have been widely noted, such as his aged bearing, costume, and frequent appearance in conch or tortoise shells, but there has been little interest in the

relation of this deity to the natural world. It is becoming increasingly evident that the agricultural cycle was of great importance in Classic Maya religion, and deities of maize, rain, and lightning are commonplace. God N is frequently found with Chac in Classic Maya scenes. An example is the aforementioned Early Classic vessel depicting Chac with the God K lightning axe (Fig. 35a). This scene is actually placed on the conch worn by God N, who appears on the opposite side of the vessel (see M. Coe 1982: no. 33). One Late Classic vase represents a veritable orgy of music and drink, with four God N figures being accompanied by young women and four Chacs within a cave (M. Coe 1978: vase 11). The identification of God N with Chac continues in the Post-Classic period. On Dresden page 41b there are two separate scenes of God N and Chac, each deity surrounded by beads of water, probably rain. In the texts immediately above, both are described as *pauahtun chac.* On Dresden page 37a,

God N stands in rain as he holds an axe, the characteristic lightning weapon of Chac.

The association of God N with Chac is entirely consistent with contemporary Maya conceptions of the Mam. J. Eric S. Thompson (1930) notes that in the village of San Antonio, Belize, the Mams are merged with the Chacs and the gods of wind. They are four in number, and their domain is the mountains and the underworld: "The Mams are gods of the mountains, of the plains, of the underground, of thunder and lightning, and, by extension, of the rain" (Thompson 1930: 57). The contemporary Chol also consider the aged *lak mam* as lightning, or *chajk* (Cruz Guzman, Josserand, and Hopkins 1986). However, the sons of *lak mam* are stronger, and, whereas these youths frequently throw lightning, *lak mam* is best known for his thunder (Cruz Guzman, Josserand, and Hopkins n.d.: 42).

Both the San Antonio Maya and the Chiapas Chol consider the principal Mam to be extremely old, and this belief is also found with the Kekchi, in the intermediate region of Alta Verapaz. In one Kekchi tale, the thunder god is extremely old and lives in thirteen green hills; his harsh bellowing is thunder (Gordon 1915: 108). Erwin Dieseldorff (1926) posits that the Kekchi have two distinct sets of gods in complementary opposition, one being the Tzultacaj, the young gods of lightning, and the other, the aged Mam. The Kekchi Mam is essentially malevolent and dangerous, and the thundering at the onset of the rains is thought to be Mam trying to escape his bonds in the underworld. E. Michael Mendelson (1959) makes a similar case for the Tzutuhil of Santiago Atitlan. In this case, the young benevolent god of rain and lightning is San Martin, and the aged god is known as Mam or Maximon. As with the Kekchi, the Maximon Mam idol is worshiped for five days of Holy Week. This widespread concept of young and old gods of lightning and thunder may be pre-Hispanic. Whereas Chac is the young axe-wielding god of lightning, the Pauahtun Mam is an aged thunder deity. But although the Chacs and Pauahtuns may thematically overlap, there is no evidence that they are simply young and old aspects of the same god. The Pauahtuns,

rather than the Chacs, are inevitably depicted as the world bearers.

The Huastec Maya of Veracruz also have a widespread belief in the Mamlab, aged and malevolent gods of thunder. Guy Stresser-Péan (1952) states that there are actually two forms of Mamlab, young and robust forms and old, degenerate types known as Ocel. Janis Alcorn (1984: 58–59) mentions that in the Huastec community of Teenek Tsabal, the principal Mam is Muxi', who undergoes a process of aging over the solar year:

> Muxi' miraculously becomes a newborn baby at the beginning of the year when the sun once again "moves" away from the South. During the year he ages and by year's end he is an old man as the sun reaches the winter solstice.

According to Stresser-Péan (1952), the Mamlab greatly love dance, drink, and music and have great parties in mountain caves with their female frog consorts. Even when floating down rivers as spent Ocel, they drum upon the bloated stomachs of drowned beasts. Stresser-Péan records that the Mamlab are the souls of ancestors drowned in the last creation. This is quite similar to the description by Alcorn (1984: 57) of four drowned men who support the earth; as they age and break, they are replaced by another four at the new year. These drowned men eventually go to the eastern realm of Muxi'. Among the neighboring Sierra Totonac, there is a similar aged thunder god known as San Juan, or Aktsini'. Like the Huastec Mam, he is an aged god associated with mountains, thunder, and drowned humans. Moreover, he is the most important of the four thunder gods who support the world (Ichon 1973: 45, 123, 130, 137).

Michael Coe (personal communication, 1984) notes that Kaminaljuyu Stela 17 appears to be a Late Preclassic rendering of God N (Fig. 49a). An old bearded man bent over his serpentine walking stick, the figure wears the diagnostic rolled cloth headdress of God N. In addition, the rear part of the headdress contains a bulbous netted element resembling the "spangled turban" frequently found at the base of Classic God N headdresses (e.g., Coe 1973: nos. 17, 70). Although I know of

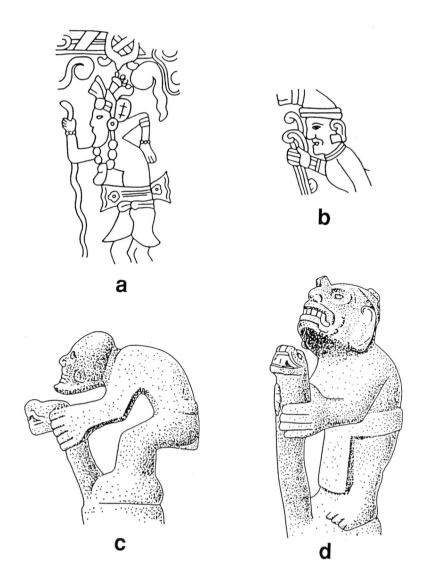

a

b

c

d

Fig. 49 The aged Mam, comparison of stone sculpture from Guatemala and the Gulf Coast.

(a) Stela 17, Kaminaljuyu, a Late Preclassic representation of God N; note bound cloth headdress and undulating staff in right hand (drawn after Parsons 1986: fig. 50)

(b) Detail of Late Classic scene from Mound of the Building Columns, El Tajin, aged figure with staff and rolled cloth headdress of Maya god N (redrawn after Kampen 1972: fig. 34c)

(c) Post-Classic Huastec sculpture of Mam bent over serpent lightning staff (drawn after de la Fuente and Gutiérrez Solana 1980: pl. CCXXXVII)

(d) Version of Huastec Mam figure with serpent lightning staff, face of Mam replaced with that of Tlaloc, the Central Mexican god of rain and lightning (drawn after Anton 1969: pl. 182).

no example of God N carrying a staff in Classic Maya art, there is an interesting Late Classic relief from El Tajín, Veracruz. A detail from a cylindrical bas-relief column, the scene represents an aged male holding a staff. With his wrapped-cloth head-dress, he is almost identical to Classic Maya representations of God N (Fig. 49b).

The El Tajín figure seems to be an early form of an important genre of Post-Classic Huastec sculpture—an aged male leaning over his walking stick (Figs. 49c–d). Stresser-Péan (1971: 596) identifies this common sculptural type as the Mam, "the old god of the earth and of thunder, lord of the year, ancestor of the Huastec." In strong support of this interpretation, one example has a wrinkled face of Tlaloc, the Central Mexican god of rain and lightning (Fig. 49d). A recent account of the chief Huastec Mam could serve as a vivid description of the pre-Hispanic sculptures: "Muxi' is generally thought of as a dangerous, powerful old man bent over his walking stick of ak' " (Alcorn 1984: 59). The stick held by the pre-Hispanic Mam figures can either be a simple shaft or a serpent. The latter variety probably alludes to a thunderbolt; it has been frequently noted in this study that the snake is a widespread symbol of lightning in Mesoamerica. Although somewhat eroded, it is quite possible that the undulating staff carried by the Kaminaljuyu figure is also a serpent.

Summary

The cited ethnographic material from Veracruz is strikingly similar to contemporary and ancient lore of the Maya region. In both areas, there is an old and often malevolent mountain god, a quadripartite supporter of the world identified with thunder, music, drunkenness, and the old year. The Huastec even call him Mam, the same name used for the deity in Guatemala, Belize, and Yucatan. This god appears to be of considerable antiquity and can be found on the Late Preclassic Stela 17 of Kaminaljuyu. Representations of Pauahtun are frequent in Classic Maya iconography, and in many scenes he is found in the sky or serves as a sky bearer. The tortoise shell and conch commonly worn by this being may refer to the association of this god with thunder, since both the conch and tortoise carapace are used as instruments to imitate the sound of thunder. Like the *tzitzimime* of Post-Classic Central Mexico, God N is not only a world supporter but also a malevolent god that threatens the world at particular calendrical and celestial events. The Post-Classic Pauahtun seems to have differed little from the Classic god, and it appears that forms of this deity are still being worshiped in both the Maya region and Veracruz.

Goddess O

As I have mentioned in the discussion of Goddess I, this deity corresponds to the Goddess O described by Günter Zimmermann (1956: pl. 7). Along with being aged, she is, in the Codex Dresden, frequently depicted with a red body. Moreover, her name is usually given with the T109 *chac* prefix, signifying "red" or "great" in Yucatec (Figs. 50a–c).

The entire name glyph of Goddess I tends to be written as T109.145:612, the two latter glyphs being the *h* and *l* of the Landa alphabet. Pronounced in Spanish, these letters are read *hache* and *ele*. In addition, Landa also glosses T612 as *le* (see Tozzer 1941: 169–170). Yuri Knorozov (1958: 471, no. 27, and 475) reads the entire compound as *chac ch'el(e)*. However, there is no indication that the second word is glottalized. Thus Kelly (1976: 69) suggests that the name is to be read *chac chel*, noting that in the *Ritual of the Bacabs* there is mention of a Chacal Ix Chel and a Zacal Ix Chel (see Roys 1965: 53). Michael Coe (1977: 329) notes that the old creator couple of the sixteenth-century Pokoman were Xchel and Xtamna, clear cognates of the Yucatec Ix Chel and Itzamna. The phonetic reading of the Goddess O name glyph strongly suggests that this aged goddess is Ix Chel, just as Seler (1904a: 50) originally suggested.

In Yucatec, the term *chel* or *cheel* signifies rainbow (Barrera Vásquez 1980: 89). Although in popular Western thought, rainbows are considered beautiful and auspicious, contemporary Yucatec regard them with a certain dread:

> The rainbow (chel) is spoken of as "the flatulence of the demons" (u ciz cizinob), because it is thought to arise out of dry wells (x-lah-chen), and these are, as it were, the ani of Metnal. From these wells the rainbow spreads across the sky. (Redfield and Villa Rojas 1934: 206)

In the Maya region, caves are commonly considered to be sources of sickness, and among the Yucatec, the rainbow also seems to be identified with disease. Thus two chants from the Colonial

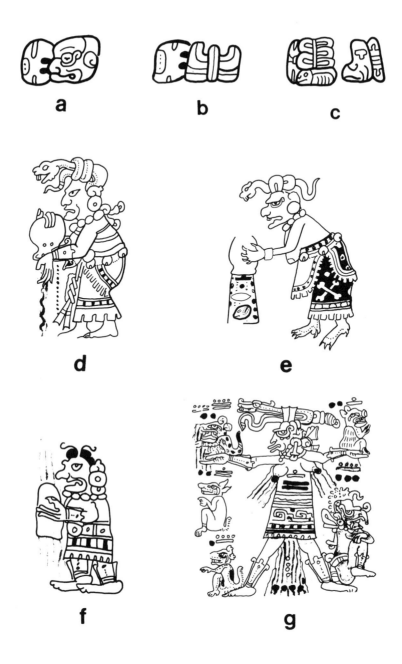

Fig. 50 The Post-Classic Goddess O, the aged genetrix; note serpent headdress in d, e, and g.

(a) Portrait glyph of Goddess O prefixed by *chac* sign, Dresden page 43b
(b) Name glyph of Goddess O, composed of elements *chac* and *che,* probably referring to name *chac chel,* Dresden page 39b
(c) Appellative phrase of Goddess O, probably to be read *chac chel chac,* Madrid page 10b
(d) Goddess O with outpouring jar of water, Dresden page 39b

(e) Goddess O with clawed hands and feet, detail of flood scene on Dresden page 74
(f) Goddess O with inverted jar and falling water, Madrid page 10b
(g) Goddess O with water pouring from loins and armpits, Madrid page 30b.

Ritual of the Bacabs describe the "fire-colored rainbow" (*ix kaak tan chel*) as the mother of certain seizures (Roys 1965: 7, 10). This phrase recalls the name of Goddess O, Chac Chel, and in fact, Chacal Ix Chel is another name mentioned in the *Ritual of the Bacabs* (Roys 1965: 146). However, in the Colonial Yucatec San Francisco dictionary, *cheel* also signifies "término, por fin" (Barrera Vásquez 1980: 89). Thus the name Chac Chel could also be glossed as "great (*chac*) end." Both meanings of rainbow and termination are consistent with Goddess O, for she appears to be a goddess of the flood and world destruction.

Far from a kindly old grandmother, Goddess O is of fearful aspect. She frequently appears clawed and fanged and wears a skirt marked with crossed bones and other death symbols (Figs. 50e, 51b–d). In one Late Classic vessel scene she is portrayed as part jaguar, and bears a jaguar ear as well as the spotted Ix eye (Fig. 51c). This representation compares closely with the depiction of the Goddess O on Dresden page 67a (Fig. 51d). In the Dresden scene, the goddess also has prominent claws and the jaguar eye commonly found on the day sign Ix. The crossed-bone skirt worn by the Late Classic Goddess O is also found with Post-Classic examples, such as on Dresden page 74 (Fig. 50e). The same crossed-bone skirt is worn by a probable skeletalized version of Goddess O at Early Post-Classic Chichen Itza (Fig. 51b). This example appears with God N as a supporting Atlantean figure in the bas-relief columns of the Lower Temple of the Jaguars. She also occurs in non-skeletalized form with God N in the upper columns of the Temple of the Warriors (see Seler 1902–23, 5: 296–297, 300–301). It will be recalled that God N seems to be in part a Maya version of the Central Mexican *tzitzimitl* sky bearer, and a similar argument could be made for the aged female at Chichen. In Central Mexico, the *tzitzimitl* was often represented as a female deity. Moreover, it will be seen that Goddess O was identified with spiders, perhaps the most important animal aspect of the Aztec *tzitzimitl*.

During the Post-Classic period, Goddess O was clearly identified with storms and floods. Perhaps for this reason, in the Dresden and Madrid codices, she often wears a serpent headdress. In the Late Post-Classic murals of Tulum Structure 16, she wears the serpent headdress and holds another serpent in her hands (Fig. 51a). The significance of the snake headdress in unknown, but it may be partly due to the strong association of Goddess O with storms and water. In view of the name, Chac Chel, it is not surprising that Goddess O is closely identified with Chac, the preeminent god of lightning and rain. On Madrid page 30b, God B sits at the left foot of Goddess O, who stands with streams of blue water pouring from her loins and breasts (Fig. 50g). On Dresden page 42b, Goddess O and God B are engaged in an amorous interlude. Although badly eroded, a scene on Madrid page 61c may depict the same event. In the codices, Goddess O frequently pours water from an inverted jar (e.g., Figs. 50d–f, 51d). The most complex of these scenes is on Dresden page 74, where she appears with God L or more probably, a black God B amidst great streams of outpouring water (Fig. 50e). This page has long been interpreted as the deluge, the destruction of the world by flood (e.g., Schellhas 1904: 31; Förstemann 1906: 266; J. Thompson 1972: 99). As in the ancient mythology of highland Mexico, the flood figures prominently in the Colonial Yucatec Chilam Balam books of Chumayel (Roys 1933: 99–100), Mani (Solís Acalá 1949: 230–233), and Tizimin (Edmonson 1982: 40–41, 45–48). It is likely that the scenes of Goddess O with the outpouring vase depict her as an extremely powerful world destroyer.

Goddess O is identified with the forces of creation as well as destruction. She appears to be the great genetrix and is closely identified with divination, medicine, childbirth, and weaving. According to Hernandez, Ix Chel is the mother of the goddess Ix Chebel Yax (Saville 1921: 214). Landa (in Tozzer 1941: 129) mentions that Ix Chel was the goddess of birthing: "For their child-births they had recourse to the sorceresses, who made them believe their lies, and put under their beds an idol of a goddess called Ix Chel whom they said was the goddess of making children." During the month of Zip, the Yucatec priests opened their sacred bundles in honor of Ix Chel, who is

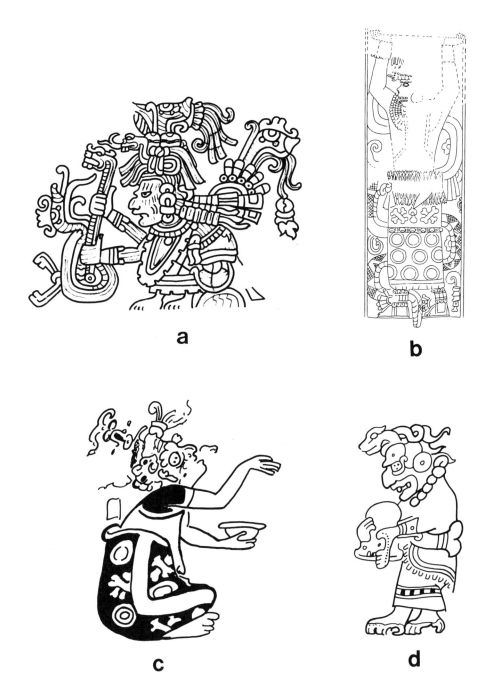

Fig. 51 Classic and Post-Classic representations of Goddess O.

(a) Goddess O grasping serpent, note spindle in head-dress, detail of mural from Tulum Structure 16 (redrawn after A. G. Miller 1982: pl. 37)

(b) Detail of column from the Lower Temple of the Jaguars, Chichen Itza (after Tozzer 1957: fig. 196)

(c) Classic form of Goddess O receiving vomit or other liquid from howler monkey artisan; note jaguar ear and spotted Ix eye (redrawn after Clarkson 1978)

(d) Post-Classic Goddess O with inverted water vessel; note clawed feet and Ix eye, Dresden 67a.

described by Landa as "the goddess of medicine" (Tozzer 1941: 154).

It is probable that Goddess O represents the aged female curer and diviner. In Mesoamerica, aged women frequently serve as midwives and curers. Tozzer (1941: note 598) cites two Colonial accounts describing the presence of aged female curers among the Yucatec Maya.

As a goddess of creation, divination, and curing, Ix Chel was also closely identified with the spider. Landa (Tozzer 1941: 154) states that along with small representations of Ix Chel, the Yucatec curers had ritual bundles containing stones used in divinatory sortilege. These stones were called *am,* the Yucatec word for spider. In the *Ritual of the Bacabs* there is an incantation in which the *am* spider is addressed: "four days were you beneath the garden plot. The cochineal of your grandmother, the virgin Ix Chel, Chacal Ix Chel, Sacal Ix Chel is the symbol of the back of the green spider of wood, the green spider of stone" (Roys 1965: 53). This passage not only identifies Ix Chel with spiders but also describes her as an aged grandmother, or *chich.* Brinton (1895: 40) suggests that Ix Kanleom, or "lady spider web" is the same as Ix Chel. According to Cogolludo, the Yucatec goddess of weaving was Ix Azal Uoh; with little justification, J. Eric S. Thompson (1939: 132) emends this term to Ix Zacal Nok. However, the original transcription may well be correct, as the root *uoh* seems to signify "tarantula." Common Yucatec terms for this creature are *chiuoh* and *cohuoh* (Barrera Vásquez 1980: 340), which could be roughly paraphrased as "fanged *uoh.*" Moreover, in the *Ritual of the Bacabs,* the genetrix of asthma is described as a biting *uoh:* "Who is his mother? The *uoh* in the sky, the *uoh* in the clouds. The biter in the sky, the biter in the clouds" (Roys 1965: 23). Although not an orb weaver, the tarantula does produce silk. In view of her identification with spiders, it is not surprising that Goddess O is often found weaving or with spools of cotton in her headdress (Figs. 50g, 51a).

In many parts of Mesoamerica and especially the American Southwest, the spider is identified with weaving, childbirth, divination, creation, and war (Taube 1983). Among the contemporary Sierra Popoluca of Veracruz, the spider of the east weaves the navel of the infant (Ichon 1973: 74, 173–174). During the creation of the fetus, the spider is the assistant to grandmother Natsi'itni, the creator goddess whom Ichon (1973: 122) compares to Toci-Tlazolteotl of Post-Classic Mexico. Toci, the aged aspect of Tlazolteotl, was the supreme genetrix of the Aztec pantheon, a deity identified with world creation as well as destruction. Sahagún (1950–71, bk. 1: 15) describes her as the goddess of diviners, midwives, and curers. Like the spider, Toci was also identified with weaving. During the festival of Ochpaniztli, an impersonator of Toci spun and wove maguey fiber (Durán 1971: 232). In her roles and attributes Goddess O compares closely to Toci-Tlazolteotl, a deity identified with creation and curing as well as spiders and divination.

On Dresden page 42a, Goddess O sits upon a pyramidal structure holding a mirror bowl containing the face of God C (Fig. 52a). Although somewhat effaced, the compound *chel* appears as the second glyph in the accompanying text. With the circular mirror, the figure recalls highland Mexican stone monuments depicting female figures holding disks to their abdomens (Figs. 52b–c). Both the illustrated examples wear zoomorphic headdresses, which, in a recent study, I identify as the head of the War Serpent (Taube n.d.b). I also argue that the disks represent mirrors, possibly allusions to *tlalxicco,* or the World Navel. A Contact period version of the female figure appears in the Selden Roll, here as a personified place name (Fig. 52d). The central disk contains a bird, perhaps an allusion to the birds commonly used in divination and augury.

The Selden Roll figure bears a headdress composed of two serpents—one with cloud markings and the other with flints—that cascade down either side of her swollen mountain body. The serpent headdress recalls not only Goddess O, but also a goddess appearing at Terminal Classic Bilbao. On Monument 21, an ancient woman, wearing the serpent headdress and seated upon a throne, receives sacrificial offerings (Fig. 52e). The same aged and wrinkled figure appears in the

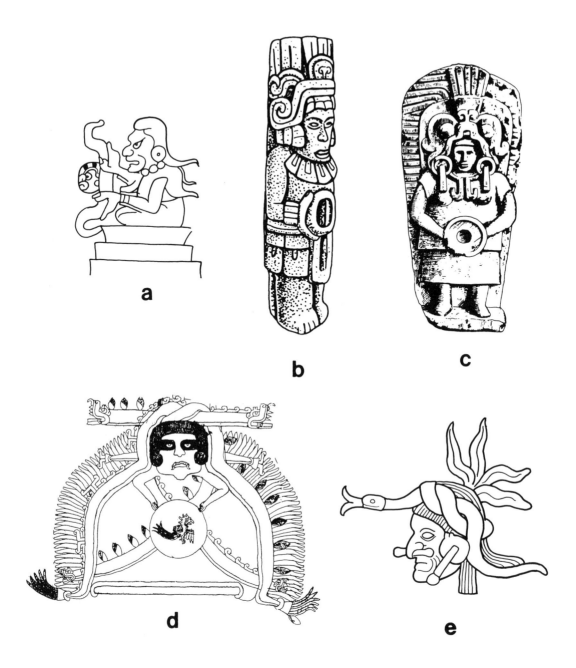

Fig. 52 Comparison of Goddess O with other goddesses of ancient Mesoamerica.

(a) Goddess O holding probable mirror bowl containing face of God C, Dresden page 42a
(b) Goddess with disk over abdomen, stone sculpture possibly from Tlaxcala area (after Nicholson and Berger 1968: fig. 18)
(c) Sculpture of goddess with disk over abdomen, reportedly from Xochicalco (after Nicholson and Berger 1968: fig. 15)

(d) Fanged goddess with serpent headdress and disk over abdomen, detail of Selden Roll
(e) Terminal Classic aged goddess with serpent headdress, detail of Bilbao Monument 21 (drawn after Parsons 1969: pl. 31).

upper portion of Bilbao Monument 8 (see Parsons 1969: pl. 33a). In both cases, her bound-serpent headdress is virtually identical to that worn by Goddess O. According to J. Eric S. Thompson (1950: 83), Goddess O may be equivalent to the aged Aztec goddess Cihuacoatl, also known as Quilaztli and Ilamatecuhtli. Thompson notes that the term Cihuacoatl signifies "Serpent Woman," and thus recalls the serpent headdress of Goddess O. In the Florentine Codex, Cihuacoatl is described as a *tecuani*, a Nahuatl term signifying a stinging or devouring beast (Sahagún 1950–71, bk. 1: 11). This term recalls not only the serpent headdress of Goddess O, but her clawed hands and feet, which are those of a fierce beast, as well. Moreover, the *tzitzimime* were also considered as devouring beasts.

Summary

Goddess O is a powerful, aged woman identified with not only birth and creation but death and probably world destruction as well. In the codices, she is usually referred to as *chel* or *chac chel,* a term signifying "rainbow" or "end" in Yucatec. It is probable that this old goddess, rather than Goddess I, corresponds to the Ix Chel of ethnohistoric literature. During both the Late Classic and Post-Classic periods, Goddess O appears with feline attributes, most notably, the Ix jaguar eye and clawed hands and feet. Like God N, Goddess O may be a Maya version of the Post-Classic Central Mexican *tzitzimitl* sky bearers, fierce demons that threaten the world at certain calendrical and celestial events. Goddess O commonly wears a twisted-serpent headdress, and clear analogues can be seen in other regions of Mesoamerica. J. Eric S. Thompson (1950) suggests that Goddess O may be equivalent to the Central Mexican Cihuacoatl. The Selden Roll and Bilbao figures support Thompson's comparison, although these images also suggest that the concept of an aged goddess with a serpent headdress is fairly widespread and is by no means limited to only the Yucatec Maya and the Valley of Mexico. Among the Maya, this goddess is associated with weaving, curing, and divination and thus shares many traits with Toci, Quilaztli-Cihuacoatl, and other aged goddesses of Post-Classic highland Mexico.

God Q

In my brief discussion of God F, I mentioned that Schellhas confused three distinct deities under the rubric of God F. One of the deities, God A', has already been described with God A. J. Eric S. Thompson (1950: 131) termed the other two divinities Gods Q and R. The primary identifying element of God Q is the curving band passing down his forehead to the back of his cheek (Fig. 53). This band can appear either as a solid line or a series of dots; dotted lines frequently appear on the body as well. The facial band also appears in the name glyph of God Q, which is usually prefixed with a coefficient of ten (Figs. 53a–d). In the Dresden and Madrid codices, this coefficient of two vertical bars is frequently topped with a single dot, suggesting that the coefficient is to be read eleven rather than ten. However, Thompson (1950: 131) points out that the dot does not allude to the number one, but rather to a death sign—a disembodied eyeball. Thus in the Codex Madrid, the element is often clearly rendered as an eye. Moreover, in the Madrid and Paris codices, the prefixed coefficient of ten can appear without the dot (Fig. 53d).

In terms of the attributes and associations of God Q, the coefficient of ten is entirely apt. It will be recalled that for the Classic period, the skeletal death deity God A was the personified head variant for the numeral ten. In the Codex Dresden, the numeral ten is identified with another death-related god. On Dresden page 47, the Venus God 10 Sky, or Lahun Chan, is rendered much like a skeletalized Chac, with a bone jaw and prominent fleshless ribs. It is possible that the association of the number ten with death is phonetic in origin. Whereas the Yucatec word for ten is *lahun, lah* signifies "fin o cabo" (Barrera Vásquez 1980: 430). Thus the skeletal death head and bone jaw may refer to completion, or *lah*.

Schellhas (1904: 27) is the first to note the wide-

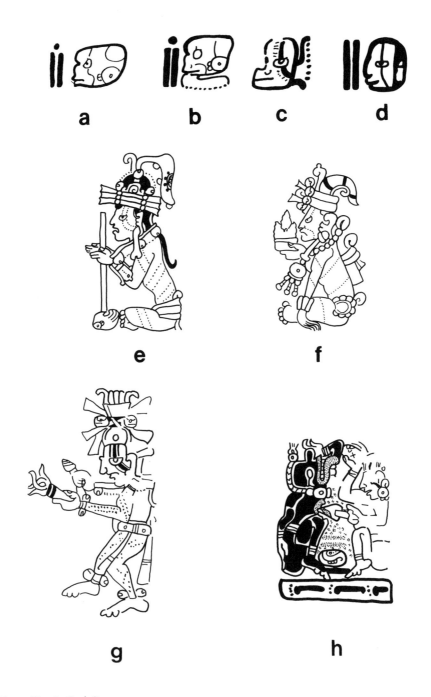

Fig. 53   The Post-Classic God Q.

(a) Portrait glyph of God Q with numeral ten prefix, Dresden page 6b
(b) Name glyph of God Q with T116 *ni* suffix, Dresden page 8c
(c) God Q appellative glyph with T116 *ni* postfix, Madrid page 84c
(d) God Q appellative with numeral ten prefix, Paris page 8

(e) God Q drilling fire, Dresden page 6b
(f) God Q holding offering of cacao, Dresden page 10b
(g) God Q with burning torch and sacrificial blade, Madrid page 84c
(h) God Q attacking God M on road with T528 stone and hafted blade, Madrid page 50a.

spread association of God Q with God A in the Codex Madrid. A clear example occurs on Madrid pages 84c to 88c (Fig. 53g). Whereas the god appearing on 84c is God Q, the two following scenes represent composites of Gods A and Q, with the final scenes on pages 87c and 88c being the death god, God A. On Madrid page 63c, God A appears with the appellative glyph of God Q, and in many scenes Gods A and Q appear together. Thus J. Eric S. Thompson (1950: 131) notes that on Madrid page 76, Gods A and Q flank a slain victim in the region corresponding to the north. In accord with his close association with God A, God Q frequently exhibits elements of death and sacrifice. Thus God Q often appears with death eyes, the death collar, and a knotted headband of cloth or paper (e.g., Fig. 53e). This knotted headband is the same device Peter Joralemon (1974) has described for Classic scenes of sacrificial bloodletting.

In the Codex Madrid, God Q is frequently shown in the guise of an executioner. The sacrificial scene on Madrid page 76 has already been described. In the aforementioned passage occurring on Madrid pages 84c to 88c, Gods A and Q hold flint weapons in their hands (Fig. 53g). Moreover, on Madrid pages 50a, 54c, and 84a, God Q is shown attacking and slaying the black merchant deity, God M (Fig. 53h). On Madrid pages 50a and 54c, this violent event occurs on a road, and it appears that in these scenes, God Q embodies the dangers faced by merchants on their travels.

It is possible that the facial patterning as well as the acts and accouterments of God Q refer to death and sacrifice. In the Post-Classic codices, the curving line passing through the face of God Q can either be solid black or dotted. The same lines tend to be found crossing the body in the form of diagonal bands. In the Codex Madrid, identical body markings frequently appear with God A. Schellhas (1904: 25) notes that the curving line on the face of God Q resembles the facial line of the Late Post-Classic Xipe Totec (Fig. 54a).

From at least as early as the Early Classic period, Xipe Totec, "our lord the flayed one," is commonly found with a similar line curving down the brow and across the cheek. This facial feature is a diagnostic element of the Classic Zapotec Xipe, and Alfonso Caso and Ignacio Bernal (1952: 249–257) have pointed out many examples on Classic ceramic urns. It is possible that in the form of Caso's Glyph P, this deity can be traced back to the Monte Alban 1, and the Formative beginnings of Zapotec writing (Caso and Bernal 1952: 249). An excellent Early Classic representation of Xipe was discovered upon a mural fragment in the Zacuala compound at Teotihuacan (Fig. 54b). The face is clearly dead, with shut eyes and pulled back lips. A similar Early Classic example was excavated in Burial 10 at Tikal (Fig. 54c). This figure is rendered in pure Teotihuacan style and, like the Zacuala example, the lips are widely open to expose the teeth. It is possible that this curious treatment of the mouth may allude to the tightly fitting mask of flayed human skin. When worn, the lips of flayed Xipe masks stretched widely around the mouth of the impersonator (see Pasztory 1983: pl. 199, 267, 298).

Claude Baudez (1985: 204, 210) notes a possible Classic Maya representation of Xipe on Copan Stela 3 (Fig. 55a). The figure appears twice on the monument, in both instances with a vertical band crossing the shut eye and crosshatching over the center of the face. According to Baudez, this entity is a Classic form of God Q. Baudez also mentions that the human hand over the jaw region of one of the faces probably refers to death, because the sign of completion or zero is a human face with a hand-covered jaw (Figs. 55e–f).

The hand-covered jaw appears at Palenque on a shield containing an explicitly flayed human face. This shield can be found on the Palace Tablet and the Tablet of the Slaves with an eccentric flint, possibly a form of the "flint-shield" war expression discussed by Houston (1983). Although these shields clearly depict flayed human faces, they are curiously spotted in the region of the mouth (Figs. 55b–c). Another example occurs on a sculpted stucco fragment discovered in the Palace (see Schele and Mathews 1979: no. 71). In this case the spots near the mouth clearly resemble the print of an outstretched hand. This is confirmed

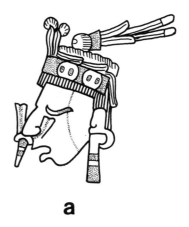

a

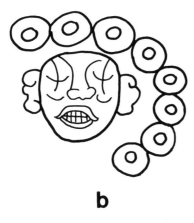

b

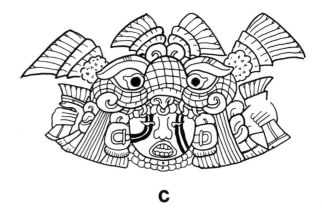

c

Fig. 54   Classic and Post-Classic representations of the flayed god, Xipe Totec.

(a) Late Post-Classic depiction of Xipe Totec, Codex Borgia page 25
(b) Early Classic depiction of Xipe with bared tooth mouth, Teotihuacan mural fragment (redrawn after Séjourné 1959: fig. 6)

(c) Early Classic Xipe figure with bared teeth, detail of vessel from Tikal Burial 10 (redrawn after W. Coe 1967: 102).

by an epigraphic form of the face shield from the Sarcophagus Lid, which shows the spots to be the print of a hand stretched across the face (Fig. 55d).

A human face shield with a hand over the mouth also occurs on Tonina Monument 91, here in a form of the flint-shield expression (see Becquelin and Baudez 1982: fig. 130). This sign and the other images from Copan and Palenque reveal that the occurrence of the human hand over the mouth of a flayed human face is quite widespread during the Late Classic period. Also

displaying the hand over the mouth, the personified variant of zero may be a Classic Maya form of Xipe Totec. In a number of instances, the zero head variant seems to be wearing a mask, possibly of flayed human skin (Fig. 55e).

Although there seems to have been a form of flayed god among the Classic Maya, it is not certain that this entity is identical to God Q. In the subsequent discussion of Central Mexican gods, it will be seen that, although Xipe Totec figures are relatively common in Late Post-Classic Yucatan, they do not display the facial markings of God Q.

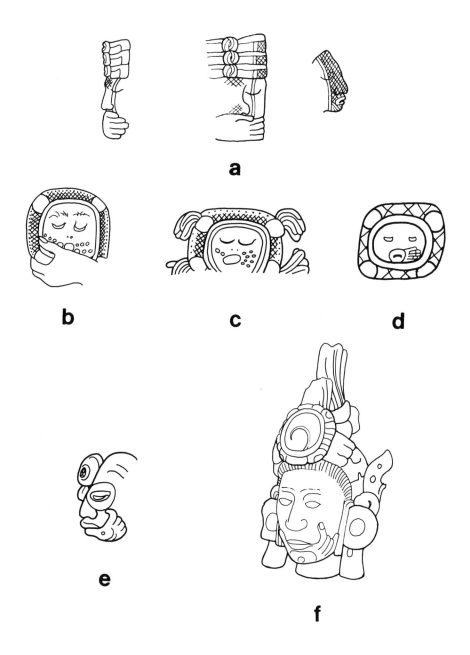

Fig. 55 Flayed figures and the head variant of zero in Classic Maya epigraphy and art.

(a) Probable flayed faces from Copan Stela 3, left and center images constitute two views of same face (redrawn after Baudez 1985: fig. 3)

(b) Flayed human face stretched over shield, note hand print across mouth, Tablet of the Slaves, Palenque

(c) Flayed face on shield with hand print across mouth, Palace Tablet, Palenque

(d) Flayed face on shield with hand over mouth, detail of Pacal name phrase from sarcophagus lid of the Temple of the Inscriptions, Palenque

(e) Head variant of zero, Copan Stela 1

(f) Monumental sculpture, representing head variant of zero, Copan (drawn after L. Schele and M. E. Miller 1986: pl. 110).

There is no clear indication that God Q is actually wearing human skin: the mouth is not stretched open, nor are there signs of cut or hanging skin at the wrists or ankles.

It is possible that the curving facial band of God Q does not refer to human skin, but to stone. Rendered in either lines, solid bands, or strings of dots, the banding is almost identical to Classic and Post-Classic Maya depictions of stone. Late Classic flint blades are frequently depicted with similar markings (Fig. 56a). The T528 *tun* or *cauac* sign for stone is usually supplied with a band and a parallel series of dots. It is possible that this beaded banding refers to hard, stone-like materials. Thus this same marking also appears on the day sign Eb, signifying "tooth" in a number of highland Maya languages. Post-Classic and early Colonial versions of this sign exhibit a facial patterning almost identical to God Q, save that the curving line and dots terminate in a point as they pass down the cheek (Fig. 56b). Although the Edznab marking is a more common means of delineating flint, stone blades are often marked with bands in the Codex Madrid (e.g., Figs. 53g–h). On Madrid pages 50a and 54c, God Q wields both a stone blade and a T528 stone sign in the other hand (Fig. 53h).

An important variant of God Q occurs on Madrid page 60c (Fig. 56d). Although the figure is somewhat eroded, it can be seen that he holds a T528 stone sign in his hand and the "stacked bow tie" paper device on his head; the accompanying text explicitly labels him God Q. On close inspection, it can be seen that the binding covers the eye region as well as the forehead.

The Madrid figure is very similar to the Venus God appearing on Dresden page 50 (Fig. 56e). An aspect of Venus as the morning star, the Dresden example has the same stacked bow tie blindfold across the eyes, and in addition, he displays the diagonal dotted-band body markings found on Dresden representations of God Q. Seler (1963, 2: 251), J. Thompson (1942: 50; 1950: 220), and Reise (1982) identify this figure as a Maya form of Tezcatlipoca-Itzlacoliuhqui-Ixquimilli, the Central Mexican god of stone, cold, and castigation, who usually wears the same knotted device across

his eyes. In a later work, J. Eric S. Thompson (1972: 69) points out that the Dresden figure appears to wear a pair of heron feathers. This heron feather bunch, known as *aztaxelli* in Nahuatl, frequently occurs with the Central Mexican god (e.g., Fig. 56f). Seler (1963; 2: 251) points out yet another striking feature shared between the Dresden figure and the Central Mexican god: the red-tipped, hafted flint point projecting out of the top of the Dresden headdress (Fig. 56e). The Mexican god Tezcatlipoca-Itzlacoliuhqui-Ixquimilli is often found with a stone-tipped dart piercing his headdress (Figs. 56g–h). The Dresden figure is almost surely a Maya form of the Mexican deity.

Although Tezcatlipoca-Itzlacoliuhqui-Ixquimilli frequently appears with the horizontal facial banding of Tezcatlipoca, in many instances, his facial marking is formed by vertical curving bands passing from the brow down across the cheek; in other words, the patterning is quite similar to that of God Q (Figs. 56f–h). Seler (1902–03: 261–262) suggests that this patterning refers to the banding found on such stones as "chert, flint, or ribbon agate." The Central Mexican Codex Cospi provides support for this identification. On the lower portion of Cospi page 12, corresponding to the north, Tezcatlipoca-Itzlacoliuhqui-Ixquimilli stands on jagged stones with similar patterning (Fig. 56c). As a personification of stone, this deity was closely identified with castigation and execution. For the Aztec, stoning was the form of punishment for adultery (Seler 1902–03: 262). The same custom was present among the protohistoric Yucatec Maya. Landa (in Tozzer 1941: 124) notes that stoning was the usual means of executing male adulterers. As a god of stone, God Q may have been identified not only with sacrifice but also with execution, the meting out of punishment to guilty individuals.

Summary

God Q is a god of violent death and execution characterized by a curving band of solid or dotted lines passing from the brow to the cheek. The same banded pattern usually appears on the limbs of the god as well. Baudez has suggested that a

Fig. 56 Stone markings, God Q, and the Central
Mexican blindfolded god of stone and castigation.

(a) Classic Maya representation of stone axe, detail of
codex style vessel (drawn after Robicsek and
Hales 1981: vessel 19)

(b) Stone markings on day sign Eb, from Landa manuscript (redrawn after Thompson 1950: fig. 8–68)

(c) Late Post-Classic Central Mexican representation of
stone, Codex Cospi page 12

(d) Blindfolded figure holding stone, epigraphically
named God Q in accompanying text, Madrid
page 60c

(e) Blindfolded god with body markings of God Q;
note flint at top of headdress, Dresden page 50

(f) Tezcatlipoca-Itzlacoliuhqui-Ixquimilli; compare pair
of heron feathers in headdress to Dresden example
(Fig. 56e), Vaticanus B page 39

(g) Tezcatlipoca-Itzlacoliuhqui-Ixquimilli; note broken
dart in headdress, Borgia page 69 (after Danzel
1923: pl. 49)

(h) Aztec representation of Tezcatlipoca-Itzlacoliuhqui-
Ixquimilli; note dart piercing headdress, Telleri-
ano Remensis, fol. 16, v. 17 (after Danzel 1923:
pl. 32).

Classic form of God Q appears on Copan Stela 3. Although this is a distinct possibility, the only certain representations of this god are limited to the Post-Classic codices. Quite frequently, a stacked series of paper knots appears on the brow of God Q. On Madrid page 60c and Dresden page 50, this knotted device actually covers the eyes of the figures. These two examples are probably Maya forms of the Central Mexican god of stone and execution, Tezcatlipoca-Itzcoliuhqui-Ixquimilli. A personification of the stone of castigation and sacrifice, the face of the Central Mexican deity is often marked by vertical curving lines. The face of God Q is similarly marked, and these curved markings commonly denote stone in pre-Hispanic Maya epigraphy and art. In the Codex Madrid, God Q commonly wields flint blades and the T528 sign for stone. Just as God Q appears with north on Madrid page 76, Tezcatlipoca-Itzcoliuhqui-Ixquimilli is identified with the north in the Central Mexican codices (e.g., Cospi page 12, Borgia page 50, Fejérváry-Mayer page 33). The facial markings and attributes of God Q do indeed point to a Central Mexican derivation. However, rather than being a Maya version of Xipe Totec, God Q may well derive from the Central Mexican god of stone and execution.

God R

The diagnostic mark of God R and his appellative glyph is a single prominent Caban curl that passes from the brow to the lower cheek (Fig. 57). Present in the day signs Caban and Cib, the Caban curl is the Maya sign for earth. For this reason J. Eric S. Thompson (1950: 131) considers God R to be the deity of the earth and maize. Thompson (1950: 135) also notes that in the Codex Madrid, the same curl appears not only with the portrait glyph of God R, but occasionally with the maize deity, God E, as well. In the Codex Madrid, the God R appellative is frequently prefixed by the same bead element found in the glyph of God H (Figs. 57b–c). In fact, the illustrated example on Madrid page 96d is entirely identical to the God H appellative. However, considering how little is known of Gods H and Q, it

is difficult to determine if they are aspects of the same god or even closely associated.

An important clue to the identity of God R may lie in the coefficient frequently prefixed to the portrait glyph (Figs. 57a–b). Composed of a dot and two bars, the coefficient is clearly eleven, or *buluc* in Yucatec. The Classic period head variant of the numeral eleven possesses the same facial curl found with God R and for this reason, J. Eric S. Thompson (1950: 135) tentatively suggests that the numerical head variant is the Classic antecedent of the codical deity. In view of the shared facial patterning and association with the number eleven, this is a likely identification (Fig. 58a). However, Classic representations of God R are not limited to the numeral eleven head variant. Thompson (1961: 14) mentions a probable Late Classic example on the well-known bloodletting scene on the Huehuetenango Vase (Fig. 58b). Engaged in the act of phallus perforation, the youthful figure displays a prominent Caban curl on the cheek.

This figure wears the Ahau cloth headband conventionally appearing with the Headband Twins—Classic forms of Hunahpu and Xbalanque. Indeed, Hunahpu appears on the same vase, also wearing the Ahau headband. It is possible that God R is an aspect of Hunahpu. A Late Classic codex style vessel depicts a pair of youthful figures, one with Caban curl markings and the other with an Ahau headband and a jaguar ear (Fig. 58c). The latter youth is probably Xbalanque, who frequently appears with jaguar attributes and the Ahau headband. It is thus possible that the accompanying figure is Hunahpu, although here with Caban curls and other black markings substituting for the conventional black spots of Hunahpu. The Caban curls and black spots at times have similar if not identical meanings. The vessel figure has not only two Caban curls upon his body, but also a third before his face. In another Late Classic codex-style scene, Hunahpu appears with a similar Caban curl in front of the face but with spots upon his body (Fig. 58d).

Classic epigraphy provides the clearest examples of the Caban marking substituting for the

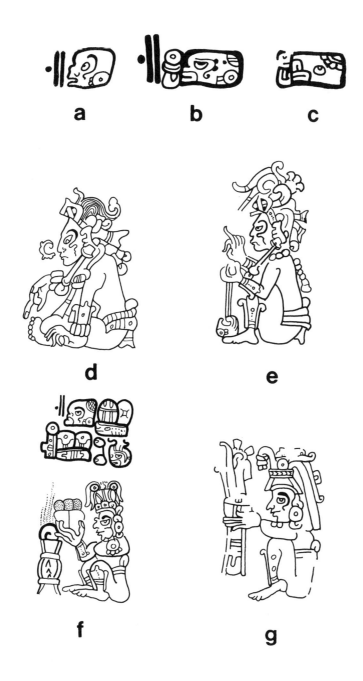

Fig. 57 The Post–Classic God R.

(a) Portrait glyph of God R with numeral eleven prefix, Dresden page 5b
(b) God R portrait glyph with numeral eleven prefix and bead-like element found with name glyph of God H, Madrid page 104b
(c) God H appellative serving as name glyph of God R, Madrid page 96d

(d) God R, Dresden page 6a
(e) God R drilling fire, Dresden page 5b
(f) God R with offerings, Madrid page 107b
(g) God R holding maize offering, Madrid page 65b.

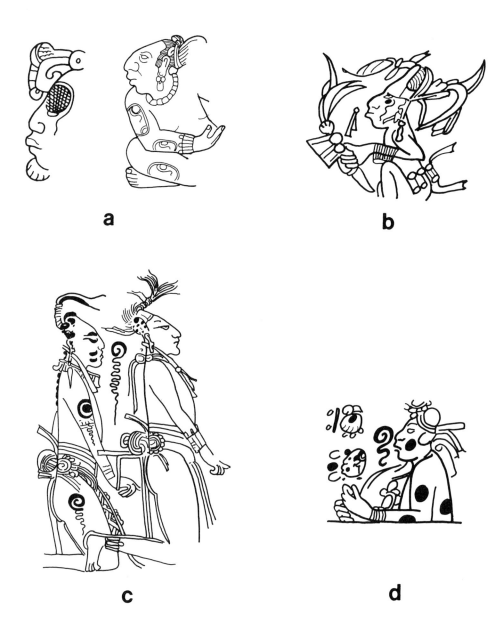

Fig. 58 Classic figures possessing Caban curl markings of God R.

(a) Personified variant of the numeral eleven, Yaxchilan Lintel 48, Palenque Palace Tablet
(b) Personified variant of the numeral eleven with perforator and Ahau headband, detail of Late Classic vase (redrawn after Gordon and Mason 1925–28: no. 27)

(c) Pair of young lords, one with Caban markings, the other with jaguar ear and Ahau headband, detail of codex style vessel (drawn after roll-out photograph courtesy of Justin Kerr)
(d) Spotted Ahau Hero Twin with Caban curl in front of face, detail of codex style vessel (drawn after Robicsek and Hales 1981: vessel 82).

Hunahpu spot. A personified variant of the Tikal emblem glyph features an Ahau head displaying both the headband and the facial spot. However, a Caban curl can appear in place of the Ahau spot (Fig. 59a). Moreover, the Caban curl also appears in conventional examples of the T1000 Ahau sign, here with clear *ahau* phonetic complements (Figs. 59b–c). The use of the Caban curl for the Ahau sign facial marking is widespread during the Late Classic period and appears at Chichen Itza, in the northern Maya lowlands, as well as in the central Peten.

a

b   **c**

Fig. 59 The spotted Ahau Hero Twin and substitutions between the Ahau facial spot and the Caban curl.

(a) Personified variant of the Tikal emblem glyph marked with Ahau spot or Caban curl, from Lintels 2 and 3 of Tikal Temple IV (redrawn after Jones and Satterthwaite 1982: figs. 73, 74)
(b) Ahau sign marked with Caban curl, Ixtutz Stela 4 (redrawn after I. Graham 1980, 2: 181)
(c) Ahau sign with Caban curl marking, Casa Colorada, Chichen Itza (redrawn after Maudslay 1889–1902, 3: pl. 24).

Summary

Although appearing both in Classic and Post-Classic iconography, God R is a relatively rare and poorly understood god. During both the Classic and Post-Classic periods he is identified with the numeral eleven, and in Classic epigraphy serves as the head variant of this numeral. His most striking attribute is the Caban curl marking, which appears on his face and body. It has been noted that these same markings can substitute for the black spots of the spotted Headband Twin, the Classic form of Hunahpu. However, although conventional forms of spotted Headband Twin do appear in the Codex Dresden, it remains to be seen whether God R is actually an aspect of this being.

God S

Although the use of the Caban curl in the facial marking of the Ahau Headband Twin suggests that the codical God R may be a version of Hunahpu, God R would not be the only form of Hunahpu in the Post-Classic codices. In an unpublished compilation of Maya god iconography and epigraphy circulated in 1985, Linda Schele notes the Post-Classic presence of the spotted Hunahpu on Dresden pages 2a, 3a, and 50a. The spotted figures on pages 2a and 50a are both accompanied by a portrait glyph featuring a spot on the cheek and a cartouche at the back of the head ringed with black circular tabs (Figs. 60d, e). In both cases the appellative is prefixed by the coefficient of 1. This appellative is virtually identical to the Classic name glyph of the spotted Headband Twin, who evidently was known as *hun ahau*, or 1 Ahau (Figs. 60a–c). In Classic Maya script, the spotted Headband Twin commonly appears as the personified form of the Ahau day sign (see Thompson 1950: 17–28, 36, fig. 11).

Although Linda Schele is surely correct in the identification of the spotted Headband Twin on Dresden pages 2a and 50a, the figure cited for page 3a is clearly Xbalanque, or God CH, with a portrait glyph prefixed with the numeral one (Fig. 28b). However, a somewhat eroded representation of the spotted Headband Twin does appear in the upper left corner of the same scene. Like the example from page 2a, this figure is bound and decapitated. Thus, on page 3a, both Hero Twins are represented in a single scene.

Along with depicting Xbalanque and Hu-

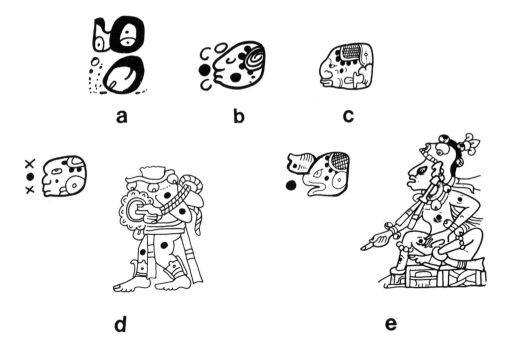

a   b   c

d   e

Fig. 60 Classic and Post-Classic examples of the appellative phrase 1 Hunahpu, the pre-Hispanic name of Hunahpu.

(a) Classic appellative phrase of spotted Headband Twin, detail of Late Classic vessel (drawn after Robicsek and Hales 1981: vessel 186)

(b) Classic name glyph of spotted Headband Twin, detail of Late Classic bowl (drawn after Robicsek and Hales 1981: vessel 117)

(c) Classic name glyph of spotted Headband Twin, detail of Late Classic vase (drawn after Robicsek and Hales 1981: fig. 41a)

(d) Post-Classic form of spotted Headband Twin with accompanying name glyph, Dresden page 2a

(e) Spotted Headband Twin with accompanying name glyph, Dresden page 50.

nahpu, the scene on Dresden page 3a also includes God E, the god of corn. God E also appears with the spotted Headband Twin in the other two cited scenes, Dresden pages 2a and 50. The appearance of Hunahpu with the maize god is consistent with Classic Maya imagery pertaining to the *Popol Vuh*. In the discussion of God E, I noted that the Tonsured Maize God was the Classic version of Hun Hunahpu, the father of Hunahpu and Xbalanque (see Taube 1985).

In the three Dresden scenes, the spotted Headband Twin has clear connotations of death and sacrifice. Thus, he is decapitated on Dresden pages 2a and 3a, whereas on page 50a, he wears a skull headdress. Moreover, the spots found on the figure are undoubtedly the "death spots" found on God A, God A', and other death fig-

ures. According to Landa, Hunhau, or 1 Ahau, was the preeminent lord of the underworld: "They maintained that there was in this place [Metnal] a devil, the prince of all the devils, whom all obeyed, and they call him in their language Hunhau" (Tozzer 1941: 132). In the Colonial Yucatec *Ritual of the Bacabs,* Uaxac Yol Kauil and Ix Hun Ahau are mentioned at the entrance to the underworld (Roys 1965: 9). J. Eric S. Thompson (1950: 299–300) notes that in the Chilam Balam books, the day 1 Ahau is identified with putrescence and the underworld.

In both the Dresden codex and the ethnohistorical accounts, the 1 Ahau character is strongly identified with sacrifice, death, and the underworld. These connotations are also known for the Classic period prototype, the spotted Headband Twin.

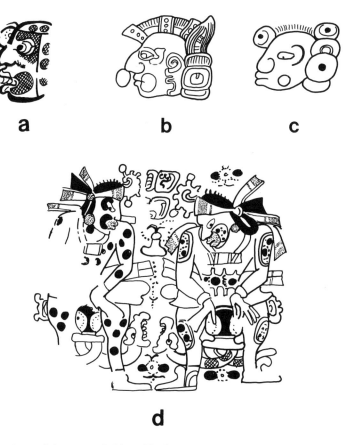

a   b   c

d

Fig. 61 A Classic variant of the spotted Ahau Headband Twin.

(a) Ahau face with markings around mouth and eyes,
Tablet of the 96 Glyphs, Palenque
(b) Early Classic example with death crest (redrawn
after Mayer 1984: pl. 27)

(c) Early Classic example with death crest and spot on
cheek (drawn after Mayer 1980: pl. 39)
(d) Spotted Headband Twin variant with Xbalanque
Headband Twin (drawn after Hellmuth 1983:
fig. 1).

Jeff Kowalski (1989) notes that the ball appearing
on the Late Classic La Esperanza ball-court
marker contains the incised head of Hunahpu, the
spotted Headband Twin. This Classic scene recalls the *Popol Vuh* episode in which Hunahpu
literally loses his head during the ball game
(Recinos 1950: 150–153). On Dresden pages 2a
and 3a, the decapitated spotted twin is represented as a bound captive. This theme also appears in Classic Maya iconography. Thus, on the
side of Tikal Altar 10, the spotted Headband
Twin appears as a hapless captive (see Jones and
Satterthwaite 1982: fig. 34b). In a Tepeu 1 vessel
scene, the spotted Headband Twin appears in another captive pose, here trampled by the Jaguar

God of the Underworld (see M. Coe 1982: 33).

Although the figure on Dresden page 50 is
named 1 Ahau, he lacks the typical facial markings found for the Classic spotted Headband
Twin. Thus rather than having a single spot upon
the cheek, this figure has markings ringing his
eye and mouth. Nonetheless, similar markings
are found with a previously unidentified Classic
aspect of the spotted Headband Twin. This spotted Headband Twin variant appears on a Tepeu 1
vessel paired with the Classic form of Xbalanque,
or God CH (Fig. 61d). Although possessing the
diagnostic headband and black body spots, the
figure displays U-shaped black elements around
the mouth and eyes. This same character also ap-

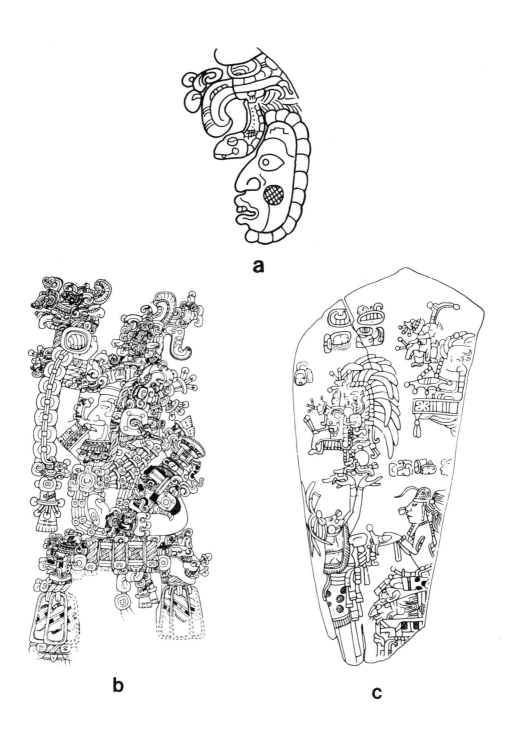

a

b

c

Fig. 62 Hunahpu with Principal Bird Diety headdress.

(a) Spotted Ahau Headband Twin wearing Principal
    Bird Deity Headdress (redrawn after Hellmuth
    1987: fig. 547)
(b) Stormy Sky as spotted Headband Twin variant;
    note headdress held in hand, Tikal Stela 31 (from
    a drawing by W. R. Coe, courtesy of the Tikal

Project, the University Museum, University of
Pennsylvania; after Jones and Satterthwaite 1982:
fig. 51c)
(c) Headband Twin receiving Principal Bird Deity
    headdress (after Taube 1987: fig. 6).

pears in Classic epigraphy, and in a number of instances the curving mouth element is replaced by the conventional check spot of the Headband Twin (Figs. 61a–c). In many examples, this entity has clear connotations of death and frequently displays a "death crest" of hair and eyeballs across the top of the head (Fig. 61b–c). The same crest appears on the skull headdress worn by the Dresden example (Fig. 60d).

One of the most ambitious portrayals of the spotted Headband Twin variant occurs on Stela 31 of Tikal (Fig. 62b). Here the Early Classic ruler Stormy Sky impersonates this being. He appears with the same eye and mouth elements and the death crest, here marked with bones. Although much eroded, it appears that the ruler upon Tikal Stela 29 is also dressed in this same aspect of the spotted Headband Twin. Thus, the same bone-marked death crest is clearly visible. In addition, a cord and large bead run down the cheek of both figures. This beaded cord is also found on the personified head variant of the Tikal emblem glyph, a sign represented with either the face of the spotted Headband Twin or the Caban curl variant (Fig. 59a).

On Stela 31, Stormy Sky wields the headdress of the Principal Bird Deity, the Classic form of Vucub Caquix, aloft in his right hand (Fig. 62b). In another Early Classic scene, the spotted Headband Twin appears actually wearing a Principal Bird Deity headdress (Fig. 62a). A finely carved bone depicts an enthroned Headband Twin with god markings receiving the bird headdress (Fig. 62c). The Principal Bird Deity appears perched in the canopy immediately above. It has been noted that this scene is very much like the accession monuments at Piedras Negras, which depict similar structures topped by the Principal Bird Deity (Taube 1987). It is quite possible that during the Classic period, the taking of the Vucub Caquix headdress by Hunahpu formed part of the mythic charter for royal accession.

Summary

The spotted Headband Twin, the pre-Hispanic form of the Quichean Hunahpu, is a rare but important god that warrants a letter designation distinct from God R. God S is an appropriate term of the Post-Classic codical entity. In the Codex Dresden, the name glyph of God S, 1 Ahau, is virtually identical to examples known for the Classic period. Moreover, many of the characteristics noted for the Dresden form are also present in the Quichean *Popol Vuh* and Classic Maya imagery. His exclusive appearance with God E agrees with Classic Maya scenes illustrating the spotted Headband Twin with the Classic form of Hun Hunahpu, the Tonsured Maize God. It is clear that for the Post-Classic period of Yucatan, Hunahpu had strong connotations of death and sacrifice. The scenes of decapitation on Dresden pages 2a and 3a almost surely correspond to the decapitation of Hunahpu mentioned in the *Popol Vuh* and illustrated in Classic Maya iconography. With his skull headdress and death crest, the figure upon Dresden page 50a has especially strong mortuary attributes and is probably a form of a Classic period Hunahpu variant.

CHAPTER 3

Foreign Gods of Post-Classic Mexico

Introduction

The majority of known Post-Classic Yucatec gods have their origins in Classic Maya iconography, although a number of divinities may have been introduced in the Post-Classic period. Possible examples are the merchant deity known as God M and God Q, who may be a Yucatec form of Tezcatlipoca-Itzlacoliuhqui-Ixquimilli. However, both these deities appear to have their own peculiarly Maya qualities, quite probably due to a syncretic merging of foreign deities with previous Maya gods inhabiting similar symbolic domains. There are a number of other deities that appear to derive directly from either the Gulf Coast or Central Mexico. These examples, many of them unique, are not found upon exotic trade goods but on locally fashioned objects. Nonetheless, their general rarity suggests that the deities portrayed were exotic and that their worship and display signaled a conscious link with foreign influence.

Tlahuizcalpantecuhtli

In an excellent study of Mayapan style *incensarios*, J. Eric S. Thompson (1957: 616–617) suggests that one censer fragment depicts Tlahuizcalpantecuhtli, a particularly baneful Mexican form of Venus as the morning star (Fig. 63a). Thompson notes that the fragment has a face marked by squares in regular zones and a fleshless mandible. Tlahuizcalpantecuhtli has almost identical facial markings and moreover, is frequently skeletal.

A column from the Northwest Colonnade at Chichen Itza depicts a probably Early Post-Classic form of the skeletal Tlahuizcalpantecuhtli (Fig. 63b). The entity appears with a fleshless face wielding an *atlatl,* the weapon par excellence of Tlahuizcalpantecuhtli. Suspended over his thigh is a rare Early Post-Classic form of the cut conch "wind jewel" of Ehecatl-Quetzalcoatl. There is good reason for Tlahuizcalpantecuhtli to display attributes of Ehecatl-Quetzalcoatl. According to the *Anales de Quauhtitlan,* Quetzalcoatl was transformed into the skeletal Tlahuizcalpantecuhtli (Seler 1904c: 359–360). The headdress of the Chichen figure bears a striking resemblance to examples worn by the Late Post-Classic Tlahuizcalpantecuhtli. Thus the series of long feathers projecting out of a shorter feather crest is also found in sixteenth-century representations of Tlahuizcalpantecuhtli (Fig. 63c). In addition, the Chichen headdress contains a series of elements lying across a headband. Similar elements are also found on the headbands of the sixteenth-century Tlahuizcalpantecuhtli (Fig. 63c).

In a recent study, Gordon Whittaker (1986: 57) posits the phonetic spelling of *tawisical* on the Dresden Venus page 48. Whittaker notes that this reading corresponds closely to the first syllables of the Nahuatl name Tlahuizcalpantecuhtli. However, the deity portrayed bears no direct resemblance to the Mexican Tlahuizcalpantecuhtli. Instead, it appears to be the Howler Monkey artisan, as previously identified by Michael Coe (1977: 341, 345). As of yet, there is no clear reason why the Howler Monkey artisan would be identified with either Tlahuizcalpantecuhtli or the morning star.

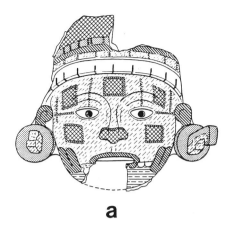

a

b

c

Fig. 63 Representations of Tlahuizcalpantecuhtli in Post-Classic Yucatan.

(a) Fragmentary effigy censer from Mayapan; note spots on face and fleshless lower jaw (after Thompson 1957: fig. 2e)

(b) Skeletal Tlahuizcalpantecuhtli from Northwest Colonnade, Chichen Itza (redrawn after Tozzer 1957: fig. 183)

(c) Aztec representation of Tlahuizcalpantecuhtli, Codex Borbonicus page 9.

Xipe Totec

In the previous discussion of God Q, it was noted that a form of flayed god was present among the Classic Maya. Landa (in Tozzer 1941: 120) mentions a Late Post-Classic Yucatec variant of the Xipe rite of donning the skin of the slain victim: ". . . they threw the body, now dead, rolling down the steps. The officials below took it and flayed it whole, taking off all the skin with the exception of the feet and hands, and the priest, all bare, covered himself, stripped naked as he was, and all others danced with him." Thompson (1957: 612) notes that Xipe Totec appears no fewer than six times in the corpus of Chen Mul deity censers from Late Post-Classic Mayapan (Fig. 64a). Five of the examples were fragmented heads from Structure Q-208, and along with these sherds, there were also limbs clearly wearing a suit of cut human skin (Thompson 1954: 78; 1957: 612–613, figs. 2a–b). The Mayapan incensario examples all appear with shut crescent eyes and an open, slack mouth, quite like examples of flayed figures known for the Classic Maya and highland Mexico. Robert Smith (1971: fig. 37d, legend) notes yet another Xipe example from Mayapan exhibiting these facial features (Fig. 64b). In this case, however, the figure is not an effigy incensario, but a hollow, mold-made figurine.

The same shut eye and slack, open mouth appear on a number of miniature ceramic masks at Mayapan (Fig. 64c). Because of their facial characteristics, Smith (1971: fig. 34) suggests that they may represent Xipe Totec. Averaging some 7 cm in height, these masquettes were clearly not to be worn. In scale, they are entirely comparable to two gold masquettes found in the Sacred Cenote at Chichen Itza (Fig. 64d). These faces, of hammered sheet gold, also possess slack mouths and shut eyes. Eight other examples of still smaller size were also found in the Sacred Well, and these too resemble the flayed face of Xipe Totec (see Lothrop 1952: fig. 50). The small ceramic masks at Mayapan may have been votive copies or poor man's versions of the sheet-gold masquettes found in the Sacred Cenote.

One of the larger Chichen Itza gold masquettes bears a crosslike device on each eyelid (Fig. 64e). Lothrop (1952: 64) notes that this element is identical to the Aztec symbol for gold, and in addition, mentions that Xipe Totec was the patron god of Aztec goldsmiths. Thus according to Francisco Clavigero, Xipe Totec was the god of precious metal workers (Robelo 1980: 779). In part, this may be due to his flayed suit. In one Contact period Nahuatl song, the flayed skin is compared

to a "suit of gold" (Seler 1963, 1: 128). It is quite possible that the Chichen Itza masquettes are the actual faces placed upon elite bags in Late Classic and Terminal Classic Maya iconography. On Uxmal Stela 14, Lord Chac holds such a bag, which displays an inverted face with shut eyes and an open, slack mouth (Figs. 4e, 64f). Other examples occur at Late Classic Piedras Negras, and it is intriguing that some of these bags have the same interlace cross sign serving as the Post-Classic Mexican sign for gold (Fig. 64g). However, it is by no means certain that gold was even present at Late Classic Piedras Negras. Nonetheless, for Post-Classic Yucatan, it is quite likely that the cited gold masquettes refer to Xipe Totec and his golden garment of human skin.

Tlazolteotl

J. Eric S. Thompson (1957: 614) identifies the face of another Mayapan incensario as that of Tlazolteotl, the Mexican goddess of earth and fertility (Fig. 65a), Thompson notes that the mouth region is blackened. This is a diagnostic attribute of Tlazolteotl, who may be found with a blackened mouth in the Late Classic sculpture of Veracruz (see M. E. Miller 1986: illus. 70).[9] This feature is especially common in Post-Classic representations of Tlazolteotl, both in Central Mexico and Veracruz (Figs. 65b–c). Thompson also states that the Mayapan fragment has a series of U-shaped elements on the brow as well. According to Thompson, these elements are a symbol of cotton and frequently appear on the costume of Tlazolteotl (Fig. 65c). Dienhart (1986: 53) agrees with the cotton signification of these U-shaped elements and notes that this identification was previously made by Seler (1902–23, 1: 166). However, it is by no means certain that all U-shaped elements represent cotton. Larger and thicker examples found with Tlazolteotl are often lunate in form, and it is quite possible that these refer to the moon (e.g., Fig. 52c). In fact, the examples from

[9] The cited figure not only has the black facial marking but also hanks of twisted cotton on the headdress and through the ears. In addition, she wears a serpent belt. In Post-Classic Mexico, Tlazolteotl is found wearing serpent belts as well as unwoven cotton (e.g., Codex Laud page 19).

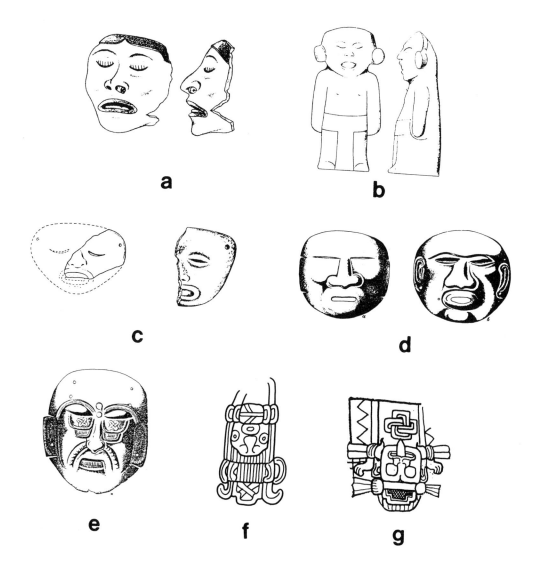

Fig. 64 Representations of Xipe Totec and flayed faces in Late Classic and Post-Classic Maya art.

(a) Late Post-Classic Xipe Totec face from effigy censer, Mayapan (after Smith 1971: fig. 32i; courtesy of the Peabody Museum of Archaeology and Ethnology)

(b) Hollow mold-made figurine of Xipe Totec, Mayapan (after Smith 1971: fig. 37d; courtesy of the Peabody Museum of Archaeology and Ethnology)

(c) Ceramic masquettes of Xipe Totec, Mayapan (after Smith 1971: fig. 34b, c; courtesy of the Peabody Museum of Archaeology and Ethnology)

(d) Gold masquettes from Sacred Cenote, Chichen Itza (after Lothrop 1952: fig. 48)

(e) Sacred Cenote gold masquette with Central Mexican symbol for gold on eye lids (after Lothrop 1952: fig. 46a)

(f) Pouch decorated with possible gold masquette or flayed human face, Uxmal Stela 14

(g) Pouch decorated with possible flayed face; note Central Mexican sign for gold, Piedras Negras Stela 7 (redrawn after Maler 1901: pl. 16).

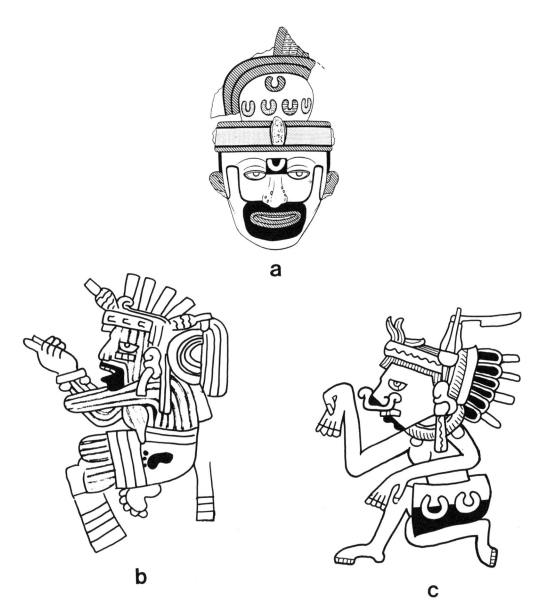

Fig. 65 Depictions of Tlazolteotl in Post-Classic Mesoamerica.

(a) Fragmentary Mayapan effigy censer; note black marking around mouth and U-shaped elements (after Thompson 1957: fig. 2c)

(b) Tlazolteotl, Vaticanus B page 30
(c) Tlazolteotl, note U-shaped elements, Borgia page 23.

the Mayapan sculpture most closely resemble this latter form. However, although the Mayapan devices may not represent cotton, they nevertheless support the Tlazolteotl identification, as Tlazolteotl is commonly found with the larger lunate sign (e.g., Codex Borbonicus page 13). It is noteworthy that neither Goddess I nor Goddess O occurs with the black facial paint or the U-shaped element. It appears that the Mayapan fragment depicts an entirely foreign introduction, possibly from Veracruz or Central Mexico.

Huehueteotl and Xiuhtecuhtli

In his discussion of God D *incensarios*, Thompson (1957: 604) identifies the upper portion of one Mayapan specimen as a depiction of Itzamna (Fig. 66a). However, this figure is not the Maya Itzamna but Huehueteotl, the aged fire god frequently occurring in the Classic sculpture of Central Mexico and the Gulf Coast. With its high cheek bones and almost senile grin, the face is highly suggestive of Huehueteotl. However, the broad headband provides the most important identifying feature of the Mexican god. Supplied with a series of quincunxes, it is virtually identical to the urn rims of many Huehueteotl *incensarios* (Fig. 66c). For the Aztec, the quincunx represented turquoise, *xiuitl,* an important morpheme in the name Xiuhtecuhtli, a closely related fire god.

Another Late Post-Classic Maya effigy *incensario* of Huehueteotl was discovered at Ichpaatun, a Late Post-Classic site situated slightly north of Chetumal, Quintana Roo (Fig. 66b). In this case, the fragment corresponds to only the uppermost part of the urn, with just the left eye and headband intact. This headband, however, is clearly composed of two quincunxes and is nearly identical to the Mayapan example. Although fragmentary, the remaining portion of the eye orbit is sunken, suggesting that the face had aged and craggy features (for a similar treatment of eye orbit, see Fig. 68c).

According to Sahagún (1950–71, bk. 1: 29), Huehueteotl was an epithet of the fire god Xiuhtecuhtli. However, whereas Huehueteotl is invariably rendered as an aged and decrepit being, Xiuhtecuhtli appears relatively youthful, with none of the characteristics of infirm old age. Named turquoise (*xiuitl*) lord (*tecuhtli*), this entity was an important god of rulership as well as of fire (see Sahagún 1950–71, bk. 6).

It has been recently noted that Xiuhtecuhtli appears as one of the deities in the Dresden Venus pages (Taube and Bade 1991). The deity occurs on Dresden page 49 as the fearful manifestation of the morning star at heliacal rising. Like the Late Post-Classic Xiuhtecuhtli of highland Mexico, this figure displays horizontal facial banding and wears a form of the *xiuhuitzolli* crown with the *xiuhtototl* bird brow-piece (Fig. 67a). The medallion worn on the chest of the figure is the same device worn on the headdress of Quetzalcoatl on Dresden page 4a (Fig. 27a). In the discussion of God H, it was stated that this is the Aztec sign for turquoise, or *xiuitl.* In the iconography of Late Post-Classic Central Mexico, Xiuhtecuhtli commonly appears wearing forms of turquoise chest pieces (e.g., Borgia pages 14, 50; Vaticanus B page 68; Borbonicus page 9).

The appellative glyph accompanying the Dresden figure provides strong phonetic evidence that this entity is Xiuhtecuhtli (Fig. 67b). The glyph compound is composed of a T109 *chac* prefix, the T1048 *xi* skull, a T277 *ui* suffix, followed by a sign identified by Whittaker (1986: 58) as *te* in the Landa alphabet, and finally, T679, Landa's *i*. With the recently proposed reading of the T1048 beaded skull as *xi* (Stuart 1987b: 37), the entire compound can be read *chac xiu(i)tei,* a close gloss for the Nahuatl Xiuhtecuhtli (Taube and Bade 1991). With the appellative compound and the attendant iconography, it is clear that this entity is a Maya interpretation of the Nahuatl Xiuhtecuhtli.

Aside from the figure on Dresden page 49, there is one other possible depiction of Xiuhtecuhtli from Late Post-Classic Yucatan (Fig. 67d). Mural 5 from Tulum Structure 1-sub depicts an entity with horizontal facial banding in yellow and blue (see A. G. Miller 1982, pl. 21). The facial patterning strongly resembles that of Xiuhtecuhtli (Fig. 67c). However, there is an additional detail: the three blue bands running across the forehead, nose, and chin are each broken into a craze of circles and fine lines. The effect is clearly to depict turquoise, with the many short fine lines representing smaller tesserae among larger disks of stone. It appears that the figure is depicted wearing a turquoise mosaic mask of Xiuhtecuhtli. The God K headdress worn by the figure may also allude to fire. It has been previously noted that God K was closely identified with fire and lightning. On Paris page 9a, the head of God K lies within a cartouche of flames.

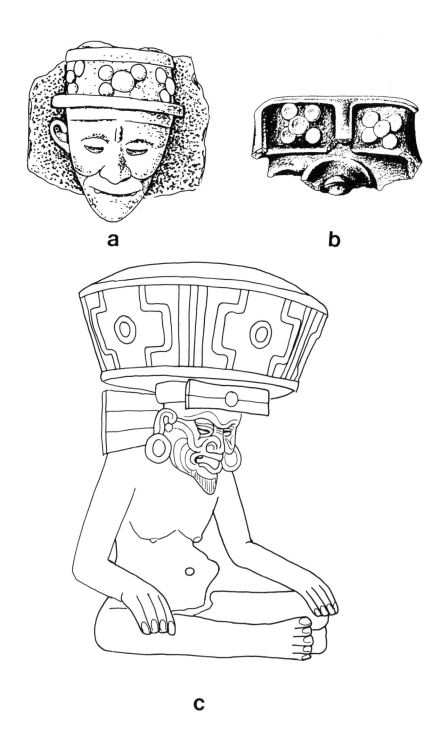

a

b

c

Fig. 66 Depictions of Huehueteotl.

(a) Fragmentary Mayapan effigy censer of Huehueteotl with quincunx headband (redrawn after Thompson 1957: fig. 4a)

(b) Fragmentary effigy censer of Huehueteotl from Ichpaatun, Quintana Roo (after Sanders 1960: fig. 8b, no. 32)

(c) Huehueteotl effigy censer from Cerro de las Mesas; note quincunx elements at rim of urn (redrawn after Ramírez Vásquez 1968: 136).

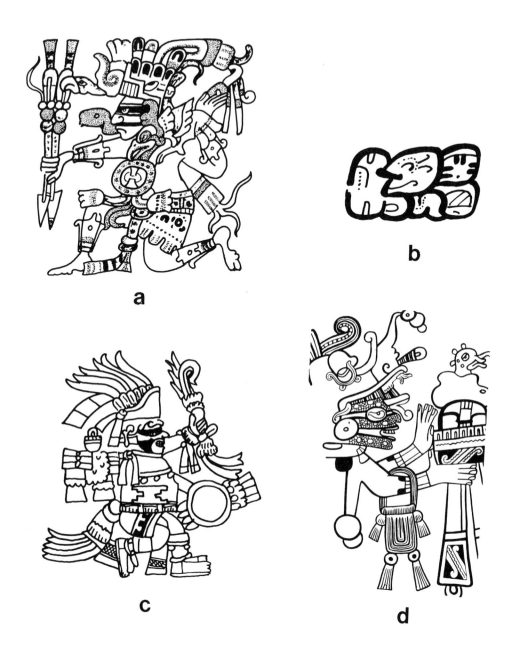

Fig. 67   Representations of Xiuhtecuhtli.

(a) Xiuhtecuhtli, Dresden page 49
(b) Appellative glyphic compound accompanying Dresden Xiuhtecuhtli, read *chac xiu(i)tei*
(c) Aztec representation of Xiuhtecuhtli, Vaticanus A
(d) Xiuhtecuhtli with turquoise mosaic mask, Tulum (after Miller 1982: illus. 157).

The Two-Horned God

In the Museum of the American Indian, New York, there is a Late Post-Classic Mayapan style *incensario* representing an aged deity (Fig. 68c). Mary Ellen Miller (1986: 189) attributes the piece to San Antonio, Quintana Roo. Like the majority of Late Post-Classic effigy burners, the figure wears the cloth "miter" headdress associated with priests and Itzamna. However, the figure also wears two projecting maize cobs on either side of the headdress. This figure is very much like an entity appearing in an Aztec group of stone sculptures from Tenochtitlan (Fig. 68d). Termed the Two-Horned God by Debra Nagao (1985), the Aztec figure is seated, usually with the arms crossed and placed over the upraised knees. The aged figure is provided with two projecting elements at the top of the head; at times, these devices are clearly corn cobs (Nagao 1985: 12). The Aztec Two-Horned God invariably has two projecting teeth, giving the impression of a snaggle-toothed mouth. The Maya example also has a prominent pair of teeth, as well as a probable beard. The Aztec Two-Horned God may also be bearded, although facial hair was not a common trait. The limited context in which he occurs makes identification of the Aztec Two-Horned God uncertain. Among the possible identities of this deity are Tonacatecuhtli, Tepeyolotl, Huehueteotl, and Xiuhtecuhtli (see Nicholson and Keber 1983; Nagao 1985; López Austin 1987).

Two Fine Orange effigy vessel fragments from the Monjas at Chichen Itza may depict a Terminal Classic or Early Post-Classic form of the Two-Horned God (Figs. 68a–b). The vessel fragments represent a human head with two horn-like elements projecting from the sides of the skull. The more intact specimen appears to be aged, with peaked features and wrinkled lips (Fig. 68c). Both display curving bands around the eyes, which recall the eye cruller of the Classic Maya Jaguar God of the underworld, also known as the numerical seven head variant. The bewhiskered Late Post-Classic effigy censer also suggests the jaguar, and it will be recalled that beards are a jaguar attribute in Classic and Post-Classic Maya iconog-raphy. The Chichen Itza and San Antonio examples of two-horned deities suggest that the Aztec Two-Horned God may actually be Tepeyolotl, the jaguar god of the earth's interior.

The Tlaltecuhtli Earth Deity

One of the major figures of Late Post-Classic Aztec sculpture is a monstrous anthropomorphic figure in a splayed and squatting posture (see Pasztory 1983: pls. 97, 98, 109, 113, 115, 117, 130, 216, color pl. 46). The splayed position of the limbs has given rise to the term of *hocker,* a German word signifying a squatting position. It is generally believed that the Aztec figure, frequently supplied with claws and an open, fanged mouth, is a representation of Tlaltecuhtli, the female earth goddess (see Klein 1976: 55–56; Nicholson and Keber 1983: 61).

At Mayapan, there is a sculpture that closely resembles the Aztec Tlaltecuhtli figure (Fig. 69a). Carved from a fine limestone block roughly 90 × 85 cm, the sculpture was discovered in a small shrine (Structure H-18a) next to a round temple (Chowning 1956). The piece represents a splayed anthropomorphic figure with the arms and legs bent at right angles and, like the Aztec sculptures, skulls appear at the knees and elbows. Citing Proskouriakoff, Chowning (1956: 453) notes the similarity of this piece to the Aztec earth monster. The earth figure overlies two intertwined serpents, which recalls the Aztec *Histoire du Mechique* account of creation. In this episode, Quetzalcoatl and Tezcatlipoca tear Tlaltecuhtli in half by transforming themselves into two great serpents (Garibay 1979: 108). However, although clearly influenced by Mexican iconography, the sculpture may also derive from Maya traditions. The Classic Altar T of Copan represents a large caiman, a well-known earth symbol, in a similar *hocker* position (Fig. 69c).

A probable reference to the Tlaltecuhtli creation episode appears in Mural 7 of Tulum Structure 16 (Fig. 69b). In this mural scene there is a figure in typical splayed Tlaltecuhtli stance: squatting with arms upraised. The entity is transfixed by a pair of twisting elements that pass through

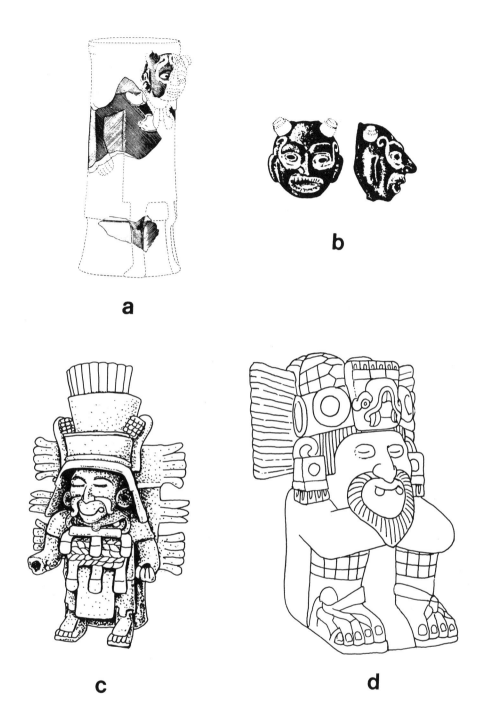

a

b

c

d

Fig. 68 The aged two-horned god in Post-Classic Mesoamerica.

(a,b) Fragmentary Fine Orange vessels from Monjas group, Chichen Itza (after Brainerd 1958: fig. 79d,f)

(c) Effigy censer of aged bearded male with two maize cobs projecting from top of headdress band (drawn after M. E. Miller 1986: illus. 155)

(d) Aztec two-horned god, "horns" formed by pair of tortoise carapaces doubling as maize cobs (drawn after Nicholson and Keber 1983: no. 25).

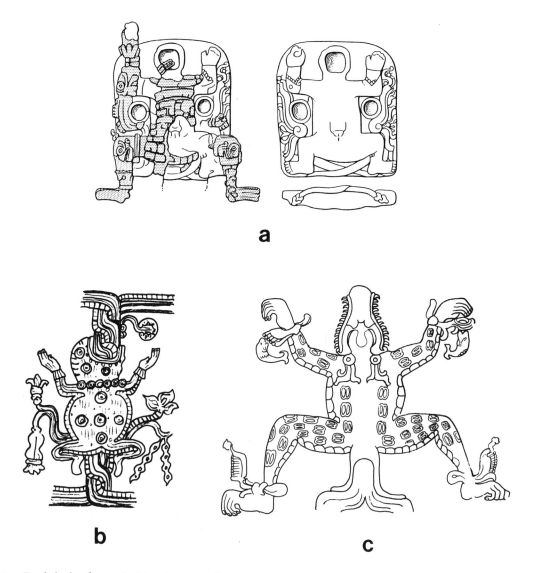

a

b

c

Fig. 69 Earth *hocker* figures in Maya iconography.

(a) Stone sculpture from Structure H-18a, Mayapan, gray portion represents overlying plaster; note skulls placed at joints (after Chowning 1956: figs. 1b,c)

(b) Squatting zoomorphic figure transfixed by pair of twisting serpents, detail of mural from Tulum Structure 16 (redrawn after A. G. Miller 1982: pl. 34)

(c) Late Classic caiman with fish tail, a probable early form of Itzam Cab Ain, Copan Altar T (redrawn after Maudslay 1889–1902, 1: 95c).

its mouth and posterior. In the Structure 16 murals, these twisting elements are rendered as serpents (see A. G. Miller 1982: pls. 37–40). Arthur Miller (1982: pl. 94, legend) describes Mural 7 entity as "an earth monster-like creature spewing forth serpentine borders." Rather than vomiting serpents, I suspect that, as Tlaltecuhtli, this entity is being pierced and torn apart by the two cosmic serpents.

A number of scenes from Chichen Itza may

represent a still older Early Post-Classic version of the *Histoire du Mechique* creation episode (Figs. 70a–c). In these scenes, a pair of serpents emerges out of the abdomen of a reclining woman. The heads of the serpents are provided with blades, as if they had slashed open her abdomen. According to Coggins (1984: 160), this female figure represents the earth. In view of the prominent pair of serpents, her identification appears to be correct. Thus the Chichen motif depicts the same *Histoire du Mechique* Tlaltecuhtli episode illustrated by the Mayapan sculpture and the mural from Tulum Structure 16.

In another Aztec creation account, here appearing in the *Historia de los Mexicanos por sus pinturas*, Quetzalcoatl and Tezcatlipoca transform themselves into a pair of trees to raise the heavens (Garibay 1979: 32). In the two columns from the North Temple of the Great Ball Court at Chichen Itza, trees covered with flowering vines emerge from the navel of the recumbent goddess (Figs. 70b–c). These columns immediately recall Mexican scenes of world trees growing out of the abdomens of reclining figures, frequently Tlaltecuhtli (Figs. 70d–e). It is probable that the North Temple columns represent two creation events: the sacrifice and dismemberment of the earth goddess and the raising of the heavens by the world trees.

Mural 1 of Tulum Structure 5 may represent a Late Post-Classic version of the North Temple scenes (Fig. 71). Here a pair of twisted serpents form three flowering columns that support the prominent sky band immediately above. The heads of the serpents appear at the far left and right. One displays the head of God B and the other, God K. In the lowest portion of the scene, there is a pair of God B serpents in what appears to be water. Thus they are flanked by a probable conch on the left and a coiled snake on the right. In the center of this scene, between the twisted serpents, there is a clawed entity that appears to be swimming. Quite possibly, this figure represents the Tlaltecuhtli monster. Unfortunately, considerable erosion prohibits its precise identification.

The discussed Tlaltecuhtli imagery from Mayapan, Chichen Itza, and Tulum indicates that a form of the Tlaltecuhtli myth was well known in Post-Classic Yucatan. In this suggested creation myth, the earth goddess was killed by a pair of cosmic serpents who then, as world trees, raised the heavens. Such an episode is consistent with ethnohistoric creation accounts appearing in the Chilam Balam books of Mani, Tizimin, and Chumayel (Craine and Reindorp 1979: 118–119; Edmonson 1982: 40–41; Roys 1933: 101). In the Mani and Tizimin passages, the earth caiman, Itzam Cab Ain, is slain to make the earth. Along with mention of Itzam Cab Ain, the three creation accounts also describe the erection of trees to sustain the heavens (Craine and Reindorp 1979: 119; Edmonson 1982: 49; Roys 1933: 100–102).

Martínez Hernández (1913: 165–166) compares the Itzam Cab Ain episode to the killing of Cipactli in the Aztec *Historia de los Mexicanos por sus pinturas*. In the Aztec account, Cipactli is equated with Tlaltecuhtli: ". . . hicieron del peje Cipactli la tierra, a la qual dijeron Tlaltecuhtli, y píntalo como dios de la tierra, tendido sobre un pescado, por haberse hecho de él" (Garibay 1979: 26). Following the creation of the earth, the *Historia* describes the raising of the heavens by Tezcatlipoca and Quetzalcoatl in the form of trees (Garibay 1979: 32). In view of the North Building of the Great Ball-Court at Chichen Itza, it would appear that the dismemberment of Tlaltecuhtli by a pair of serpents and the raising of the heavens by trees is an ancient creation account antedating the Late Post-Classic Aztec.

Tlaloc

One of the oldest known deities of the Mexican pantheon, Tlaloc can be traced as early as the Late Preclassic ceramics of Tlapacoya (Barba de Piña Chan 1956). Known for their goggle eyes and large jaguar teeth, the images of this god are widespread at Early Classic Teotihuacan (Pasztory 1974) and in the later iconography of Xochicalco, Cacaxtla, and El Tajin. Representations of Tlaloc are fairly common in Classic Maya art, although Schele (1986b) notes that the Classic examples appear primarily in the context of war. However, it does appear that the Classic Maya did recognize Tlaloc as a god of rain and lightning. Thus, in

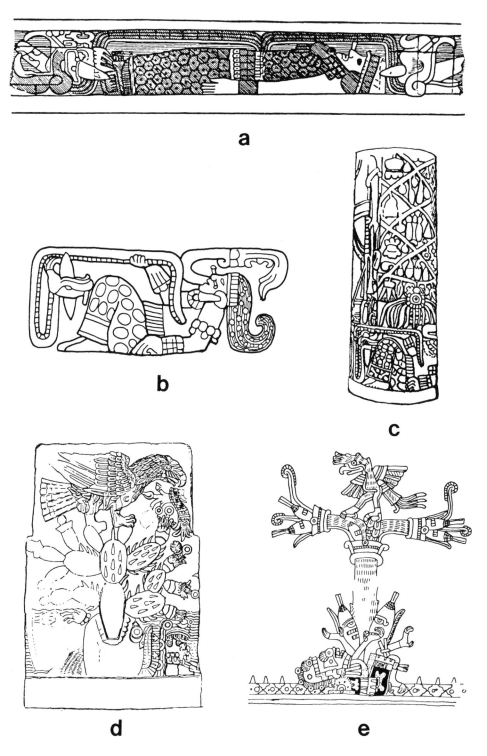

Fig. 70 Post-Classic representations of earth goddesses.

(a) Supine earth goddess with pair of bladed serpents emerging from abdomen, North Temple of the Great Ball Court (after Seler 1902–23, 5: 321)

(b) Detail of North Temple column (drawn after rubbing courtesy of Merle Greene Robertson)

(c) Lower portion of North Temple column, note vine-wrapped tree above abdomen of recumbent goddess (after Breton 1917: fig. 3)

(d) Tenochtitlan represented as nopal growing out of reclining Tlaltecuhtli (after Palacios 1929: fig. 2)

(e) Sacred *axis mundi* tree growing out of skeletal earth goddess, Borgia page 53.

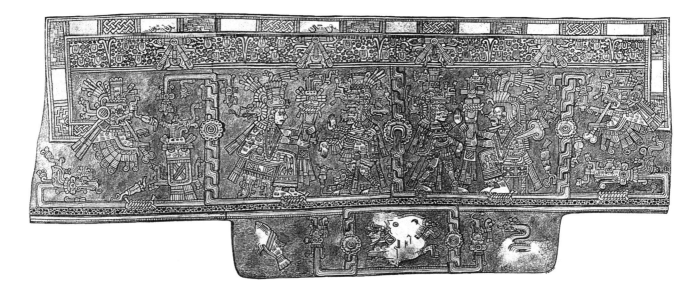

Fig. 71 Mural 1 of Tulum Structure 5, a possible representation of two cosmic serpents raising the heavens; note clawed figure in lower center of scene (after A. G. Miller 1982: pl. 28).

one Copan scene, Tlaloc with a War Serpent leg substitutes for God K, a Maya god of lightning and rain (Fig. 72a). In contrast to the anthropomorphic nose of the Teotihuacan Tlaloc, the majority of Late Classic Maya Tlaloc representations have a sharply upturning snout or lip (e.g., Fig. 72a). This same convention also occurs in the iconography of Late Classic El Tajin and other Veracruz sites (Fig. 72b) and in that of Late Post-Classic Mexico (Fig. 35b).

Depictions of Tlaloc are common in the iconography of Terminal Classic and Early Post-Classic Chichen Itza. In one scene, a Tlaloc with the upturned lip wields an undulating lightning bolt (Fig. 72c). At the outskirts of Chichen Itza, the cave of Balankanche contained a series of contemporaneous Tlaloc censers (Fig. 72d). These ceramic censers display the conventional goggle eyes, large teeth, and upturned snout of the Mexican rain god. However, these were not the only rain god censers found in the cave. Another form of censer was carved of local limestone, with full-figured gods sculpted on the sides (see Andrews

1970: figs. 22–23). Although a number of the carved figures have been identified as Xipe Totec (Andrews 1970: 32, 57), they appear with the characteristic face, headdress, and lightning weapons of Chac. Thus it appears that during the Early Post-Classic of Chichen Itza, both Chac and Tlaloc were invoked in the cave at Balankanche.

The presence of Tlaloc and Chac censers in the Balankanche cave suggests that the symbolic domain of these two gods overlapped in Post-Classic Yucatan. As early as the Terminal Classic period, Chac appears with characteristics of Tlaloc. Thus the Chac figure on Oxkintok Stela 12 displays the goggle eye of Tlaloc (Fig. 5a). During the Late Post-Classic period, the syncretic merging of Chac and Tlaloc is widespread in Yucatan. A number of Chac effigy vessels from Mayapan appear with goggle eyes and fanged mouths (Figs. 73b–d). One example bears an element at the bridge of the nose, which closely resembles the prominent nose beads of the Balankanche Tlaloc censers (Figs. 72d, 73c). The large teeth of the Mayapan Chac vessels resemble those

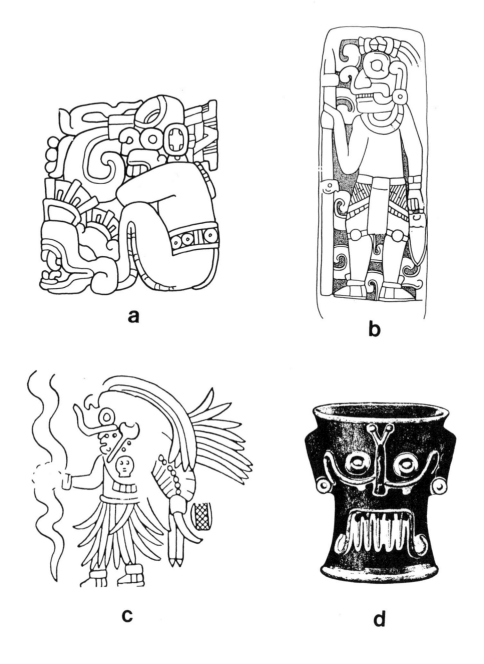

a

b

c

d

Fig. 72 Representations of Tlaloc in Late Classic and Post-Classic Mesoamerica.

(a) Full-figure glyph of Tlaloc with War Serpent foot, an allusion to God K (redrawn after Coggins 1979: fig. 3–2)
(b) Misantla Stela, Late Classic Veracruz (drawn from photograph courtesy of the Yale University Art Gallery)

(c) Tlaloc with lightning bolt, Chichen Itza (after Tozzer 1957: 219)
(d) Early Post-Classic Tlaloc censer, Balankanche (after Andrews 1970: fig. 9a; courtesy of the Middle American Research Institute, Tulane University).

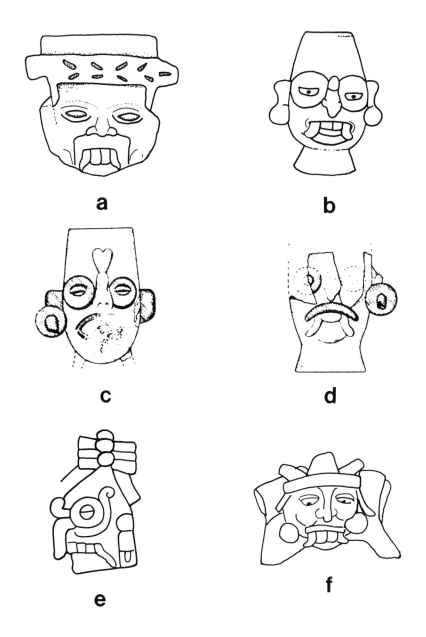

a
b
c
d
e
f

Fig. 73 Late Post-Classic composite forms of Chac and Tlaloc from the northern Maya lowlands.

(a) Tlaloc vessel, Santa Rita (redrawn after D. Chase 1985: fig. 5)
(b) Chac vessel with ring eyes and pronounced teeth of Tlaloc, Mayapan (drawn after Smith 1971: fig. 75g)
(c) Chac or Tlaloc vessel with goggle eyes and nose element found with Balankanche Tlaloc censers (see Fig. 72), Mayapan (after Smith 1971: fig. 30z)

(d) Fragmentary Chac or Tlaloc vessel, Mayapan (after Smith 1971: fig. 30aa)
(e) Chac displaying the pronounced teeth and goggle eye of Tlaloc, detail of Cozumel Stela 2 (drawn after Mayer 1984: pl. 162)
(f) Effigy vessel displaying Tlaloc teeth, Mayflower, Belize (redrawn after E. A. Graham 1985: fig. 7).

in the mouths of two Late Post-Classic effigy vessels from Santa Rita and Mayflower, Belize (Figs. 73a, f). Diane Chase (1985: fig. 5) identifies the Santa Rita example as Tlaloc; the precise identity of the second example is uncertain.

The mouths of the Mayapan, Mayflower, and Santa Rita examples all suggest the jaguar maw of Tlaloc, which is frequently supplied with long incisors and curving canines at the sides. However, such a mouth is not a characteristic of the Classic Chac (see Figs. 4–8). It appears that during the Late Post-Classic period, the elements curling out of the corner of the Chac mouth were reinterpreted in terms of canines. A transitional form appears on Stela 2 of Cozumel (Fig. 73e). In this case, the element is sinuous like the Classic examples, but appears to function as a canine in a Tlaloc mouth. Like the Mayapan examples and Oxkintok Stela 12, the Cozumel Chac displays the goggle eye of Tlaloc.

Quetzalcoatl

For the northern Maya lowlands, there is no foreign god as famous as Quetzalcoatl. In part, this is due to Central Mexican and Yucatec ethnohistorical accounts chronicling the journey of Quetzalcoatl from Tollan to Yucatan (Seler 1902–23, 1: 669–705). In the Yucatec sources, Quetzalcoatl is usually referred to as Kukulcan, meaning plumed or quetzal serpent in Yucatec. According to Landa (in Tozzer 1941: 21), Kukulcan first arrived at Chichen Itza from a region in the west. In view of his direct link with Chichen Itza, it is not surprising that images of Quetzalcoatl abound at this site. The prevalence of Quetzalcoatl imagery at Chichen Itza is especially intriguing since this site shares many specific architectural and iconographic traits with the site of Tula, Hidalgo, generally regarded to be the legendary Tollan (Jiménez Moreno 1941).

At Chichen Itza, Quetzalcoatl appears in both zoomorphic and anthropomorphic form. Thus, feathered serpents are extremely common at Early Post-Classic Chichen Itza and frequently appear in architectonic contexts upon columns, cornices, and balustrades. Where paint is preserved, the serpents are provided with the green feathers of the quetzal. In the Lower and Upper Temples of the Jaguars at Chichen Itza, the feathered serpent often accompanies a particular individual wearing a mask with clearly demarcated regions around the mouth and eyes (Fig. 74a). Remarkably, the gold portion of such a mask was found in the Sacred Well at Chichen Itza (Fig. 74b). In this case, the goggles demarcating the eye region are supplied with feathered serpents.

At Chichen Itza, either the feathered serpent or an associated human figure can appear with star markings (Figs. 74c, d). Clemency Coggins (1984) and Virginia Miller (1989) note that these star-marked figures probably refer to Quetzalcoatl as an aspect of Venus. It will be recalled that according to the *Anales de Quauhtitlan,* Quetzalcoatl was transformed into Tlahuizcalpantecuhtli, and it is likely that these figures refer to Quetzalcoatl as the morning star. A similar figure also appears in the Toltec style rock painting at Ixtapantango, in the State of Mexico (Fig. 74d). Although badly eroded, the scene represents a figure with a star-marked serpent. Another partially preserved star sign seems to cover the abdomen of the human figure, much like examples known for Chichen Itza (Fig. 74c).

At Chichen, star signs also appear against the undulating bodies of feathered serpents (Fig. 75a). The earliest known example of a plumed serpent appearing with the star sign occurs in the rock relief carving at Maltrata, Veracruz (Fig. 75b). Rendered in a style strongly reminiscent of Xochicalco, the scene probably dates to the Late Classic period. The presence of stars on feathered serpents occurs as far north as the American Southwest. In the remarkable kiva murals from Pottery Mound, New Mexico, there is a depiction of a star sign placed on the undulating body of a feathered serpent (Fig. 75c). The Pottery Mound murals date to Pueblo IV, that is, roughly equivalent to the Late Post-Classic period of Mesoamerica. Quite probably, the star-marked feathered serpents appearing at Chichen and the American Southwest derive from a single source, Classic Veracruz or Central Mexico.

Aside from Chichen Itza, anthropomorphic rep-

a

b

c

d

Fig. 74   Early Post-Classic representations of Quetzalcoatl.

(a) Masked individual backed by feathered serpent,
    Lower Temple of the Jaguars, Chichen Itza (after
    Maudslay 1889–1902, 3: pl. 49)
(b) Gold mask from Sacred Cenote (after Tozzer 1957:
    fig. 216)

(c) Feathered serpent figure with star sign (after Mor-
    ris, Charlot, and Morris 1931: pl. 124)
(d) Feathered serpent figure with star signs, detail of
    rock painting from Ixtapantango, State of Mexico
    (redrawn after Villagra Caleti 1971: fig. 27)

resentations of Quetzalcoatl are rare in the Maya
lowlands. In the discussion of God H, a striking
example was noted for Dresden page 4a (Fig.
27a). On Edzna Stela 16, a plumed serpent curls
behind a seated individual (Fig. 76a). As in the
case of Chichen Itza, it is quite possible that this
figure represents an anthropomorphic form of
Quetzalcoatl. However, zoomorphic representations of Quetzalcoatl are far more widespread in
the northern Maya lowlands. The feathered ser-

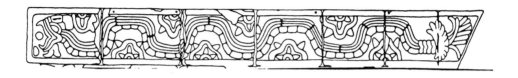

a

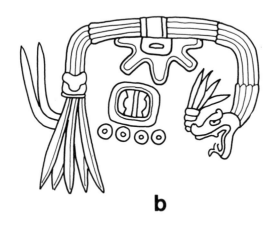

b

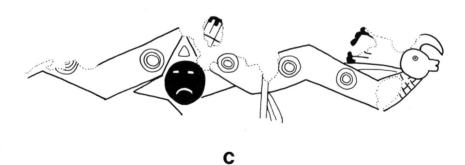

c

Fig. 75 Representations of feathered serpents with star signs, probably denoting the morning star.

(a) Feathered serpent with star signs, detail of Mercado dais, Chichen Itza (after Tozzer 1957: fig. 126)

(b) Feathered serpent with star sign, accompanied by 4 Ollin date, Maltrata, Veracruz (redrawn after Berlo 1989: fig. 25)

(c) Feathered serpent with four-pointed star, Pottery Mound, New Mexico (redrawn after Hibben 1975: 48).

pent most commonly appears as an architectural device, such as upon cornices and balustrades.

One of the most ambitious portrayals of the plumed serpent appears on the West Structure of the Nunnery Quadrangle at Uxmal. The head of

Chac appears in the mouth of this serpent, which also bears a prominent feather crest on its brow (Fig. 76b). A recently discovered pair of serpent balustrade sculptures from San Angel, Quintana Roo, appear to have been supplied originally with

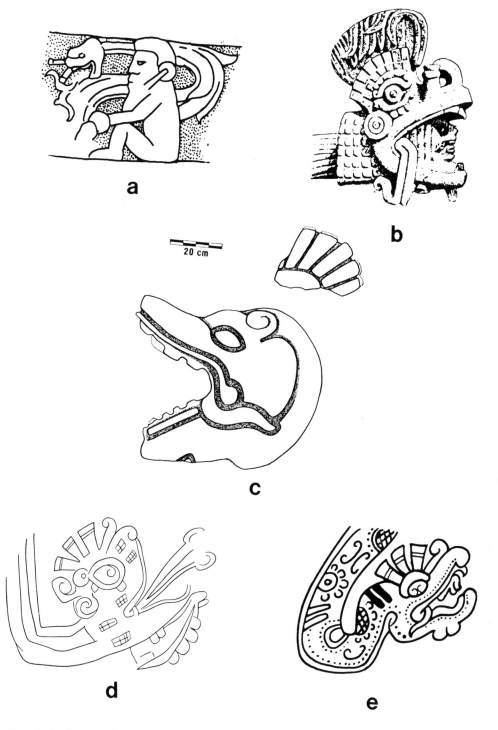

Fig. 76 Terminal Classic and Post-Classic representations of the plumed serpent in the northern Maya lowlands.

(a) Bearded figure backed by plumed serpent, detail of Edzna Stela 16 (drawn from rubbing courtesy of Merle Greene Robertson)

(b) Feathered serpent containing face of Chac in mouth, West Structure of Nunnery Quadrangle, Uxmal (after Foncerrada de Molina 1965: fig. 39)

(c) Serpent balustrade with probable feathered crest, Group B, San Angel, Quintana Roo (after Taube and Gallareta Negrón n.d., reproduced courtesy of National Geographic Society)

(d) Feathered serpent graffito, Chichen Itza (after Tozzer 1957: fig. 246)

(e) Serpent with feather crest, Codex Madrid page 18.

similar feathered crests (Fig. 76c). Rendered in stone, the crests would have been held in a hole cut in the central brow of the serpent. Supplied with this feathered crest, the San Angel sculptures are probably Late Post-Classic analogues of the well-known Early Post-Classic balustrades at Chichen Itza. However, the San Angel sculptures also recall contemporaneous representations of serpents. The crested balustrades are notably similar to a probable Late Post-Classic graffito from Chichen Itza (Fig. 76d). Manuel Perez (personal communication, 1988) notes that the San Angel examples are also like the great crested serpents stretched over pages 12 to 18 of the Codex Madrid (Fig. 76e).

Although five of the six serpents on Madrid pages 12 to 18 are supplied with prominent feather crests, their bodies are covered with serpent markings rather than feathers. Nonetheless, as in the case of the Nunnery Quadrangle example, these serpents also appear with Chac. Thus these pages are filled with gouts of water and scenes of the rain god. Quite probably, these crested serpents were considered as geniuses of water. It will be recalled from the discussion of God D that the *tzitzab* serpent-tailed aspergillum was used to sprinkle sacred water. In the mural scene of God D at Santa Rita, the serpent aspergillum is supplied with a prominent feather crest, as if it were a miniature form of the crested serpent (Fig. 14d).

During the Post-Classic period of Yucatan, there were two forms of Quetzalcoatl: one an anthropomorphic being and the other a feathered serpent. Whereas the anthropomorphic form is fairly rare outside of Chichen Itza, zoomorphic forms are common over much of Post-Classic Yucatan. It is quite possible that the human aspect of Quetzalcoatl was more closely integrated into political and historical processes in Post-Classic Yucatan. For example, the human aspect may closely reflect political titles or offices at Chichen Itza (see Lincoln n.d.). The appearance of an anthropomorphic form at Edzna may have implications for the political geography of the northern lowlands during the Terminal Classic and Early Post-Classic periods.

In contrast to the human form of Quetzalcoatl, the feathered serpent appears to embody a more generalized concept of water and agricultural fertility. Although the appearance of the feathered serpent at Mayapan, San Angel, and other sites may reflect a self-conscious evocation of Chichen Itza and perhaps even distant Tula, it is clear that this being was also identified with water and Chac. The Post-Classic crested serpent recalls the Chicchan rain serpents of the contemporary Chorti Maya, which overlap considerably with Chac of the northern lowlands (see J. Thompson 1970b: 262–265). The lake-dwelling Chicchan serpents are also similar to a serpent being of contemporary Yucatec belief. During a year of residence in the village of San Juan de Dios, Quintana Roo, I was informed of the great *noh can* serpents that at certain times fly out of the lakes of Coba.

Tonatiuh

One of the great gods of Late Post-Classic Central Mexico, Tonatiuh generally corresponds in symbolic role to God G, the sun god of Post-Classic Yucatan. However, the two deities differ widely in appearance. Thus, whereas God G tends to share physical attributes with the jaguar and God D, Tonatiuh is rendered as a youthful lord with no overt feline characteristics. In addition, Tonatiuh frequently appears within a prominent solar disk marked with pointed ray signs. Although solar disks are known for the Classic and Post-Classic Maya (e.g., Tikal Stela 1, Paris page 21), disks with pointed rays are notably rare in the Maya region. One of the earliest examples appears on El Castillo Monument 1 (Fig. 77a). Here the disk backs a male individual, probably a form of the sun god. Rendered in pure Cotzumalhuapa style, the monument probably dates to the Terminal Classic period. Rayed solar disks are also found in the Late Post-Classic murals of Santa Rita. In one scene, a human face wearing a serpent headdress peers out of the sun disk (Fig. 77b). Quite probably, this figure represents the sun god.

Figures with rayed solar disks are fairly common during the Early Post-Classic period. The

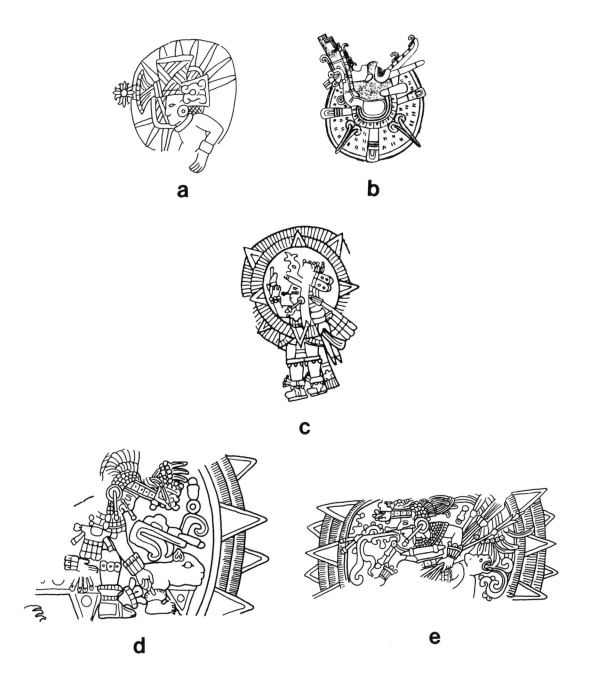

Fig. 77 Representations of solar figures in Terminal Classic and Early Post-Classic Mesoamerica.

(a) Figure backed by solar disk, El Castillo Monument 1 (redrawn after Parsons 1969: pl. 59a)

(b) Anthropomorphic head and serpent headdress within solar disk, detail of mural, Mound 1, Santa Rita (after Gann 1900: pl. xxxi)

(c) Detail of rock painting at Ixtapantango, State of Mexico (redrawn after Villagra Caleti 1971: fig. 27)

(d) Sun figure from Lower Temple of the Jaguars (redrawn after Maudslay 1889–1902, 3: pl. 50, detail)

(e) Sun figure from wooden lintel, Upper Temple of the Jaguars (redrawn after Maudslay 1889–1902, 3: pl. 35b, detail).

Toltec style rock painting at Ixtapantango, State of Mexico, depicts a standing figure surrounded by the rayed solar disk (Fig. 77c). The same figure also appears at Chichen Itza, Yucatan. As in the case of the Ixtapantango scene, the solar figure is paired with the anthropomorphic form of Quetzalcoatl (Fig. 77d, e). According to a number of researchers (e.g., A. Miller 1977: 220; Coggins 1984: 160–161), the Chichen Itza figure is portrayed as a Maya lord. Clemency Coggins (1984: 56–57, 160) notes that the figure wears Maya jade ornaments, such as the nose bar and, more importantly, the Jester God brow-piece, an important Classic Maya symbol of rulership. The element on the brow of the Ixtapantango figure is probably also a form of the Jester God. The jade collar, chest-piece, bracelets, and anklets found with the Chichen Itza figure are also typical of Terminal Classic Maya elite dress. This solar figure sits on a jaguar throne—a clear allusion to Maya rulership. Although unknown in the iconography of highland Mexico, jaguar thrones are relatively common in Classic Maya art (e.g., Tikal Stela 20, Palenque Oval Palace Tablet).

In several of the polychrome murals from the Upper Temple of the Jaguars, the Chichen Itza figure is represented with a striking iconographic trait, yellow hair (see Coggins 1984: figs. 17–19). An excellent example of the yellow-haired solar figure appears on a mural fragment from the Temple of Chacmool (Fig. 78a). The remains of the solar disk can be seen curving behind the head and shoulders of the figure. He is clearly Maya, and in fact, Ann Morris (1931: 444) uses this example to represent Maya figures in the murals. The figure wears a prominent pair of black-tipped feathers in his headdress. The same feather device appears in another Chichen Itza depiction of the solar figure, as well as in the Ixtapantango scene (Figs. 77c, 78b).

All of the important traits of the Chichen Itza solar figure can be found with the Late Post-Classic Tonatiuh of highland Mexico. Thus, along with possessing the rayed solar disk, Tonatiuh is usually golden-haired, with a prominent pair of black-tipped eagle plumes in his headdress (Figs. 78c–d). In addition, he wears a nose bar and abundant jade jewelry. His jade headband usually has a prominent zoomorphic mask on the brow. In form, this jade brow-piece is very much like the Classic Maya Jester God. It is quite possible that this Mexican device ultimately derives from Maya conventions. Although the precise origins of the Late Post-Classic brow-piece await further study, one fact seems reasonably clear: many of the attributes of the Late Post-Classic Tonatiuh derive from the Early Post-Classic solar entity appearing at Chichen Itza and Ixtapantango, a figure portrayed as a Terminal Classic Maya king.

In the Maya region, individuals appearing in rayed solar disks do not appear until the Terminal Classic period, that is, during the ninth and tenth centuries A.D. At Chichen Itza and Ixtapantango, the solar entity is paired with the anthropomorphic Quetzalcoatl. Like the Quetzalcoatl figure, the solar being may refer to a particular office or title of the Early Post-Classic period (see Lincoln n.d.). In contrast to the anthropomorphic Quetzalcoatl, the solar figure displays the costume and regalia of Terminal Classic Maya kings. However, although ethnically Maya, the solar figure bears no attributes of the Maya sun deity, God G. Instead, he is an entirely different solar being, a blending of Maya and Central Mexican iconography. It appears that this entity is the direct antecedent of the Late Post-Classic Tonatiuh. Although it is by no means certain that the Late Post-Classic Tonatiuh was considered to be a Maya prince, this would not be inconsistent with Central Mexican cosmography. In terms of Central Mexico, Yucatan corresponds to the red land of the east, the realm of Tonatiuh.

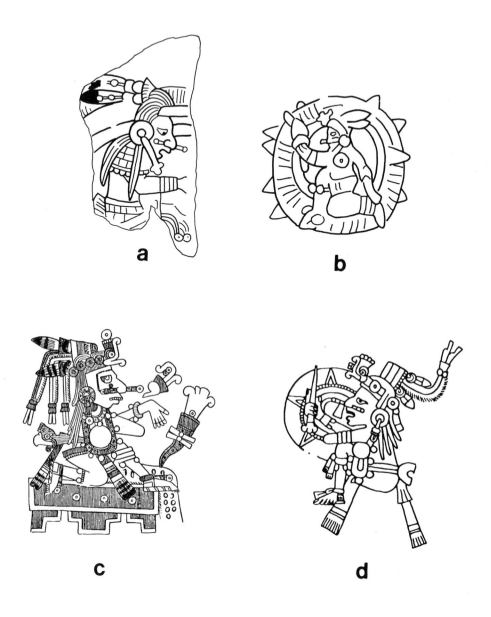

Fig. 78 The Maya solar figure and Tonatiuh.

(a) Maya sun lord backed with remains of solar disk; note eagle feathers. Mural fragment from Temple of Chac Mool, Chichen Itza (redrawn after Morris, Charlot, and Morris 1931: pl. 142c)

(b) Sun disk figure with probable eagle plumes in headdress, Temple of the Wall Panels, Chichen Itza (redrawn after Tozzer 1957: fig. 275)

(c) Tonatiuh, note eagle plumes, Codex Borgia page 70 (after Danzel 1923: pl. 50)

(d) Tonatiuh with solar disk, Codex Laud page 14.

Conclusions

In this study, I have discussed the major gods appearing in the Post-Classic iconography of Yucatan. The particular gods described are primarily those found in the Post-Classic Maya codices. Many of these figures can be related to Colonial Yucatec and Spanish ethnographic accounts. However, aside from the omnipresent Chac, most of these deities are not readily discerned among contemporary Maya peoples. It is far easier to trace the Post-Classic gods, not forward into the ethnographic present, but back to Classic Maya iconography. It has been shown that the majority of known Post-Classic Yucatec deities—Gods A, B, C, D, E, CH, G, I, K, L, N, O, R, and S—are clearly present in the preceding Classic Period. Furthermore, forms of Gods B, C, and G can be traced as early as the Late Preclassic Period. Due to the highly realistic and narrative nature of the Classic imagery—particularly that found on carved and painted vases—Classic iconography and epigraphy provide vivid insights into the meanings of particular Post-Classic deities. Thus, for example, the frequent appearance of God L with merchant staffs and bundles in Classic iconography reveals that this deity was at least in part a merchant god. Or there is the Classic occurrence of God K as the burning lightning axe of Chac—a very strong indication that God K is a lightning god.

To study the complex and all too frequently bewildering array of gods, symbolic elements, and forms appearing in pre-Hispanic Maya iconography, structured sets of recurring and predictable complexes are indispensible. Thus in the introduction it was noted that the Schellhas set of Post-Classic codical gods serves as an excellent means of distinguishing Classic deities. Of course, such sets of known entities can also be projected from the Classic period into the Post-Classic. In the present study, the Classic personified numerals have proved to be of great use in interpreting Post-Classic as well as Classic Maya gods. Thus the Classic head variant of the numeral four is God G; five is God N; eight, God E; nine, God CH; ten, God A; and eleven, God R. Furthermore, I have suggested that God H is the Post-Classic form of the youthful deity appearing as the head variant of three and the patron of the month of Mac. Far more than simply faces, these Classic personified numerals provide complex constellations of recurrent and definable traits. However, since the work of J. Eric S. Thompson (1950) there has been no systematic study of these gods. In the light of recent finds and interpretations, a detailed compilation and analysis of the Classic head variants should provide important insights into the identity and nature of the Classic and Post-Classic Maya gods.

Aside from the personified variants of numbers, there is another important form of emic classification, the Quichean *Popol Vuh*. A great many of the deities appearing in the codices can be correlated with characters of the sixteenth-century *Popol Vuh*, as well as Classic period antecedents. Thus God CH is clearly the codical form of Xbalanque. The brother of Xbalanque, Hunahpu, appears as the codical God S. During the Classic and Post-Classic periods, Hunahpu was epigraphically named 1 Ahau. In the Codex Dresden, God S is clearly identified with death, decapitation, and the maize god—attributes consistent with the Quichean and Classic Maya forms of Hunahpu. Quite possibly, God R is another aspect of Hunahpu, although his precise identification and meaning remains to be established. One Classic Maya form of God E, the Tonsured Maize God, is the prototype of the Quichean Hun Hunahpu, the father of the Hero Twins. The consistent appearance of God E with God S in the Codex Dresden suggests that God E may have had a similar role during the Post-Classic period as well.

During the Classic period, God D was identified with one of the major characters of the *Popol Vuh* creation epic, the monster bird, Vucub Caquix. Often referred to as the Principal Bird Deity, this being appears to be no less than an avian aspect of God D. Paris page 11 suggests that the Principal Bird Deity was similarly related to God D in Late Post-Classic Yucatan. Considering the ignominious defeat of Vucub Caquix, it is curious that the omnipotent God D is so closely identified with this being. Nonetheless, it does appear that the relations between God D and the Hero Twins were not always amicable. In the aforementioned Classic vessel scene illustrating Hunahpu as a captive, the Hero Twin lies before an enthroned God D (see Coe 1982: 33).

Maya epigraphy constitutes one of the most important tools for the identification and interpretation of ancient Maya gods. For one, the god appellatives serve as an extremely direct and elegant means of identifying particular gods. At times, these name glyphs serve to link physically disparate entities with conventional forms of a god. An example occurs on Dresden page 4a, where a form of Quetzalcoatl is epigraphically labeled as God H. But aside from logographic signs, the phonetic component of the Maya script presents explicit information regarding the actual names and characteristics of the ancient gods. Thus it is now known that God A was termed Cizin by the writers of the Codex Madrid. Maya epigraphy also reveals that from the beginnings of the Classic period, Chac was the uttered name of God B, as it continues to be to this day. Through epigraphic research, it is now known that God C was referred to as Ku or Ch'u, God D as Itzamna, God G as Kinich Ahau or Ahau Kin, God K as Kauil, God N as Pauahtun, and Goddess O as Chac Chel. Nonetheless, however satisfying these

readings may be, it should be borne in mind that each ancient god probably had a series of epithets that varied according to context.

The phoneticism of Maya script also provides secondary characteristics to Maya gods, providing depth and character to otherwise poorly known figures. Thus in the Codex Dresden, God A is provided with the epithet *xib,* a term bearing strong connotations of fright and death in Mayan languages. The cited reading by David Stuart of God D as an *ah dzib,* or "scribe" at Xcalumkin indicates that God D was a patron of the scribal arts by as early as the Terminal Classic period. In the codices, God G frequently bears the title of Ahau, or lord, and it is clear that he was closely tied to the office of rulership.

Through ethnohistorical accounts, Maya epigraphy, and scenes in ancient Maya art, it is possible to discern something of the social domains of particular gods. Thus, for example, from at least the Classic period to the early Colonial era, God D was considered as a scribe. However, during the Classic period, he was also portrayed as paramount lord presiding over lesser divinities. During the Post-Classic and Colonial eras, however, he appears more often in the role of a priest, frequently with the ritual accouterments of priests. Commonly bearing the title of lord, or Ahau, it is clear that God G was considered as a powerful king. During the Classic period, Gods E and N appear to have been identified less with rulership than with subsidiary positions in the elite court. Thus in one Classic aspect of God E, the Tonsured Maize God often appears as a courtly artist and entertainer. Although also an entertainer, God N appears more in the role of mummer or buffoon than an elegant dancer. Both Gods L and M are depicted as merchants, frequently with staffs and carrying packs. It would appear that for the Classic period, God L was considered as a merchant king, a wealthy and powerful owner of riches.

The two major female divinities, Goddess I and Goddess O, represent distinct roles of Maya women. The lovely Goddess I appears to embody a youthful wife and to preside over matters of marriage, human fertility, and physical love. Goddess O, on the other hand, appears as an old woman. Rather than appearing as a wife coupled with various gods, Goddess O is portrayed as an aged female diviner and curer.

Considering the social roles of various gods, it is clear that old age is not antithetical to power. Thus both the aged God D and Goddess O are portrayed as extremely powerful beings. At least in part, their power appears to derive from wisdom in the form of learned esoteric knowledge. The identification of aged people with power and respect is also consistent with contemporary Maya conceptions. For example, a common Yucatec term for an old individual is *nohoch mac,* meaning "great person."

In many instances, the social roles of particular gods correspond to specific religious functions. For example, Gods L and M are depicted as merchants because they were gods of commerce and trade. Similarly, it is probable that God G bears the title of kings because he embodied the concepts of elite power and rulership. However, it is also true that the social roles of deities serve as indicators of relative rank and power. Thus the Classic period Itzamna appears as a paramount lord not because he was the god of kings, but because he was the king of gods. Careful attention to such distinctions in rank could provide considerable insights into the structure of the ancient Maya pantheon.

In viewing the gods of the ancient Maya, what one sees is striking continuity over at least a millennium. Despite the Classic collapse and strong Mexican influence in Post-Classic Yucatan, the Post-Classic pantheon is remarkably similar to that of the Classic period. The process of change can be considered more in the nature of gradual, natural drift rather than episodes of sharp disjunction by internal innovation or acculturation from foreign influence. Of the discussed major codical gods, only two can be considered as being relatively late Mexican introductions. These are God M, the Maya version of Yacatecuhtli, and God Q, a possible form of Tezcatlipoca-Itzlacoliuhqui-Ixquimilli, or less likely, Xipe Totec. Of the markedly foreign gods appearing in Post-Classic Yucatan, most tend to be quite localized in occur-

rence and are primarily at Chichen Itza and Mayapan—sites that seem to have intentionally displayed foreign Mexican traits.

It appears that the most geographically restricted Mexican gods are those representing specific political offices or titles. Examples are the anthropomorphic Quetzalcoatl and Maya Tonatiuh at Chichen Itza. In contrast, Mexican gods associated with agricultural fertility seem to have been more readily incorporated into Post-Classic Maya religion. Thus the feathered serpent appears with Chac as a deity of water, whereas attributes of the Mexican rain god Tlaloc frequently merge with the Maya Chac.

In order to understand the particular processes and events that created the special character of the Maya gods it is necessary to recognize the Maya as active participants in the greater co-tradition of Mesoamerica. Many Mexican gods are functionally equivalent to the major Maya deities. Clear examples are the death gods, Mictlantecuhtli and God A, and the gods of rain and lightning, Tlaloc and God B. Due to the underlying meanings of these gods, particular attributes were readily exchanged. Thus the Post-Classic Mictlantecuhtli displays elements first found with the Classic God A, whereas during the Late Post-Classic period, Chac frequently appears with characteristics of Tlaloc. However, certain shared traits do not appear to be direct borrowing but rather seem to derive from older, shared traditions common throughout Mesoamerica. These basic concepts can also offer important clues to the meaning and significance of particular gods. For example, the widespread identification of lightning with serpents and axes in Mesoamerica provides important insights into the agricultural roles of Gods B and K.

Aside from the Maya gods I have described, there may be other important deities not represented in the Post-Classic corpus of iconographic imagery. In discussions of pre-Hispanic Maya gods, we are limited to what has survived and, in addition, to what the ancient Maya chose to have rendered. Thus, it is possible that there is also a supreme omnipotent god analogous to Ometeotl in Central Mexico, a deity that is not readily identifiable in the iconographic record. However, this calls attention to another issue: the varied Post-Classic deities have a wide range of thematic meanings and offices that vary according to context. For example, Itzamna, or God D, may at times represent the omnipotent creator, whereas in other instances he may be identified with agricultural fertility, curing, or the esoteric knowledge of priests. Many of the more subtle meanings of the ancient gods, such as their relation to the moral code or philosophy are largely unknown. There has been greater success in identifying the more material aspects of the Maya gods, especially their roles in the natural world. Thus it is possible to note the maize component of God E and describe the association of God B and God K with rain and lightning. Moreover, many of the Maya gods can be identified with particular social positions, such as occupations and offices. Gods L and M appear with merchant bundles and staffs, making them, at least partially, merchant gods. In terms of political offices, it has been seen that in Classic imagery God D is frequently portrayed as an omnipotent ruler seated on his throne. In Post-Classic Yucatan, this being is often found as an *ah kin* priest. However rich or complex these many associations may appear, it should be always borne in mind that we are seeing only a small part of the entire spectrum of meanings associated with the ancient Maya gods.

TABLE. Summary of Attributes and Associations of Deities Appearing in the Revised Schellhas God List

Deity	Yucatec names	Classic counterparts	Primary significance	Counterparts in social world	Associated animals and plants	Personified numbers	Popol Vuh counterparts	Nahuatl counterparts	Conflated with other Maya gods
A	Cizin Cimi Uac Mitun Ahau	Present Cimi (?)	God of death and underworld			10	Hun Came (?)	Mictlantecuhtli	
A'		Present	God of violent death and sacrifice						
B	Chac Chac xib Chac	Chac Chac xib Chac GI (variant)	God of rain and lightning	Warrior Sacrificer Fisherman	Serpent Fish			Tlaloc	God K
C	Ku	Ku Ch'u	Personification of sacredness		Maize				God D God E
D	Itzamna	Itzamna	Creator god God of writing and esoteric knowledge	Ruler Scribe Priest	Caiman Principal Bird Deity Ceiba Maize		Vucub Caquix	Tonacatecuhtli	God C God E God G God H
E	Uaxac-Yol-Kauil (?) Nal (?)	Hun Nal (?) Foliated maize god Tonsured maize god	God of maize	Court artisan Prince	Maize Deer (?)	8	Hun Hunahpu	Cinteotl Xochipilli	God C God D God K
G	Kinich Ahau	GIII Kinich Ahau	Sun God	Ruler Warrior	Jaguar	4		Tonatiuh	God D God K (rare)
H		God of number 3 (?)	God of wind (?)	Youthful priest	Serpent	3 (?)		Quetzalcoatl	God D

CH	Zip (variant)	Headband Twin Xbalanque	Hero Twin Monster slayer	Hunter	Jaguar Maize	9	Xbalanque	Xochiquetzal	God E
I		Moon goddess (?)	Goddess of women, marriage, and sensual love	Wife		1 (?)	Xquic (?)		Goddess O
K	Kauil Bolon Dzacab	Kauil GII	God of lightning, fertility, and dynastic descent		Serpent Maize		Tohil Huracan	Tezcatlipoca (?)	God B God E God G (rare)
L	Moan Chan (?)	Moan Chan (?)	God of underworld God of merchants and trade	Ruler Merchant	Jaguar Moan Owl				God M
M	Ek Chuah	Absent	God of merchants and trade	Merchant	Jaguar Moan Owl				God L
N	Pauahtun Mam	Pauahtun	World bearer God of thunder and mountains	Court official Buffoon	Opossum Turtle Snail Spider Monkey	5		Tzitzimitl Sky bearer	God L (rare)
O	Chac Chel	Present	Aged genetrix Goddess of curing	Curer	Jaguar Serpent		Grandmother of Hero Twins (?)	Toci	Goddess I
Q		Absent	God of stone and castigation	Executioner				Itzlacoliuhqui-Ixquimilli	God A
R		Hunahpu (variant)				11	Hunahpu		
S	Hun Ahau	Hun Ahau Spotted Headband Twin Personified *ahau* sign	Hero Twin Monster slayer	Ruler		11 (?) (variant)	Hunahpu		

Bibliography

ALCORN, JANIS B.
  1984 *Huastec Mayan Ethnobotany.* University of Texas Press, Austin.
ANDERS, FERDINAND
  1963 *Das Pantheon der Maya.* Akademische Druck, Graz.
ANDREWS IV, E. WYLLYS
  1970 *Balankanche, Throne of the Tiger Priest.* Middle American Research Institute, Pub. 32. Tulane University, New Orleans.
ANDREWS, IV, E. WYLLYS, and E. WYLLYS ANDREWS V
  1980 *Excavations at Dzibilchaltun, Yucatan, Mexico.* Middle American Research Institute, Pub. 48. Tulane University, New Orleans.
ANTON, FERDINAND
  1969 *Ancient Mexican Art.* Thames and Hudson, London.
AULIE, H. WILBUR, and EVELYN W. DE AULIE
  1978 *Diccionario Ch'ol-Español, Español-Ch'ol.* Instituto Lingüistico de Verano, Mexico City.
BARBA de PIÑA CHAN, BEATRIZ
  1956 *Tlapacoya: Un sitio preclasico de transición.* Acta Antropológica, ép. 2, 1 (1).
BARRERA VÁSQUEZ, ALFREDO (ED.)
  1980 *Diccionario Maya Cordemex: Maya-Español, Español-Maya.* Ediciones Cordemex, Merida.
BARTHEL, THOMAS S.
  1952 Der Morgensternkult in den Darstellungen der Dresdener Mayahandschrift. *Ethnos* 17: 73–112.
  1968 El Complejo Emblema. *Estudios de Cultura Maya* 7: 159–193.
BAUDEZ, CLAUDE F.
  1985 The Knife and the Lancet: The Iconography of Sacrifice at Copan. In *Fourth Palenque Round Table, 1980* (Merle Greene Robertson, gen. ed.): 203–210. Pre-Columbian Art Research Institute, San Francisco.
BECQUELIN, PIERRE and CLAUDE F. BAUDEZ
  1982 *Tonina, une cité Maya du Chiapas, 3.* Centre d'Etudes Mexicaines et Centroaméricaines, Paris.
BERJONNEAU, GERALD, EMILE DELETAILLE, and JEAN-LOUIS SONNERY
  1985 *Rediscovered Masterpieces of Mesoamerica: Mexico-Guatemala-Honduras.* Editions Arts, Bologne.
BERLIN, HEINRICH
  1963 The Palenque Triad. *Journal de la Société des Américanistes* 52: 91–99.

BERLIN, HEINRICH, and DAVID H. KELLEY
  1961 *The 819 Day Count and Color-Direction Symbolism Among the Classic Maya.* Middle American Research Institute, Pub. 26: 9–20. Tulane University, New Orleans
BERLO, JANET CATHERINE
  1989 Early Writing in Central Mexico: In Tlilli, in Tlapalli, before A.D. 1000. In *Mesoamerica after the Decline of Teotihuacan, A.D. 700–900* (Richard A. Diehl and Janet Catherine Berlo, eds.): 19–47. Dumbarton Oaks, Washington, D.C.
BERNAL, IGNACIO
  1965 Brasero ceremonial. *Boletín del Instituto Nacional de Antropología e Historia* 22: 1–2. Mexico.
BEYER, HERMAN
  1931 Mayan Hieroglyphs: The Variable Element of the Introducing Glyphs as Month Indicator. *Anthropos* 26: 99–108.
  1933 A Discussion of the Gates Classification of Maya Hieroglyphs. *American Anthropologist* 35: 659–694.
  1937 *Studies on the Inscriptions of Chichen Itza.* Carnegie Institution of Washington, Pub. 483, no. 21. Washington, D.C.
BLAIR, ROBERT, and REFUGIO VERMONT-SALAS
  1965 *Spoken Yucatec Maya I.* University of Chicago Library, Chicago.
BLOM, FRANS
  1950 A Polychrome Plate from Quintana Roo. *Notes on Middle American Archaeology and Ethnology,* no. 98. Carnegie Institution of Washington, Washington, D.C.
BOLZ, INGEBORG
  1975 *Meisterwerke altindianischer Kunst.* Aurel Bongers, Recklinghausen, Germany.
BRAINERD, GEORGE W.
  1958 *The Archaeological Ceramics of Yucatan.* University of California, Anthropological Records, no. 19. Berkeley.
BRASSEUR DE BOURBOURG, CHARLES E.
  1869– *Manuscrit Troano: Etudes sur le système graph-
  70 ique et la langue des Mayas.* Imprimerie Impériale, Paris.
BRAY, WARWICK
  1977 Maya Metalwork and Its External Connections. In *Social Process in Maya Prehistory: Studies in Honour of Sir Eric Thompson* (Norman Hammond, ed.): 365–403. Academic Press, London.

BRETON, ADELA C.

1917 Preliminary Study of the North Building (Chamber C), Great Ball Court, Chichen Itza, Yucatan. *19th International Congress of Americanists:* 187–194. Washington, D.C.

BRICKER, VICTORIA R.

1986 *A Grammar of Maya Hieroglyphs.* Middle American Research Institute, Pub. 56. Tulane University, New Orleans.

BRINTON, DANIEL GARRISON

1895 *A Primer of Mayan Hieroglyphs.* University of Pennsylvania Series in Philology, Literature, and Archaeology 3 (2). Philadelphia.

CAMPBELL, LYLE

1984 The Implications of Mayan Historical Linguistics for Glyphic Research. In *Phoneticism in Mayan Hieroglyphic Writing* (John S. Justeson and Lyle Campbell, eds.): 1–16. Institute for Mesoamerican Studies, State University of New York at Albany, Albany.

CARLSON, JOHN B.

1981 Olmec Concave Iron-Ore Mirrors: The Aesthetics of a Lithic Technology and the Lord of the Mirror. In *The Olmec and Their Neighbors: Essays in Memory of Matthew W. Stirling* (Elizabeth P. Benson, ed.): 117–147. Dumbarton Oaks, Washington, D.C.

1983 The Grolier Codex: A Preliminary Report on the Content and Authenticity of a Thirteenth-Century Maya Venus Almanac. In *Calendars in Mesoamerica and Peru: Native Computations of Time* (Anthony F. Aveni and Gordon Brotherston, eds.): 27–57. BAR, Oxford.

CASO, ALFONSO

1971 Calendrical Systems of Central Mexico. In *Handbook of Middle American Indians* (Robert Wauchope, gen. ed.) 10 (1): 333–348. University of Texas Press, Austin.

CASO, ALFONSO and IGNACIO BERNAL

1952 *Urnas de Oaxaca.* Memorias del Instituto Nacional de Antropología e Historia, 2. Mexico City.

CHASE, ARLEN F.

1985 Postclassic Peten Interaction Spheres: The View from Tayasal. In *The Lowland Maya Postclassic* (Arlen F. Chase and Prudence M. Rice, eds.): 184–205. University of Texas Press, Austin.

CHASE, DIANE Z.

1985 Ganned But Not Forgotten: Late Postclassic Archaeology and Ritual at Santa Rita Corozal, Belize. In *The Lowland Maya Postclassic* (Arlen F. Chase and Prudence M. Rice, eds.): 104–125. University of Texas Press, Austin.

CHOWNING, ANN

1956 A Round Temple and Its Shrine at Mayapan. *Current Reports* 34: 443–461. Carnegie Institution of Washington, Washington, D.C.

CLARKSON, PERSIS B.

1978 Classic Maya Pictorial Ceramics: A Survey of Content and Theme. In *Papers on the Economy and Architecture of the Ancient Maya* (Raymond Sidrys, ed.): 86–141. Institute of Archaeology, University of California, Los Angeles.

COE, MICHAEL D.

1973 *The Maya Scribe and His World.* The Grolier Club, New York.

1975 *Classic Maya Pottery at Dumbarton Oaks.* Dumbarton Oaks, Washington, D.C.

1977 Supernatural Patrons of Maya Scribes and Artists. In *Social Process in Maya Prehistory* (Norman Hammond, ed.): 327–347. Academic Press, London.

1978 *Lords of the Underworld: Masterpieces of Classic Maya Ceramics.* Princeton University Press, Princeton.

1981 Religion and the Rise of Mesoamerican States. In *The Transition into Statehood in the New World* (Grant D. Jones and Robert R. Kautz, eds.): 157–171. Cambridge University Press, Cambridge.

1982 *Old Gods and Young Heroes: The Pearlman Collection of Maya Ceramics,* The Israel Museum, Jerusalem.

1984 *Mexico,* 3rd ed. Thames and Hudson, London.

1989 The Hero Twins: Myth and Image. In *The Maya Vase Book* (Justin Kerr, ed.) 1: 161–184. Kerr Associates, New York.

COE, WILLIAM R.

1967 *Tikal: A Handbook of the Ancient Maya Ruins.* University Museum, University of Pennsylvania, Philadelphia.

COGGINS, CLEMENCY C.

1975 *Painting and Drawing Styles at Tikal: An Historical and Iconographic Reconstruction.* Ph.D. dissertation, Harvard University. University Microfilms, Ann Arbor.

1979 A New Order and the Role of the Calendar: Some Characteristics of the Middle Classic Period at Tikal. In *Maya Archaeology and Ethnohistory* (Norman Hammond and Gordon R. Willey, eds.): 38–50. University of Texas Press, Austin.

1984 The Cenote of Sacrifice: Catalogue. In *Cenote of Sacrifice: Maya Treasures from the Sacred Well at Chichen Itza* (Clemency Chase Coggins and Orrin C. Shane III, eds.): 23–265. University of Texas Press, Austin.

1988 The Manikin Scepter: Emblem of Lineage. *Estudios de Cultura Maya* 17: 123–158.

COGGINS, CLEMENCY C., and ORRIN C. SHANE III (EDS.)

1984 *Cenote of Sacrifice: Maya Treasures from the Sacred Well at Chichen Itza.* University of Texas Press, Austin.

CORTEZ, CONSTANCE

1986 The Principal Bird Deity in Preclassic and Early Classic Maya Art. M.A. thesis, Department of art history, University of Texas at Austin.

COTO, FRAY TOMAS DE

1983 *Thesaurus Verborum: Vocabulario de la lengua Cakchiquel y Guatemalteca, nuevamente hecho y* recopilado con sumo estudio, trabajo y erudición (René Acuña, ed.). Universidad Nacional Autónoma de México, Mexico City.

CRAINE, EUGENE R., and REGINALD C. REINDORP
1979   The Codex Pérez and the Book of Chilam Balam of Mani. University of Oklahoma Press, Norman.

CRUZ GUZMAN, AUCENCIO, J. KATHRYN JOSSERAND, and NICHOLAS A. HOPKINS
n.d.   T'an ti Wajali: Cuentos Choles Antiguos. Unpublished manuscript in possession of the author.

DANZEL, THEODOR-WILHELM
1923   Mexiko I: Bilderhandschriften. Folkwang-Verlag, Germany.

DAVIES, NIGEL
1977   The Toltecs until the Fall of Tula. University of Oklahoma Press, Norman.

DELHALLE, JEAN-CLAUDE, and ALBERT LUYKX
1986   The Nahuatl Myth of the Creation of Humankind: A Coastal Connection? American Antiquity 51 (1): 117–121.

DIENHART, JOHN M.
1986   The Mayan Hieroglyph for Cotton. Mexicon 8 (3): 52–56.

DIESELDORFF, ERWIN P.
1926   El Tzultacá y el Mam, los dioses prominentes de la religión Maya. Anales de la Sociedad de Geografía e Historia (Guatemala), Año 2 (2): 378–386.

DURÁN, FRAY DIEGO
1971   Book of the Gods and Rites and the Ancient Calendar (Doris Heyden and Fernando Horcasitas, trans. and eds.). University of Oklahoma Press, Norman.

EDMONSON, MUNRO S.
1965   Quiché-English Dictionary. Middle American Research Institute, Pub. 30. Tulane University, New Orleans.
1982   The Ancient Future of the Itza: The Book of Chilam Balam of Tizimin. University of Texas Press, Austin.

EUW, ERIC VON
1977   Itzimte, Pixoy, Tzum. Corpus of Maya Hieroglyphic Inscriptions 4 (1). Peabody Museum of Archaeology and Ethnology, Harvard University, Cambridge, Mass.
1978   Xultun. Corpus of Maya Hieroglyphic Inscriptions 5 (1). Peabody Museum of Archaeology and Ethnology, Harvard University, Cambridge, Mass.

FEWKES, WALTER J.
1894   A Study of Certain Figures in a Maya Codex. American Anthropologist 7: 260–274.
1895   The God "D" in the Codex Cortesianus. American Anthropologist 8(3): 205–222.

FONCERRADA DE MOLINA, MARTA
1965   La escultura arquitectónica de Uxmal. Imprenta Universitaria, Mexico City.
1980   Mural Painting in Cacaxtla and Teotihuacan

Cosmopolitanism. In Third Palenque Round Table, 1978, Part 2 (Merle Greene Robertson, ed.): 183–198. University of Texas Press, Austin.

FÖRSTEMANN, ERNST WILHELM
1886   Erläuterung zur Mayahandschrift der Königlichen öffentlichen Bibliothek zu Dresden. Dresden.
1898   Die Tagesgotter der Maya. Globus 73 (9): 137–140, 162–164.
1901   Der Mayagott des Jahresschlusses. Globus 80: 189–192.
1906   Commentary on the Maya Manuscript in the Royal Public Library of Dresden. Papers of the Peabody Museum of Archaeology and Ethnology 4 (2): 49–269. Harvard University, Cambridge, Mass.

FOUGHT, JOHN G.
1972   Chorti (Mayan) Texts. University of Pennsylvania Press, Philadelphia.

FOX, JAMES A., and JOHN S. JUSTESON
1984   Polyvalence in Mayan Hieroglyphic Writing. In Phoneticism in Mayan Hieroglyphic Writing (John S. Justeson and Lyle Campbell, eds.): 17–76. Institute for Mesoamerican Studies, State University of New York at Albany, Pub. 9, Albany.

DE LA FUENTE, BEATRIZ, and NELLY GUTIÉRREZ SOLANA
1980   Escultura Huasteca en Piedra. Universidad Nacional Autónoma de México, Mexico City.

GANN, THOMAS
1900   Mounds in Northern Honduras. Nineteenth Annual Report of the Bureau of American Ethnology, 1897–98, Part 2: 655–692. Washington, D.C.

GARIBAY, ANGEL MARÍA
1979   Teogonia e historia de los Mexicanos: Tres opúsculos del siglo XVI. Editorial Porrua, Mexico City.

DE LA GARZA, MERCEDES
1983   Relaciones histórico-geográficas de la gobernación de Yucatán, 2 vols. Universidad Nacional Autónoma de México, Mexico City.

GIRARD, RAFAEL
1966   Los Mayas. Libro Mex, Mexico City.

GLASS, JOHN B., and DONALD ROBERTSON
1975   A Census of Native American Pictorial Manuscripts. In Handbook of Middle American Indians (Robert Wauchope, gen. ed.) 14: 81–252. University of Texas Press, Austin.

GOODMAN, J. T.
1897   The Archaic Maya Inscriptions. Appendix to A. P. Maudslay, Biologia Centrali-Americana: Archaeology. R. H. Porter and Dulau and Company, London.

GORDON, GEORGE B.
1915   Guatemala Myths. The Museum Journal 6: 103–144.

GORDON, GEORGE B., and J. ALDEN MASON
1925–   Examples of Maya Pottery in the Museum and
28   Other Collections. University Museum, University of Pennsylvania, Philadelphia.

GOSSEN, GARY H.
1974 A Chamula Solar Calendar Board from Chiapas, Mexico. In *Mesoamerican Archaeology: New Approaches* (Norman Hammond, ed.): 217–253. University of Texas Press, Austin.

GRAHAM, ELIZABETH A.
1985 Facets of Terminal to Postclassic Activity in the Stann Creek District, Belize. In *The Lowland Maya Postclassic* (Arlen F. Chase and Prudence M. Rice, eds.): 215–229. University of Texas Press, Austin.

GRAHAM, IAN
1978 *Naranjo, Chunhuitz, Xunantunich. Corpus of Maya Hieroglyphic Inscriptions* 2 (2). Peabody Museum of Archaeology and Ethnology, Harvard University, Cambridge, Mass.
1979 *Yaxchilan. Corpus of Maya Hieroglyphic Inscriptions* 3 (2). Peabody Museum of Archaeology and Ethnology, Harvard University, Cambridge, Mass.
1980 *Ixkun, Ucanal, Ixtutz, Naranjo. Corpus of Maya Hieroglyphic Inscriptions* 2 (3). Peabody Museum of Archaeology and Ethnology, Harvard University, Cambridge, Mass.
1982 *Yaxchilan. Corpus of Maya Hieroglyphic Inscriptions* 3 (3). Peabody Museum of Archaeology and Ethnology, Harvard University, Cambridge, Mass.

GRAHAM, IAN, and ERIC VON EUW
1975 *Naranjo. Corpus of Maya Hieroglyphic Inscriptions* 2 (1). Peabody Museum of Archaeology and Ethnology, Harvard University, Cambridge, Mass.
1977 *Yaxchilan. Corpus of Maya Hieroglyphic Inscriptions* 3 (1). Peabody Museum of Archaeology and Ethnology, Harvard University, Cambridge, Mass.

GRAHAM, JOHN A.
1971 A Maya Hieroglyph Incised on Shell. *Contributions to the University of California Research Facility*, no. 14: 155–160.

HELLMUTH, NICHOLAS M.
1983 Iconographic Amendments to Andrea Stone's "Recent Discoveries from Naj Tunich." *Mexicon* 5 (3): 45–46.
1986 *Die Oberflache der Unterwasserwelt: Iconographie der Maya-Gottheiten der Fruhklassischen Kunst der Maya im Peten Guatemala.* Ph.D. dissertation in art history, Karl-Franzens-Universität, Graz.
1987 *Monster und Menschen in der Maya-Kunst.* Akademische Druck- und Verlagsanstalt, Graz.

HIBBEN, FRANK C.
1975 *Kiva Art of the Anasazi at Pottery Mound.* KC Publications, Las Vegas.

HOLLAND, WILLIAM R.
1963 *Medicina maya en los altos de Chiapas: Un estudio del cambio socio-cultural.* Colección de Antropología Social 2. Instituto Nacional Indigenista, Mexico City.

HOUSTON, STEPHEN D.
1983 A Reading for the Flint Shield Glyph. In *Contributions to Maya Hieroglyphic Decipherment* (Stephen D. Houston, ed.): 13–15. Human Relations Area Files, New Haven.
1988 The Phonetic Decipherment of Maya Glyphs. *Antiquity* 62 (234): 126–135.
1989a Archaeology and Maya Writing. *Journal of World Prehistory* 3 (1): 1–32.
1989b *Maya Glyphs.* British Museum Publications, Ltd., London.

HOUSTON, STEPHEN D., and DAVID STUART
1989 The *Way* Glyph: Evidence for "Co-essences" among the Classic Maya. *Research Reports on Ancient Maya Writing*, no. 30.

HOUSTON, STEPHEN D., DAVID STUART, and KARL A. TAUBE
1989 Folk Classification of Classic Maya Pottery. In *American Anthropologist* 91 (3): 720–726.

HUMBERTO RUZ, MARIO (ED.)
1986 *Vocabulario de lengua Tzeldal segun el orden de Copanabastla* (original by Domingo de Ara). Universidad Nacional Autónoma de México, Mexico City.

HVIDTFELDT, ARILD
1958 *Teotl and Ixiptlatli: Some Central Conceptions in Ancient Mexican Religion.* Andreassen & Co., Copenhagen.

ICHON, ALAIN
1973 *La religión de los Totonacas de la sierra.* Instituto Nacional Indigenista, Mexico City.

JIMENEZ MORENO, WIGBERTO
1941 Tula y los Toltecas segun las fuentes históricas. *Revista Mexicana de estudios antropólogicos* 5: 79–83.

JONES, CHRISTOPHER, and LINTON SATTERTHWAITE
1982 *The Monuments and Inscriptions of Tikal: The Carved Monuments.* University Museum Monograph 44. University Museum, University of Pennsylvania, Philadelphia.

JORALEMON, PETER DAVID
1971 *A Study of Olmec Iconography.* Studies in Pre-Columbian Art and Archaeology 7, Dumbarton Oaks, Washington, D.C.
1974 Ritual Blood-Sacrifice Among the Ancient Maya: Part I. In *Primera Mesa Redonda de Palenque, Part II* (Merle Greene Robertson, ed.): 59–75. The Robert Louis Stevenson School, Pebble Beach.

JOYCE, THOMAS A.
1927 *Maya and Mexican Art.* The Studio, London.

JUSTESON, JOHN S.
1984 Interpretations of Maya Hieroglyphs. Appendix B in *Phoneticism in Mayan Hieroglyphic Writing* (John S. Justeson and Lyle Campbell, eds.): 315–362. Institute for Mesoamerican Studies, State University of New York at Albany, Pub. 9, Albany.

JUSTESON, JOHN S., and LYLE CAMPBELL (EDS.)
1984 *Phoneticism in Mayan Hieroglyphic Writing.*

Institute for Mesoamerican Studies, State University of New York at Albany, Pub. 9, Albany.

JUSTESON, JOHN S., WILLIAM M. NORMAN, and NORMAN HAMMOND

1988   The Pomona Flare: A Preclassic Maya Hieroglyphic Text. In *Maya Iconography* (Elizabeth P. Benson and Gillett G. Griffin, eds.): 94–151. Princeton University Press, Princeton, N.J.

KAMPEN, MICHAEL E.

1972   *The Sculptures of El Tajín, Veracruz, Mexico.* University of Florida Press, Gainesville.

KELLEY, DAVID H.

1965   The Birth of the Gods at Palenque. *Estudios de Cultura Maya* 5: 93–134.

1972   The Nine Lords of the Night. In *Contributions of the University of California Archaeological Research Facility* 5 (16): 53–68.

1976   *Deciphering the Maya Script.* University of Texas Press, Austin.

KERR, JUSTIN

1989   *The Maya Vase Book, 1.* Kerr Associates, New York.

1990   *The Maya Vase Book, 2.* Kerr Associates, New York.

KIDDER, ALFRED II, and CARLOS SAMAYOA CHINCHILLA

1959   *The Art of the Ancient Maya.* Thomas Y. Crowel, New York.

KLEIN, CECELIA F.

1976   *The Face of the Earth: Frontality in Two-Dimensional Mesoamerican Art.* Garland Publishing, New York.

KNOROZOV, YURI V.

1958   New Data on the Maya Written Language. *Proceedings of the 32nd International Congress of Americanists* 32: 467–475, Copenhagen.

1967   *The Writing of the Maya Indians* (Sopie Coe, trans.) Peabody Museum of Archaeology and Ethnology, Russian Translation Series 4. Cambridge, Mass.

KNOWLES, SUSAN MARIE

1984   *A Descriptive Grammar of Chontal Maya (San Carlos Dialect).* Ph.D. dissertation, Department of anthropology, Tulane University, New Orleans.

KOWALSKI, JEFF KARL

1985   A Historical Interpretation of the Inscriptions of Uxmal. In *Fourth Palenque Round Table, 1980* (Merle Greene Robertson, gen. ed.): 235–247. Pre-Columbian Art Research Institute, San Francisco.

1989   The Mythological Identity of the Figure on the La Esperanza ("Chinkultic") Ball Court Marker. *Research Reports on Ancient Maya Writing,* no. 27.

KUBLER, GEORGE

1969   *Studies in Classic Maya Iconography.* Memoirs of the Connecticut Academy of Arts and Sciences 18. New Haven.

LAUGHLIN, ROBERT M.

1975   *The Great Tzotzil Dictionary of San Lorenzo Zincantan.* Smithsonian Contributions to Anthropology 19, Smithsonian Institution, Washington, D.C.

1977   *Of Cabbages and Kings: Tales from Zinacantan.* Smithsonian Contributions to Anthropology 23, Smithsonian Institution, Washington, D.C.

LEE, THOMAS

1985   *Los Códices Mayas.* Universidad Autónoma de Chiapas, Tuxtla Gutierrez.

LENKERSDORF, CARLOS

1979   *B'omak'umal tojol ab'al—Kastiya: Diccionario Tojolabal-Español,* 1. Editorial Nuestro Tiempo, Mexico City.

LINCOLN, CHARLES E.

n.d.   Dual kingship at Chichen Itza. Paper presented at the 53rd Annual Meeting of the Society for American Archaeology, Phoenix, 1988.

LOMBARDO DE RUIZ, SONIA (COOR.)

1987   *La pintura mural Maya en Quintana Roo.* Instituto Nacional de Antropología e Historia, Chetumal.

LÓPEZ AUSTIN, ALFREDO

1987   The Masked God of Fire. In *The Aztec Templo Mayor* (Elizabeth Hill Boone, ed.): 257–291. Dumbarton Oaks, Washington, D.C.

LOTHROP, SAMUEL K.

1952   *Metals from the Cenote of Sacrifice, Chichen Itza, Yucatan.* Memoirs of the Peabody Museum of American Archaeology and Ethnology 10 (2). Harvard University, Cambridge, Mass.

LOUNSBURY, FLOYD

1973   On the Derivation and Reading of the "Ben-Ich" Prefix. In *Mesoamerican Writing Systems* (Elizabeth P. Benson, ed.): 99–143. Dumbarton Oaks, Washington, D.C.

1985   The Identity of the Mythological Figures in the Cross Group Inscriptions of Palenque. In *Fourth Palenque Round Table, 1980* (Merle Greene Roberston, gen. ed.): 45–58. Pre-Columbian Art Research Institute, San Francisco.

1982   Astronomical Knowledge and Its Uses at Bonampak, Mexico. In *Archaeoastronomy in the New World* (Anthony F. Aveni, ed.): 143–186. Cambridge University Press, Cambridge.

LOVE, BRUCE

1989   Yucatec Sacred Breads Through Time. In *Word and Image in Maya Culture: Explorations in Language, Writing, and Representation* (William F. Hanks and Don Rice, eds.): 336–350. University of Utah Press, Salt Lake City.

LUMHOLTZ, CARL

1900   *Symbolism of the Huichol Indians.* Memoirs of the American Museum of Natural History 2 (1). American Museum of Natural History, New York.

MALER, TEOBERT

1901 *Researches in the Central Portion of the Usumatsintla Valley.* Memoirs of the Peabody Museum of American Archaeology and Ethnology 2 (1). Harvard University, Cambridge, Mass.

1908– *Explorations in the Department of Peten, Guate-*
10 *mala, and Adjacent Region.* Memoirs of the Peabody Museum of American Archaeology and Ethnology 4. Harvard University, Cambridge, Mass.

MARCUS, JOYCE

1978 Archaeology and Religion: A Comparison of the Zapotec and Maya. *World Archaeology* 10 (2): 172–191.

MARTÍNEZ HERNÁNDEZ, JUAN

1913 La creación del mundo según los Mayas. Páginas inéditas del manuscrito Chumayel. *Proceedings of the XVIII International Congress of Americanists:* 164–171, London.

MATHEWS, PETER

1980 Notes on the Dynastic Sequence of Bonampak, Part 1. In *Third Palenque Round Table, 1978,* Part 2 (Merle Greene Robertson, ed.): 60–73. The University of Texas Press, Austin.

MAUDSLAY, ALFRED P.

1889– Archaeology. In *Biologia Centrali-Americana,* 5
1902 vols. R. H. Porter and Dulau, London.

MAURER-AVALOS, EUGENIO

1979 El concepto del mal y del poder espiritual en el mundo Maya-Tzeltal. *Journal de la Société des Américanistes* 66: 219–233.

MAYER, KARL HERBERT

1980 *Maya Monuments: Sculptures of Unknown Provenance in the United States* (Sandra L. Brizee, trans.). Acoma Books, Ramona, Calif.

1983 Gewölbedecksteine mit dekor der Mayakultur. *Archiv für Völkerkunde* 37: 1–62.

1984 *Maya Monuments: Sculptures of Unknown Provenance in Middle America.* Karl-Friedrich von Flemming, Berlin.

1989 *Maya Monuments: Sculptures of Unknown Provenance, Supplement 2.* Verlag von Flemming, Graz.

MEANS, PHILIP AINSWORTH

1917 *History of the Spanish Conquest of Yucatan and of the Itzas.* Papers of the Peabody Museum of Archaeology and Ethnology 7. Harvard University, Cambridge, Mass.

MENDELSON, E. MICHAEL

1959 Maximon: An Iconographical Introduction, *Man* 59: 57–60.

MILES, SUZANNA W.

1957 The Sixteenth Century Pokom-Maya. *Transactions of the American Philosophical Society* 47 (4): 735–781.

MILLER, ARTHUR G.

1977 Captains of the Itzá: Unpublished Mural Evidence from Chichén Itzá. In *Social Process in*

Maya Prehistory: Studies in Honour of Sir Eric Thompson (Norman Hammond, ed.): 197–225. Academic Press, New York.

1982 *On the Edge of the Sea: Mural Painting at Tancah-Tulum, Quintana Roo, Mexico.* Dumbarton Oaks, Washington, D.C.

MILLER, MARY ELLEN

1986 *The Art of Mesoamerica from Olmec to Aztec.* Thames and Hudson, New York.

MILLER, VIRGINIA E.

1989 Star Warriors at Chichen Itza. In *Word and Image in Maya Culture: Explorations in Language, Writing, and Representation* (William F. Hanks and Don S. Rice, eds.): 287–305. University of Utah Press, Salt Lake City.

MOLLER, HARRY

1989 Cacaxtla: Vuelve a hablar. *Mexico Desconocido* 153: 10–14.

MONTEJO, VICTOR DIONICIO

1984 *El Kanil, Man of Lightning.* Signal Books, Carrboro, N.C.

MORA-ECHEVERRÍA, JESÚS IGNACIO

1984 Prácticas y conceptos prehispánicos sobre espacio y tiempo. *Boletín Bibliográfico de Antropología Americana* 9: 5–46.

MORLEY, SYLVANUS G.

1920 *The Inscriptions at Copan.* Carnegie Institution of Washington, Pub. 219. Washington, D.C.

MORLEY, SYLVANUS G., GEORGE W. BRAINERD, and ROBERT R. SHARER

1983 *The Ancient Maya,* 4th ed. Stanford University Press, Stanford.

MORRIS, ANN AXTEL

1931 Murals from the Temple of the Warriors and Adjacent Structures. In *The Temple of the Warriors at Chichen Itza* (Earl H. Morris, Jean Charlot, and Ann Axtel Morris): 347–485. Carnegie Institution of Washington, Pub. 406. Washington, D.C.

MORRIS, EARL H., JEAN CHARLOT, and ANN AXTEL MORRIS

1931 *The Temple of the Warriors at Chichen Itza.* Carnegie Institution of Washington, Pub. 406. Washington, D.C.

MOSER, CHRISTOPHER L.

1975 Cueva de Ejutla: Una cueva funeraria Postclasica? *Boletín del Instituto Nacional de Antropología e Historia* 15: 25–36.

NAGAO, DEBRA

1985 The Planting of Sustenance: Symbolism of the Two-Horned God in Offerings from the Templo Mayor. *Res: Anthropology and Aesthetics* 10: 5–27.

NASH, JUNE

1970 *In the Eyes of the Ancestors: Belief and Behavior in a Mayan Community.* Yale University Press, New Haven.

NICHOLSON, HENRY B.

1971 Religion in Pre-Hispanic Central Mexico. In *Handbook of Middle American Indians* (Robert

Wauchope, gen. ed.) 10 (1): 395–446. University of Texas Press, Austin.

NICHOLSON, H. B., and RAINER BERGER

1968   *Two Aztec Wood Idols: Iconographic and Chronologic Analysis.* Studies in Pre-Columbian Art and Archaeology 5. Dumbarton Oaks, Washington, D.C.

NICHOLSON, HENRY B., and ELOISE QUINONES KEBER

1983   *Art of Ancient Mexico: Treasures of Tenochtitlan.* National Gallery of Art, Washington, D.C.

NORMAN, V. GARTH

1973   *Izapa Sculpture.* Papers of the New World Archaeological Foundation 30. Brigham Young University, Provo.

PALACIOS, ENRIQUE JUAN

1929   La piedra del escudo nacional de México. *Publicaciones de la Secretaría de Educación Pública* 22 (9). Mexico City.

PARSONS, ELSIE CLEWS

1939   *Pueblo Indian Religion,* 2 vols. University of Chicago Press, Chicago.

PARSONS, LEE ALLEN

1969   *Bilbao, Guatemala: An Archaeological Study of the Pacific Coast Cotzumalhuapa Region 2.* Publications in Anthropology 12. Milwaukee Public Museum.

1980   *Pre-Columbian Art: The Morton D. May and The Saint Louis Museum Collections.* Harper and Row, New York.

1986   *The Origins of Maya Art: Monumental Stone Sculpture of Kaminaljuyu, Guatemala, and the Southern Pacific Coast.* Studies in Pre-Columbian Art and Archaeology 28. Dumbarton Oaks, Washington, D.C.

PASZTORY, ESTHER

1974   *The Iconography of the Teotihuacan Tlaloc.* Studies in Pre-Columbian Art and Archaeology 15. Dumbarton Oaks, Washington, D.C.

1983   *Aztec Art.* Harry N. Abrams, New York.

PAXTON, MERIDETH D.

1986   *Codex Dresden: Stylistic and Iconographic Analysis of a Maya Manuscript.* Ph.D. dissertation, Department of art history, University of New Mexico at Albuquerque.

PIÑA-CHAN, ROMAN

1964   Algunas consideraciones sobre las pinturas de Mulchic, Yucatán. *Estudios de Cultura Maya* 4: 63–78.

POLLOCK, H.E.D.

1980   *The Puuc: An Architectural Survey of the Hill Country of Yucatan and Northern Campeche, Mexico.* Memoirs of the Peabody Museum of Archaeology and Ethnology 19. Harvard University, Cambridge, Mass.

PORTER, JAMES

n.d.a. The Linked Earflare Assemblage: The Distribution of a Maya Costume Element in Eastern and Central Mesoamerica. Unpublished manuscript in possession of the author, 1989.

n.d.b. Schellhas' God B: A Reappraisal. Unpublished manuscript in possession of the author.

PROSKOURIAKOFF, TATIANA

1950   *A Study of Classic Maya Sculpture.* Carnegie Institution of Washington, Pub. 593. Washington, D.C.

1962   The Artifacts of Mayapan. In *Mayapan Yucatan Mexico* (H. E. D. Pollock, Ralph L. Roys, Tatiana Proskouriakoff, and A. Ledyard Smith): 321–442. Carnegie Institution of Washington, Pub. 619. Washington, D.C.

1965   Sculpture and Major Arts of the Classic Lowlands. In *Handbook of Middle American Indians* (Robert Wauchope, gen. ed.) 2: 469–497. University of Texas Press, Austin.

1970   On Two Inscriptions at Chichen Itza. In *Monographs and Papers in Maya Archaeology* (William R. Bullard, Jr., ed.): 457–467. Papers of the Peabody Museum of Archaeology and Ethnology 61. Harvard University, Cambridge, Mass.

1978   Olmec Gods and Maya God-Glyphs. In *Codex Wauchope* (Marco Giardino, Barbara Edmonson, and Winifred Creamer, eds.): 113–117. Human Mosaic, Tulane University, New Orleans.

1980   Maize-God: The Symbol of *Symbols. Symbols* 8: 8–10.

PROYECTO ARQUEOLÓGICO COPAN

1983   *Introducción a la arqueología de Copan, Honduras,* Instituto Hondureno de Antropología e Historia, Tegucigalpa.

RAMÍREZ VÁSQUEZ, PEDRO

1968   *The National Museum of Anthropology, Mexico.* Harry N. Abrams, New York.

RECINOS, ADRIAN

1950   *The Popol Vuh: The Sacred Book of the Ancient Quiche Maya* (Delia Goetz and Sylvanus G. Morley, trans.). University of Oklahoma Press, Norman.

REDFIELD, ROBERT, and ALFONSO VILLA ROJAS

1934   *Chan Kom: A Maya Village.* Carnegie Institution of Washington, Pub. 448. Washington, D.C.

REISE, BERTHOLD

1982   Eine mexikanische Gottheit im Venuskapitel der Mayahandschrift Codex Dresdensis. *Société Suisse des Américanistes, Bulletin* 46: 37–39.

RINGLE, WILLIAM M.

1988   Of Mice and Monkeys: The Value and Meaning of T1016, the God C Hieroglyph. *Research Reports on Ancient Maya Writing,* no. 18.

RIVARD, JEAN-JACQUES

1965   Cascabeles y ojos del dios Maya de la muerte, Ah Puch. *Estudios de Cultura Maya* 5: 75–91.

ROBELO, CECELIO A.

1980   *Diccionaria de Mitologia Nahuatl,* 2 vols. Editorial Innovación, Mexico City.

ROBERTSON, MERLE GREENE

1986   Some Observations on the X'telhu Panels at Yaxcaba, Yucatan. In *Research and Reflections in Archaeology and History: Essays in Honor of Doris Stone* (E. Wyllys Andrews V, ed.): 87–

111. Middle American Research Institute, Tulane University, New Orleans.

ROBICSEK, FRANCIS

1978 *The Smoking Gods: Tobacco in Maya Art, History, and Religion.* University of Oklahoma Press, Norman.

ROBICSEK, FRANCIS, and DONALD M. HALES

1981 *The Maya Book of the Dead: The Ceramic Codex.* University of Virginia Art Museum, Charlottesville.

ROSNY, LEON DE

1881 Les documents écrits de l'antiquité américaine. Compte-rendu d'une mission scientifique en Espagne et en Portugal. *Mémoires de la Société d'Ethnographie* n.s. 1 (1): 57–100. Paris.

ROYS, RALPH L.

1933 *The Book of Chilam Balam of Chumayel.* Carnegie Institution of Washington, Pub. 438. Washington, D.C.

1965 *Ritual of the Bacabs.* University of Oklahoma Press, Norman.

RUZ LHUILLIER, ALBERTO

1973 *El Templo de las Inscripciones, Palenque.* Colección Cientifica, Arqueología 7. Instituto Nacional de Antropología e Historia, Mexico City.

SABLOFF, JEREMY

1970 Type Descriptions of the Fine Paste Ceramics of the Bayal Boca Complex, Seibal, Peten, Guatemala. In *Monographs and Papers in Maya Archaeology* (William R. Bullard, ed.): 357–404. Papers of the Peabody Museum of Archaeology and Ethnology 61. Harvard University, Cambridge, Mass.

SAHAGÚN, FRAY BERNARDINO DE

1950– *Florentine Codex: General History of the Things*
71   *of New Spain* (A. J. O. Anderson and C. E. Dibble, trans.). School of American Research, Santa Fe.

SANDERS, WILLIAM T.

1960 Prehistoric Ceramics and Settlement Patterns in Quintana Roo, Mexico. *Contributions to American Anthropology and History* 12 (60): 154–264. Carnegie Institution of Washington, Washington, D.C.

SANTANA SANDOVAL, ANDRES, SERGIO DE LA L. VERGARA VERDEJO, and ROSALBA DELGADILLO TORRES

1990 Cacaxtla, su arquitectura y pintura mural: Nuevos elementos para analisis. In *La epoca clasica: Nuevos hallazgos, nuevas ideas* (Amalia Cardos de Mendez, coordinator): 329–350. Museo Nacional de Antropología, Instituto Nacional de Antropología e Historia, Mexico City.

SATTERTHWAITE, LINTON

1965 Calendrics of the Maya Lowlands. In *Handbook of Middle American Indians* (Robert Wauchope, gen. ed.) 3: 603–631. University of Texas Press, Austin.

SAVILLE, MARSHALL H.

1921 Reports on the Maya Indians of Yucatan by Santiago Mendez, Antonio Garcia y Cubas, Pedro Sanchez de Aguilar and Francisco Hernandez. *Museum of the American Indian, Notes and Monographs* 9: 133–226. Heye Foundation, New York.

SCHELE, LINDA

1974 Observations on the Cross Motif at Palenque. In *Primera Mesa Redonda de Palenque, Part 1:* 41–61. Robert Louis Stevenson School, Pebble Beach.

1976 Accession Iconography of Chan-Bahlum in the Group of the Cross at Palenque. In *The Art, Iconography and Dynastic History of Palenque, Part 3* (Merle Greene Robertson, ed.): 9–34. Robert Louis Stevenson School, Pebble Beach.

1979 Genealogical Documentation on the Trifigure Panels at Palenque. In *Tercera Mesa Redonda de Palenque, Vol. IV* (Merle Green Robertson, ed.): 41–70. Herald Printers, Monterey.

1982 *Maya Glyphs: The Verbs.* University of Texas Press, Austin.

1986 Architectural Development and Political History at Palenque. In *City-States of the Maya: Art and Architecture* (Elizabeth P. Benson, ed.): 110–137. Rocky Mountain Institute for Pre-Columbian Studies, Denver.

n.d. The Tlaloc Complex in the Classic Period: War and the Interaction between the Lowland Maya and Teotihuacan. Paper presented at the symposium "The New Dynamics," Kimbell Art Museum, Fort Worth, 1986.

SCHELE, LINDA, and PETER MATHEWS

1979 *The Bodega of Palenque, Chiapas, Mexico.* Dumbarton Oaks, Washington, D.C.

SCHELE, LINDA, PETER MATHEWS, and FLOYD LOUNSBURY

1990 *The Nal Suffix at Palenque and Elsewhere.* Texas Notes on Precolumbian Art, Writing, and Culture 6.

SCHELE, LINDA, and JEFFREY H. MILLER

1983 *The Mirror, the Rabbit and the Bundle: "Accession" Expressions from the Classic Maya Inscriptions.* Studies in Pre-Columbian Art and Archaeology 25. Dumbarton Oaks, Washington, D.C.

SCHELE, LINDA, and MARY ELLEN MILLER

1986 *The Blood of Kings: Dynasty and Ritual in Maya Art.* Kimbell Art Museum, Fort Worth.

SCHELLHAS, PAUL

1886 Die Maya Handschrift der Königlichen Bibliothek zu Dresden. *Zeitschrift für Ethnologie* 18: 12–42, 49–84.

1897 *Die Göttergestalten der Mayahandschriften: Ein Mythologisches Kulturbild aus dem alten Amerika.* Verlag von Richard Bertling, Dresden.

1904 Representation of Deities of the Maya Manuscripts. *Papers of the Peabody Museum of American Archaeology and Ethnology* 4 (1). Harvard University, Cambridge, Mass.

SEDAT, GUILLERMO
 1955　*Nuevo Diccionario de las Lenguas K'ekchi' y Espa-
　　　ñola.* Chamelco, Guatemala.

SÉJOURNÉ, LAURETTE
 1959　*Un Palacio en la Ciudad de los Dioses [Teotihua-
　　　can]: Exploraciones en 1955–1958.* Instituto
　　　Nacional de Antropología e Historia, Mexico
　　　City.

SELER, EDUARD
 1886　Maya-Handschriften und Maya-Götter. *Zeit-
　　　schrift für Ethnologie* 18: 416–420.
 1887a　Entzifferung der Maya-Handschriften. *Zeit-
　　　schrift für Ethnologie* 19: 231–237.
 1887b　Über die Namen der in der Dresdener
　　　Handschrift abgebildeten Maya-Götter. *Zeit-
　　　schrift für Ethnologie* 19: 224–231.
 1898　Die Venusperiode in den Bilderschriften de
　　　Codex-Borgia-Gruppe. *Zeitschrift für Ethnolo-
　　　gie* 30: 346–383.
 1902–　*Codex Vaticanus No. 3773 (Codex Vaticanus B),*
 03　　Berlin and London.
 1902–　*Gesammelte Abhandlungen zur Amerikanischen
 23　　Sprach- und Alterthumskunde,* 5 vols. Ascher &
　　　Co., Berlin.
 1904a　The Mexican Chronology, with Special Ref-
　　　erence to the Zapotec Calendar. In *Mexican
　　　and Central Mexican Antiquities, Calendar Sys-
　　　tems, and History* (Charles P. Bowditch, ed.):
　　　11–55. Smithsonian Institution, Bureau of
　　　American Ethnology, Bull. 28. Washington,
　　　D.C.
 1904b　The Vase of Chama. In *Mexican and Central
　　　Mexican Antiquities, Calendar Systems, and His-
　　　tory* (Charles P. Bowditch, ed.): 651–664.
　　　Smithsonian Institution, Bureau of American
　　　Ethnology, Bull. 28. Washington, D.C.
 1904c　The Venus Period in the Borgian Codex
　　　Group. In *Mexican and Central Mexican Antiqui-
　　　ties, Calendar Systems, and History* (Charles P.
　　　Bowditch, ed.): 353–391. Smithsonian Institu-
　　　tion, Bureau of American Ethnology, Bull.
　　　28. Washington, D.C.
 1963　*Comentarios al Códice Borgia,* 3 vols. (M. Fenk,
　　　trans.). Fondo de Cultura Económica, Mexico
　　　City.
 1976　*Observations and Studies in the Ruins of Palen-
　　　que, 1915* (Gisela Morgner, trans.; Thomas
　　　Bartman and George Kubler, eds.) Robert
　　　Louis Stevenson School, Pebble Beach.

SHARER, ROBERT J. (GEN. ED.)
 1978　*The Prehistory of Chalchuapa, El Salvador,* 3
　　　vols. University of Pennsylvania Press, Phila-
　　　delphia.

SIEGEL, M.
 1941　Religion in Western Guatemala, a Product of
　　　Acculturation. *American Anthropologist* 43: 62–
　　　76.

SIMÉON, RÉMI
 1977　*Diccionario de la lengua Náhuatl o Mexicano.*
　　　Siglo Veintiuno, Mexico City.

SMITH, ROBERT E.
 1952　*Pottery from Chipoc, Alta Verapaz, Guatemala.*
　　　Contributions to American Anthropology
　　　and History 56. Carnegie Institution of Wash-
　　　ington, Washington, D.C.
 1958　The Place of Fine Orange Pottery in Meso-
　　　american Archaeology. *American Antiquity* 24
　　　(2): 151–160.
 1971　*The Pottery of Mayapan, Including Studies of Ce-
　　　ramic Material from Uxmal, Kabah, and Chichen
　　　Itza,* 2 parts. Papers of the Peabody Museum
　　　66. Harvard University, Cambridge, Mass.

SOLÍS ACALÁ, ERMILIO
 1949　*Códice Pérez.* Oriente, Mérida.

SOSA, JOHN ROBERT
 1985　*The Maya Sky, the Maya World: A Symbolic
　　　Analysis of Yucatec Maya Cosmology.* Ph.D. dis-
　　　sertation, Department of anthropology, State
　　　University of New York at Albany.

SPERO, JOANNE M.
 1987　*Lightning Men and Water Serpents: A Compari-
　　　son of Mayan and Mixe-Zoquean Beliefs.* M.A.
　　　thesis, Department of anthropology, Univer-
　　　sity of Texas at Austin.

SPINDEN, HERBERT J.
 1913　*A Study of Maya Art: Its Subject Matter and
　　　Historical Development.* Memoirs of the Pea-
　　　body Museum of American Archaeology and
　　　Ethnology 6. Harvard University, Cam-
　　　bridge, Mass.

SPRANZ, BODO
 1973　*Los dioses en los códices mexicanos del grupo Bor-
　　　gia: Una investigación iconográfica.* Fondo de
　　　Cultura Económica, Mexico City.

STIRLING, MATTHEW W.
 1943　*Stone Monuments of Southern Mexico.* Bureau of
　　　American Ethnology, Bull. 138. Smithsonian
　　　Institution, Washington, D.C.

STONE, ANDREA
 1983　*The Zoomorphs of Quirigua, Guatemala.* Ph.D.
　　　dissertation, Department of art history, Uni-
　　　versity of Texas, Austin.

STRESSER-PÉAN, GUY
 1952　Montagnes calcaires et sources vauclusiennes
　　　dans la religion des Indiens Huasteques de la
　　　regíon de Tampico. *Revue de l'Histoire des Reli-
　　　gions* 141: 84–90.
 1971　Ancient Sources on the Huasteca. *Handbook of
　　　Middle American Indians* (Robert Wauchope,
　　　gen. ed.) 11 (2): 582–602. University of Texas
　　　Press, Austin.

STROSS, BRIAN
 1988　The Burden of Office: A Reading. *Mexicon* 10
　　　(6): 118–121.

STUART, DAVID
 1984　Blood Symbolism in Classic Maya Iconogra-
　　　phy. *Res: Anthropology and Aesthetics* 7/8: 6–
　　　20.
 1985　A New Child-Father Relationship Glyph. *Re-
　　　search Reports on Ancient Maya Writing,* no. 2.

1987a A Variant of the *Chak* Sign. *Research Reports on Ancient Maya Writing,* no. 10.

1987b Ten Phonetic Syllables. *Research Reports on Ancient Maya Writing,* no. 14.

STUART, GEORGE

1975 Riddle of the Glyphs. *National Geographic* 148 (6): 768–795.

TATE, CAROLYN

1985 The Carved Ceramics Called Chochola. In *Fifth Palenque Round Table, 1983* (Merle Greene Robertson, gen. ed.): 123–133. Pre-Columbian Art Research Institute, San Francisco.

1986 *The Language of Symbols in the Ritual Environment of Yaxchilan, Chiapas.* Ph.D. dissertation, Department of art history, University of Texas at Austin.

TAUBE, KARL A.

1983 The Teotihuacan Spider Woman. *Journal of Latin American Lore* 9 (2): 107–189.

1985 The Classic Maya Maize God: A Reappraisal. In *Fifth Palenque Round Table, 1983* (Merle Greene Robertson, gen. ed.): 171–181. Pre-Columbian Art Research Institute, San Francisco.

1986 The Teotihuacan Cave of Origin: The Iconography and Architecture of Emergence Mythology in Mesoamerica and the American Southwest. *Res: Anthropology and Aesthetics* 12: 51–82.

1987 A Representation of the Principal Bird Deity in the Paris Codex. *Research Reports on Ancient Maya Writing,* no. 6.

1988 A Prehispanic Maya Katun Wheel, *Journal of Anthropological Research* 44 (2): 183–203.

1989a The Maize Tamale in Classic Maya Diet, Epigraphy, and Art, *American Antiquity* 54 (1): 31–51.

1989b Ritual Humor in Classic Maya Religion. In *Word and Image in Mayan Culture* (William Hanks and Donald Rice, eds.): 351–382. University of Utah Press, Salt Lake City.

n.d.a The Iconography of Mirrors at Early Classic Teotihuacan. In *Art, Polity, and the City of Teotihuacan* (Janet Catherine Berlo, ed.) Dumbarton Oaks, Washington, D.C. (in press).

n.d.b The Temple of Quetzalcoatl and the Cult of Sacred War at Teotihuacan. *Res: Anthropology and Aesthetics* (in press).

TAUBE, KARL A., and BONNIE L. BADE

1991 An Appearance of Xiuhtecuhtli in the Dresden Venus Pages. *Research Reports on Ancient Maya Writing,* no. 34.

TAUBE, KARL A., and TOMÁS GALLARETA NEGRÓN

n.d. Survey and Reconnaisance in the Ruinas de San Angel Region, Quintana Roo, Mexico. Preliminary report of the 1988 San Angel Survey Project, submitted to National Geographic Society, 1989.

TEDLOCK, DENNIS

1985 *Popol Vuh: The Definitive Edition of the Mayan Book of the Dawn of Life and the Glories of Gods and Kings.* Simon and Schuster, New York.

THOMAS, CYRUS

1882 *A Study of the Manuscript Troano.* U.S. Department of the Interior: Contributions to North American Ethnology 5: 1–237. Washington, D.C.

1888 Aids to the Study of the Maya Codices. *Sixth Annual Report of the Bureau of American Ethnology:* 253–371. Smithsonian Institution, Washington, D.C.

THOMPSON, DONALD E.

1955 An Altar and Platform at Mayapan. *Current Reports* 28: 281–288. Carnegie Institution of Washington, Washington, D.C.

THOMPSON, J. ERIC S.

1930 *Ethnology of the Mayas of Southern and Central British Honduras.* Anthropological Series 17 (2). Field Museum of Natural History, Chicago.

1934 *Sky Bearers, Colors, and Directions in Maya and Mexican Religion.* Carnegie Institution of Washington, Pub. 436, Contrib. 10. Washington, D.C.

1938 Sixteenth and Seventeenth Century Reports on the Chol Mayas. *American Anthropologist* n.s. 40 (4): 584–604.

1939 The Moon Goddess in Middle America with Notes on Related Deities. *Contributions to American Anthropology and History* 5 (29): 121–173. Carnegie Institution of Washington, Washington, D.C.

1942 Representations of Tezcatlipoca at Chichen Itza. *Notes on Middle American Archeology and Ethnology* 12. Carnegie Institution of Washington, Division of Historical Research, Cambridge, Mass.

1950 *Maya Hieroglyphic Writing: An Introduction.* Carnegie Institution of Washington, Pub. 589. Washington, D.C.

1954 A Presumed Residence of the Nobility at Mayapan. *Current Reports* 19. Carnegie Institution of Washington, Department of archaeology, Cambridge, Mass.

1957 Deities Portrayed on Censers at Mayapan. *Current Reports* 40. Carnegie Institution of Washington, Department of archaeology, Cambridge, Mass.

1961 A Blood-drawing Ceremony Painted on a Maya Vase. *Estudios de Cultura Maya* 1: 13–20.

1962 *A Catalog of Maya Hieroglyphs.* University of Oklahoma Press, Norman.

1970a The Bacabs: Their Portraits and Glyphs. *Papers of the Peabody Museum of American Archaeology and Ethnology* 61: 471–485. Harvard University, Cambridge, Mass.

1970b *Maya History and Religion.* University of Oklahoma Press, Norman.

1972 *A Commentary on the Dresden Codex.* American Philosophical Society, Philadelphia.

1975   The Grolier Codex. *Contributions of the University of California Research Facility* 27: 1–9.

THOMPSON, J. ERIC S., and FRANCIS B. RICHARDSON (EDS.)

1939   *Gesammelte Abhandlungen zur Amerikanischen Sprach- und Alterthumskunde, Vols. I–V by Eduard Seler, Berlin, 1902–1923.* Carnegie Institution of Washington, Cambridge, Mass.

THOMPSON, RAYMOND H.

1962   Un espejo de pirita con respaldo tallado de Uayma, Yucatán. *Estudios de Cultura Maya* 2: 239–249.

TOZZER, ALFRED M.

1907   *A Comparative Study of the Mayas and the Lacandones.* Archaeological Institute of America, Macmillan, London.

1941   Landa's Relación de las Cosas de Yucatan. *Papers of the Peabody Museum of American Archaeology and Ethnology* 18. Harvard University, Cambridge, Mass.

1957   *Chichen Itza and Its Cenote of Sacrifice: A Comparative Study of Contemporaneous Maya and Toltec.* Memoirs of the Peabody Museum of American Archaeology and Ethnology 11–12. Harvard University, Cambridge, Mass.

TRIK, AUBREY

1963   The Splendid Tomb of Temple 1 at Tikal, Guatemala. *Expedition* 6 (1): 2–18.

TROIKE, NANCY P.

1978   Fundamental Changes in the Interpretations of the Mixtec Codices. *American Antiquity* 43 (4): 553–568.

VALLADARES, LEON A.

1957   *El hombre y la maíz: Etnografía e etnopsicología de Colotenango, Guatemala.* Guatemala City.

VILLAGRA CALETI, AGUSTÍN

1971   Mural Painting in Central Mexico. In *Handbook of Middle American Indians* (Robert Wauchope, gen. ed.) 10: 135–156.

VOGT, EVON Z.

1976   *Tortillas for the Gods: A Symbolic Analysis of Zinacanteco Rituals.* Harvard University Press, Cambridge, Mass.

WESTHEIM, PAUL, ALBERTO RUZ, PEDRO ARMILLAS, RICARDO DE ROBINA, and ALFONSO CASO

1969   *Cuarenta siglos de plástica Mexicana.* Editorial Herrero, Mexico City.

WHITTAKER, GORDON

1986   The Mexican Names of Three Venus Gods in the Dresden Codex. *Mexicon* 8 (3): 56–60.

WILKERSON, JEFFREY K.

1980   Eighty Centuries of Veracruz. *National Geographic* 158 (2): 203–231.

WINNING, HASSO VON

1968   *Pre-Columbian Art of Mexico and Central America.* Harry N. Abrams, New York.

1982   A Procession of God-bearers: Notes on the Iconography of Classic Veracruz Mold-impressed Pottery. In *Pre-Columbian Art History: Selected Readings* (Alana Cordy-Collins, ed.): 109–118. Peek Publications, Palo Alto.

ZIMMERMANN, GÜNTER

1956   *Die Hieroglyphen der Maya-Handschriften.* Cram, de Gruyter, Hamburg.